THE GOD JUGGERNAUT and HINDUISM in INDIA

THE GOD JUGGERNAUT and HINDUISM in INDIA

From a Study of their Sacred Books and more than 5,000 Miles of Travel in India

JEREMIAH ZIMMERMAN, D.D., LL.D.

GYAN

Published by

GYAN

Gyan Publishing House
5, Ansari Road
Daryaganj, New Delhi-110002
Phone: 011-47034999, 9811692060
E-mail: books@gyanbooks.com

Distribution Network
gyanbooks.com
India, USA, Canada, UK, Australia, France

ISBN: 978-81-212-8698-5 (PB)
First Published, 1914

2nd Impression 2023

Printed at: Gyan Press, Delhi.

THE GOD JUGGERNAUT AND HINDUISM IN INDIA
Author: Jeremiah Zimmerman

THE FESTIVAL OF THE JUGGERNAUT CAR

The God Juggernaut *and* Hinduism in India

From a Study of their Sacred Books and more than 5,000 Miles of Travel in India

By
JEREMIAH ZIMMERMAN, D.D., LL.D.

NEW YORK CHICAGO TORONTO
Fleming H. Revell Company
LONDON AND EDINBURGH

To my Wife the
Companion of my Travels

Preface

I HAVE written this book because of my love for world-wide humanity, and my intense interest in the study of the religious beliefs of the human race. There is no subject in which universal humanity has been so profoundly interested through every generation, and among the most diverse peoples, as that of religion. The history of mankind cannot be written apart from the religious element, for it has been inseparable from man and constituted the most dominant factor in moulding his thoughts, determining his conduct and shaping his destiny. This fact is clearly borne out in the study of archæology and anthropology, and the ancient coins of Greece and Rome, which bear the ideal effigies of their gods and goddesses, are the contemporary monuments that testify to the prevailing religious character and life of the people, and which even entered into the organization and control of their political institutions. Not only has religion been universal and instinctive among mankind, but often uncontrollable, for the religious consciousness has been most potent in producing deeds in conformity with convictions; for in our thoughts we live and move and have our being, and as a man thinketh within himself so he is and acts.

Some anthropologists once held that what we call the religious instinct was due to education, and that the earlier races of man were without religion, but recent archæological discoveries in Egypt have furnished unmistakable evidence that not only through the long period of history, but far back in prehistoric times—to at least 10,000 years ago—man was a religious being, as the ancient remains of articles buried with him in the innumerable graves abundantly show. The ancient Egyptians approached very near to the monotheistic faith, and they held firmly to their belief in the immortality of the soul and the eternal life hereafter.

That religion is innate may be inferred from the universality of worship, and man's conscious helplessness and dependence upon a higher power, which lead him instinctively to make his appeal to a Supreme Being for help, whilst the universal supremacy of conscience is the irresistible power and echo of that divine inner voice.

It is true that no being has been so misunderstood and misrepresented as that Supreme Being whom we call God, and who is the loving Father of us all, for the grossest superstitions, the most extraordinary delusions and vagaries of the human mind, and even shocking crimes have been associated with various forms of religious development; but these do not deny but rather accentuate the fact of the irresistible power that religion has exerted upon the human race, irrespective of culture and social standing. In the history of religious thought among ancient and mediæval civilizations we find some of the most extraordinary beliefs that ever influenced the minds of a people, and neither expense nor personal sacrifice prevented them from following their deep religious convictions. I need but mention the enormous labour and cost of the Egyptians in preparing their dead so as to make their future existence doubly secure, or the shocking self-inflicted tortures of the flagellants.

We look at everything relatively or by way of comparison. It is the instinctive method of every thoughtful observer, and it is inseparable from our study of human thought, philosophy and religion as outwardly expressed in the habits, customs, social and political life of a people through many centuries. Within recent years the comparative study of religions has been pursued in accordance with scientific methods, and it has a prominent place in the minds of cultured people generally, whilst it has come to the fore in our great institutions of learning. But there is also a deep and growing interest among all inquiring minds as evidenced in literary circles and clubs, where the subject is freely discussed; but especially in all the churches, and Woman's Missionary Societies of every denomination, for they have seriously taken up the study of Christianity in its relation to other world religions.

My personal experiences in educational work with these various classes have made me acquainted with their deepest interests, doubts and perplexing difficulties, and the many questions that they ask in view of contradictory and often extravagant statements made by superficial tourists and Swamis from India respecting the comparative character and actual fruits of certain religions. These earnest souls, with inquiring minds and desire to know of things as they exist in India, I have had in view in writing this book, which has been a labour of love as well as of research. I have conscientiously endeavoured to write a reliable work, in a straightforward and readable style such as I employ in my lectures, and as far as possible I have avoided all dry abstractions and technical detail.

I have introduced much of the human element which is of universal interest and value, and in order to vitalize and give vivid realism to the religious thought of India, and its effect upon the practices and customs and life of the people as effected by the dominant religion of Hinduism. In other words, I have endeavoured to write so that the reader might be able to see the things about which I have written. After having studied the Sacred Books of India I resolved to visit the country where for so many centuries they had swayed the minds of the countless millions of followers, for I wanted to see the effect of those teachings in their influence upon the people, and then judge them according to their fruits, after being tested for many generations. Some of the results of my studies of their sacred writings, and profound impressions made upon me from careful personal observation gained during more than five thousand miles of travel, I have embodied in this work. Often I went beyond the beaten track of tourists as when I visited Puri, the home of the god Juggernaut, and where millions have made the pilgrimage to the sacred shrine of their Lord of the world, and which intensified my enthusiasm to witness and study the psychological phenomenon of religious devotion gone mad.

I have written with a sympathetic spirit, for my inherent love for humanity is world-wide, but this has not blinded me to facts nor made me cover the sins and gross defects connected with any religion, not even the perversions and abuses of the Christian religion, for we should be less tolerant and compromising with these.

My regret is that, owing to my absence in Egypt for research, I am unable to read the proof of my book, for the author always finds some forms of expression that he would revise, if not the thought or particular statement of fact. But I am reluctantly compelled to forego this privilege.

Contents

I

INTRODUCTION

INDIA has the preëminent distinction of being the paradise of the oriental gods, and with the exception of Confucianism, it has been the battle-field of the world-religions. Each one of these has been engaged in the most aggressive efforts, and with characteristic missionary zeal and method, for the mastery. Christianity has won its way among the dominant faiths, and with a mighty host of devoted workers, has been earnestly striving for the moral and spiritual supremacy, although Hinduism and Mohammedanism are easily in the ascendency, so far as numerical strength is concerned.

There are many reasons why we are interested in India, for it was into the northern portion, now known as the Punjab, that the Aryans, the descendants of our common ancestors, came from their northwestern home after many centuries of migration, and here they established themselves and gradually extended their conquests southward. Here the ancient Vedas had their origin, and here Brahmanism arose and became a mighty priestly power; and here Buddha was born and began his reforms as a reaction against the abuses and usurpations of the Brahmanical priests.

Buddhism encountered opposition, but it grew in power, and especially under the tremendous influence and personal support of King Asoka, for under his reign it spread rapidly, and in time extended throughout the greater portion of India, and almost completely supplanted Brahmanism. Strange as it may seem, that reform movement began suddenly to wane, and after some centuries it declined as speedily as it once grew, in part owing to the shrewd device of the influential and unyielding Brahmans, who foresaw the only way for their self-preservation. That was to make a compromise of Brahmanism with Buddhism, and from this fusion there has been evolved that degenerate and amorphous amalgam of heterogeneous beliefs known as Hinduism. To-day there are but several hundred thousand followers of Buddha in India proper, although there are several hundred millions of followers in other countries, and more than ten millions in Burma, a portion of the Indian empire.

It was in India that a small remnant of the followers of Zoroaster found an asylum when the conquering Mohammedan invader threatened them with utter extermination or the alternative of absorption into the Islamitic faith. Little did they know that in fleeing from the bitter persecutions of the conqueror of their own country, and escaping into a neighbouring land of strangers, they were really coming among a people whose distant ancestors belonged to a branch of the same stock, and once speaking the same Indo-European language; and that by this event the two streams that had been separated in remote ages were brought together, and who at that very day were actually speaking a related language. It is an interesting fact that whilst the entire number of Parsees do not exceed 126,000, no less than 100,000 are living in the Presidency of Bombay, and the vast majority of them live within the city, and they are numbered among the most influential, public spirited and progressive of all the people of India, and they claim a greater antiquity for their sacred book, the Persian Avesta, than Hinduism can claim for the Veda.

It was India that the warlike Mohammedans invaded, and in their fanaticism made converts by the power of the sword, and to-day the Prophet has more than twice as many followers in India as in the Ottoman empire, or no less than sixty-three millions. The Hindus are vastly in the majority, and number more than two hundred millions, if we include all the nondescript outcastes; for the religion of Hinduism is so elastic that it is their boast that it includes every shade of belief and worship, and the theist, pantheist, materialist, or idealist do not seem to discover any incongruity in a religious system that embraces all these diverse doctrines of faith and irreconcilable contradictions; and there is no trial for heresy and no persecution so long as they do not commit the unpardonable sin of violating the law of caste, and while they recognize the Brahmanical supremacy.

While there is a great variety in the multiform religious beliefs and practices among the Hindus, this will not seem so strange when we remember that India has the most extensive pantheon of any country in the history of mankind, and in comparison with which the polytheism of ancient Babylon, Egypt, Greece and Rome was insignificant, so far as numbers are concerned. Among this multitudinous host of Hindu divinities, that even exceeds their vast population, there is the greatest variety of character and grade as well as distinctive sphere of action and special service, that each one is supposed to render to the one who seeks its favour, for as celestial bodies in the planetary system are not all of the same magnitude so there are greater and lesser gods in the diversified system of Hinduism to attend to the varied interests of the people. Whilst each one selects one of the three chief gods, he enjoys the liberty of choosing as many of the less potential local gods or goddesses as he may desire. Some of the gods are attractive in appearance, but others are repulsive, such as Juggernaut (Jagannath), Kali, and Ganesa with his elephantine head; for whilst the cultured and art loving Greeks made their gods beautiful the Oriental has often given hideous shape to some of his, as though he had no eye nor love for the beautiful, for at times the outward expression is more demoniacal than divine and hideous enough to frighten the children and give the nightmare to adults.

Among the innumerable gods there are some startling monstrosities that are a caricature of the human form and are without the remotest suggestion of the divine, except as they may represent certain ideas or attributes of strength or cunning. When we look upon some of these strange caricatures it is difficult for us to understand how these distorted figures (some too grotesque to be taken seriously by a Western observer) can appeal to the minds and hearts of the natives and give comfort and help in time of their sorrow, for they do not seem to have any suggestion of love, tenderness, mercy and help, and yet these hideous and often repulsive images are the outward expression of personified beings that have been enthroned among the deities of the vast pantheon of Hinduism.

One thing is most evident throughout India: that man is an intensely religious being, and often intoxicated by his belief to such a degree as to carry him beyond the bounds of all reason; but every age and nation has been preëminently religious, for man is not only a religious being but his religious nature and wants are both intensive and imperative and cannot be satisfied by any substitute, and hence the greatest sacrifices have been made for religious convictions. The religious quest of the human soul is inseparable from the world of humanity, and no race nor people has ever been found without religious belief and practices; and hence no subject has ever been of such universal interest throughout the entire history of humanity, among all races and in every age, as that of religion. We cannot write the history of any nation without its religion, for the deep and controlling religious element has been the most dominant factor in moulding the thoughts, directing the energies and shaping the destinies of nations as well as of individuals.

The ancient Egyptians were an eminently religious people and the distinguished French archæologist Maspero remarked in the famous museum in Cairo that "The vast majority of their literature was of a religious character, and the same was true of their monuments, so that we might infer that the country was inhabited by the gods, and had only men and animals sufficient to attend to the religious services of the temples and for sacrifices." The same may be said of Greece and Rome, and of the former the eminent authority Farnell states in his recent work on Greece and Babylon that "No other religious people of which we have any record was so political as the Hellenic, not even the Romans. In the organized and complex Greek societies every institution of the state—the assembly, the council, the law-courts, the agrarian economy,—all the regulations of the family and clan were consecrated by the supervision of some deity." The "Greek religion had no sacred books or authoritative cosmogony to oppose to the dawn and the development of scientific inquiry." Everywhere in the Mediterranean area "We observe the blood sacrifice of animals, and the frequent offering of fruits and cereals." "The sacrificial ritual of Leviticus does not differ in any essential trait from that which commended itself to the Greeks and to the other peoples of these lands."

There has been the greatest diversity of religious opinions and practices among men as seen in the history and growth of religions, but no nation nor people has been found capable of dispensing with religion. Buddha may have attempted it, but the futility of his attempt manifested itself in time, and the irony of it all was that his followers found it impossible to maintain his atheistical system, and went to the other extreme by elevating Buddha himself to a place among the gods, although he had ignored such a Supreme Being during his lifetime and would have repudiated their action in deifying him. The universal quest of the human soul has been its search after God, and Buddha's followers felt compelled to create one for their soul's need, though the founder of their religious system did not recognize that Supreme Being in theory.

To the student of religions no country affords such an extensive and varied field for study as India. I do not refer to the vast area of empire, and population, but to the great stretch of time and religious history since their early ancestors raised their altars and sacrificed to the phenomenal powers of heaven and earth as their gods, for they appeared to them as instinct with some superhuman force, and hence in those remote times they worshipped and offered prayers to trees, rocks and animals, the sky, sun and moon, dawn, fire and water as embodiments of a divine anima or spirit, for animism and fetishism swayed the minds of that primitive people before they knew of the personal gods. No wonder that the sky had the supreme place among the heavenly ones in their worship, for the crash of thunder and the lightning flash must have filled their minds with deepest awe, for without knowledge that science has revealed to us, those startling manifestations of nature were involved in impenetrable mystery, although they had an innate religious aptitude for apprehending the Divine Being, as evidenced by the appearance in their sacred book of that wonderful word—Dyaus pitar—shining heaven or sky-father.

True they may not have recognized a personal God, and whilst philologists were startled when they discovered this word as the forerunner of Zeus and Jupiter, still there was a great difference between the conception of that remote people and ours when we speak of God, our heavenly Father, as a Person of infinite love and mercy, although the original word may have been the same. That Sanskrit word meaning sky or heaven father did not convey to them the same idea that we have when we speak of Our Heavenly Father, just as the word Zeus did not convey the same meaning to the Greeks as the word God does to us, and the same is true of the god Jupiter among the Romans.

No people to-day as a whole are so thoroughly imbued with their religion as the Hindus, for they are not merely religious in thought and practice one day in the week, but three hundred and sixty-five days in the year, and their religion permeates their daily life so completely that they may be said to eat, drink, sleep and bathe religiously. They have clearly prescribed rules for such observances that they follow most scrupulously, and one of the religious requirements according to the Sacred Books is that no man shall allow his wife to eat with him, although she may stand and serve her lord while he eats, but he must not be present to see his wife eat.

Inasmuch as the religion of the majority is inseparable from the most commonplace affairs of every-day life, and has such an important place even in the culinary department owing to the supreme doctrine of caste; hence their religious history, beliefs and practices are not concealed from the public and the curious gaze of strangers; all are open before the eyes of the student who would study them in their native country and in action as outwardly expressed in the daily occupation of the people. They are not ashamed of their religion, nor to be seen living it in public and to be known as followers of their particular god, but proclaim the fact in many instances by the conspicuous and unmistakable symbols marked in colours on their forehead.

Therefore India is a favourable land for this study, for we behold in an extended and ever varying panorama the every-day workings of Hinduism in the most practical experience of the millions of followers, and not merely as a fine spun system of philosophy and religion as evolved by an academic study of their books in our library at home, but as a living and practiced religion, and instinct with tremendous activity and power in controlling the lives of more than two hundred millions who believe its teachings and whose thought and lives are moulded by it. We can examine it at close range within and without the temples, in the streets and public highways as well as in the homes of the people, and not merely in individual cases on dress parade during some annual festival and in a particular locality, but everywhere throughout India in the leading cities, towns and villages. We were excluded from a few temples but with those exceptions we were freely admitted so that we enjoyed the opportunity of seeing the faithful worshippers and the distinctive ceremonies of Hinduism, as well as its abundant fruits, borne after many centuries of unhindered freedom in testing its legitimate and unmixed character on its native soil.

Some of the practices were so extravagant as to appear bewildering to a Western observer; at times we found it difficult to adjust or to orientate ourselves to their point of view in order to see things from their particular angle, so as to view things as they viewed them and if possible get their interpretation of the symbols and ceremonies and not misunderstand them. To use an expression coined by Max Müller: "We must make full allowance for the very important intellectual parallax which no doubt renders it most difficult for a Western observer to see things and thought under exactly the same angle and in the same light as they appear to an Eastern one."

It is to be regretted that this eminent Sanskrit scholar confined his studies to their Sacred Books alone and never visited India to see what those teachings had done for the people through many centuries of undisputed sway. Had he studied them in connection with their direct influence upon the people and judged them by the fruits they bore, then he himself at times would have received a different point of view, and modified impressions, and he would have reached different conclusions as to their real character, after witnessing their practical effect upon the destiny of a nation that had believed and practiced them. That would have somewhat changed the angle of his intellectual parallax also and given him some valuable suggestions that a mere academic study of their Sacred Books in his far-away library in London could never produce. There he studied the words and their meaning, and the subtle and idealistic thought of metaphysical systems, and which have attracted some Western minds, but the supreme question respecting it all is: What is it worth as a practical working religion for the social and spiritual elevation and regeneration of the human race in India? India made the experiment with countless millions and for centuries, and what is the result? "By their fruits ye shall know them."

I am well aware that several distinguished Hindus visited Max Müller in London, but they were such choice specimens and so much elevated above the teeming millions of the depressed classes that they were by no means the logical and representative products of the Hindu religion just as Booker Washington himself would not be a true representative of the coloured race in the South; and should he visit some distinguished pundits in India, he would create a very erroneous impression were they to look upon him as a type of the American negro. This suggests a caution for us when a highly gifted and cultured Swami of India visits our country, for many have been carried away with enthu-

DR. AND MRS. ZIMMERMAN IN FRONT OF A TRAVELLERS' PALM

siasm, and fascinated by utterances that are so suggestive of the teaching of Christ, for they overlook the fact that this same Swami may be greatly indebted to the Christian schools for his education and modern culture, and especially for the many attractive phrases that have been moulded by Christian thought. Unless Christianity had familiarized them with the New Testament we would not find so much in common when they speak, for the influence of the Gospel has permeated the thought of many of the cultured classes, who instinctively employ words and ideas borrowed from the Christian religion.

Because of the multitudinous and heterogeneous variety of religious ideas and sects in India the people constitute an exceptionally interesting field for the student of comparative religions. The force of this statement is seen in the fact that the vast number of gods in the pantheon of Hinduism has been placed at no less than three hundred and thirty millions, easily outnumbering all the gods of the ancient world, and the members of the particular sects conform to the outward corresponding practices, for their religion has made them what they are.

The millions of religious mendicants, ascetics and devotees are so ubiquitous that we are ever reminded of this pernicious phase of Hinduism, and that the poor are always with us. The number of animals sacrificed at the Kalighat in Calcutta, even on an ordinary day, surpasses the seven lambs that are annually killed at the Samaritan Passover on Mount Gerizim, while the number that are sacrificed at Kalighat throughout the year almost rivals the vast number that were offered up at the yearly Jewish Passover in Jerusalem. Hence in

India where religion becomes largely exemplified in a living and varying panorama of outward ceremonies that are often of a highly spectacular character, we are permitted to see their religion in action and at work in its immediate influence upon the social and intellectual life of the people, and as it has been transmitted for several thousand years.

We are not left to any uncertainty as when studying some prehistoric specimens, and the remains found in the graves and tombs of extinct races and religions, but they are living remains—the descendants clothed in flesh and warm blood coursing through their veins—living on the same ancient soil and believing and living their religion and which has determined their destiny. For as men believe so they are and act, for in our thought and religious faith we live and move and have our being.

But perhaps in no country has it been so true that the thought and life of a people throughout their historical development have been determined by the dominating character of their religion as it is seen to-day in India and where we may behold and study the strength and weakness of a religion in its effect upon the countless millions of people for more than thirty centuries. This is due to the persistence of its distinctive features and controlling power over its followers, and the fact that it ever rises to the surface so that to a great extent we become an eye-witness to what their religion is and what it has done for them. It has been the most potent and characteristic factor in their history, and which still sways the vast majority and opposes the many needed reforms for the social elevation of the many millions whose lives have been doomed to an appalling state of degradation and for which their religion offers them no relief, and no hope for future redemption.

In Southern India we saw about the temples multitudes who bore on their forehead the distinctive symbol of their god, Vishnu or Siva, rubbed on in the early morning by the priest, and the Pharisaic Brahmans bore their marks with conspicuous pride that recalled the Pharisees of Jerusalem, who made wide their phylacteries in order to proclaim their superiority. But in one respect the Hindus surpassed those Pharisees in making an outward show of their religion for they made use of the temple elephants to proclaim their particular religion, and covered the great foreheads with the trident, the symbol of Vishnu.

In Bombay on a festival day we saw scores of religious devotees whose bare breasts, backs, arms and limbs were streaked with the sacred vermilion that had been profusely smeared over their bodies and faces. They rushed through the streets, shouting and gesticulating violently like madmen, looking as though bedlam had broken loose and that these had escaped from a bloody massacre. This is also an example of the wonderful-marked contrasts that we find in travelling over the country, for like a kaleidoscope the view is ever changing and there is such remarkable variety seen in different towns and sections of the country that we never suffer from monotony. Many things that grow tedious and commonplace after years of familiarity with them in a particular locality have all the charms of novelty, and are rich in suggestiveness as they make their first and lasting impression upon us. The contrast or comparison with other classes brings out the chief qualities in clearer relief, for there is no such thing as sameness in traversing India.

When we speak of India we do not refer to a distinct nationality and a homogeneous people who speak one common language like the Japanese or the Chinese for India is not homogeneous, neither in a political, ethnological, linguistic or religious sense, but is composed of most heterogeneous races, and speaking as many as one hundred and fifty different languages and various dialects. The population is one-fifth that of the world and more than twice that of the Roman Empire at the period of its greatest prosperity. The country has an area of one million and one-half square miles and equal to about two-thirds of the United States. It is pear shaped and the greatest length and width are about 1,900 miles. It is bounded on the north by the lofty Himalayan range that attains its greatest height on the summit of Mt. Everest more than 29,000 feet above sea level. The sacred Ganges has its source in this same vast abode of snow, some 14,000 feet higher than the Bay of Bengal into which it annually pours a far greater volume of water than that which flows from the mouth of any other river on earth.

Under British conquest and rule the empire of India expanded, until it not only included Burma, but Baluchistan where no traces of Indian culture are visible among a hardy people who seem to have taken on the stern characteristics of their rugged and forbidding physical environments. These severe and unattractive features of nature as they see it have given rise to a familiar but rather shocking native proverb: "O God! when thou hadst created Sibi and Dadhar, what object was there in conceiving hell?"

That region is in striking contrast with some of the beautiful tracts included in the empire of India, and yet the intolerable heat and frequent pestilential epidemics which the people have suffered are proverbial. Moreover they have been afflicted with such dreadful calamities as the overflowing of the Ganges, drought and famine and the memorable ones of 1896 and 1897, 1899 and 1900 when no less than five millions perished from starvation. The bubonic plague has been an unspeakable scourge and during its prevalence in the year 1896 cost the lives of 1,000,000 people.

However, great as these appalling calamities have been, the awful ravages from the many cruel wars of invasion and conquest have even exceeded them, for according to Ratzel, "None of the greater nations of Asia has been so broken up, pulverized, and kneaded by conquerors as the Indian: among none has the vital marrow of independence been so destroyed. In all this push and pressure India developed no predominant nationality. Nothing but the fact that the 300,000,000 of the Anglo-Indian Empire are split up into thousands of ethnological, social and religious fragments enabled British sovereignty to spread so quickly and maintain itself."

In this connection, bearing upon the heterogeneous and diversified character and languages of a people that have so little in common, the following extract of Dr. Grierson forcibly illustrates the situation:

"*India is a land of contrasts* and nowhere are they more evident than when we approach the consideration of its *vernaculars*. There are languages whose phonetic rules prohibit the existence of more than a few hundred words, which cannot express to us what are the commonest and most simple ideas; and there are others with opulent vocabularies, rivalling English in their copiousness and in their accuracy of idea-connotation. There are languages every word of which must be a monosyllable, and there are others with words in which syllable is piled on syllable, till the whole is almost a sentence in itself. There are languages which know neither noun nor verb, and whose only grammatical feature is syntax, and there are others with grammatical systems as complete and as systematically worked out as those of Greek or Latin. There are languages with a long historical past reaching over thirty centuries, and there are others with no tradition whatever of the past. There are the rude languages of the naked savages of East Assam, which have never been reduced to writing, and there are languages with great literatures adorned by illustrious poets and containing some of the most elevated deistic sentiments which have found utterance in the East. There are languages, capable in themselves of expressing every idea, which are nevertheless burdened with an artificial vocabulary borrowed from a form of speech which has been dead for 2,000 years; and there are others, equally capable, that disdain such fantastic crutches, and every sentence of which breathes the reek of the smoke from the homesteads of the sturdy peasantry that utters it. There are parts of India that recall the plain in the land of Shinar where the tower of old was built, and in which almost each of the many mountains has its own language, and there are great plains, thousands and tens of thousands of miles in area, over which one language is spoken from end to end.

"And over all there broods the glamour of Eastern

mystery. Through all of them we hear the inarticulate murmur of past ages when the Aryans wandered with their herds across the steppes of Central Asia, when the Indo-Chinese had not yet issued from their home on the Yang-tse-kiang and perhaps when there existed the Lemurian continent where now sweep the restless waves of the Indian Ocean.

"Light comes from the East, but many years must yet be passed in unremitting quest of knowledge before we can inevitably distinguish it from the false dawn which is but a promise and not the reality. Hitherto scholars have busied themselves with the tongues and thoughts of ancient India, and have too often presented them as illustrating the India of the present day. But the true India will never be known till the light of the West has been thrown on the hopes, the fears, the beliefs, of the 300,000,000 who have been counted at the present census. For this, an accurate knowledge of the vernaculars is necessary, a knowledge not only of the colloquial languages, but also, when they exist, of the literatures too commonly decried as worthless, but when one who has studied them and loved them can confidently affirm to be no mean possession of no mean land."

When a schoolboy I was inspired with a feeling of hero worship as I read the thrilling military achievements of Alexander the Great, although my visions of him seldom extended beyond the Hellenic world; the extreme limit of his conquests in Northern India seemed too far away and the strange people were not even remotely related to us. Within recent years the relationship has become more intimate and India has been brought nearer to us by the wonderful discovery of philological research, for the comparative study of languages or "linguistic palæontology" has established the fact of the affinity of the family of languages, known as the Indo-European (or Indo-Germanic) group and including the Sanskrit of India, the Zend of Persia, the Greek, Latin, Celtic, Teutonic, etc. All these members can be traced to one common origin, and beyond all question there was once such a parent Indo-European language and there was a people who spoke it and from this original the different languages mentioned were derived, although it does not necessarily follow that all the people who speak the languages of this group are the lineal descendants of that ancient prehistoric race that once used this language.

It is far more difficult to locate the original home of the primitive Indo-European people, although we desire to know where they dwelt before the dawn of recorded history. Once there was a general agreement in assigning the Asiatic origin to somewhere in the middle of Asia, perhaps on the Caucasus or on the Hindu Kush, and that before the dawn of history there was a movement from the original habitation and one branch migrated Westward and in time settled the various countries of Europe and whose descendants we are, whilst another stream of humanity moved Southward and invaded India, and settled in the Punjab, overcoming the aboriginal inhabitants and driving them south or into the hill country.

But within recent years the tendency of most scholars of ethnology and philology has been to abandon this once favourite theory and to shift the primitive home of the Indo-Europeans Westward into Northern Europe as the most likely abode of snow referred to in the Veda. Philological research has discovered the contrary to what was once supposed, and that the Sanskrit does not represent the most archaic form of language, but rather that it has been preserved by the Letto-Lithuanians who are still found in their ancestral homes along the Baltic.

Professor Skeat's last word on the conclusions of linguistic research respecting Indo-Germanic types is contained in his posthumous work on the "Science of Etymology," in which he states that "the various Teutonic languages evidently go back to a common original, though such an original is not actually recorded, as it had its being in prehistoric times. . . . Just as Italian, Spanish, Provençal, and the rest are sister languages descended from popular Latin, so Teutonic, Celtic, Baltic, Slavonic, Latin, Greek, Sanskrit, and the rest go back to a common origin. One result of this is that they may be practically regarded as coeval, and that it is hardly safe to look upon one of these languages as being older than another. Latin is as old as Greek and the Teutonic element in English is as old as Sanskrit. The fact is that many are apt to forget the one all-essential consideration, that languages consist, properly speaking, of spoken utterances only, and that the representation of them by means of written symbols is conventional and inadequate."

Hence the pendulum of authority has swung Westward and somewhat to the chagrin of the proud Brahman and his allies who were persuaded that not only the rising sun came from the East but that all the great light of primitive knowledge, and especially religion emanated from the Far East, and that even we ourselves and the various European races are their descendants, though somewhat degenerated through time and environment. That self-gratuitous view as held by the Aryans of India placed us under tribute to them who regarded their Sanskrit as the most ancient form of language and the sacred depository of all knowledge and the source of the greatest civilization. That self-complacent view has not always been as agreeable to our Western pride as we might have desired, especially when the arrogant Swamis have been masquerading through our country with their extravagant claims of Eastern wisdom and now for the first time revealed to the West. By parading such views it became an exaggerated and aggravated example of the tail wagging the dog, an illogical and irritating category into which we were forced but to which we could not gracefully submit.

No wonder then that we have hailed with gratitude and delight the new light that has been coming from the West; for whilst the controversy has not been absolutely closed the accumulating weight of authority is sufficient to establish the highest probability and amounting to a proof that the Aryans of Iran and India came from the original cradle of the Indo-Europeans somewhere in the West and migrated to their subsequent homes in the Far East; that during the sojourn in Northern India the Sanskrit language was developed and there at different places and at widely different times the earliest hymns of the Vedas were composed. Another branch that followed them to the East separated and settled in the country known as Persia and where the Avesta, the sacred book of Iran, was composed and which Bloomfield claims to be more ancient than the Veda. Other portions remained in the West and scattered over Europe becoming the ancestors of the Greeks and Romans and various countries of Europe.

Unfortunately monumental records fail us in our endeavour to trace the remote history of India, for the archæological monuments are not so ancient as those of Assyria and Egypt and hence we lack definite historical information for penetrating the distant past. The earliest known political date does not take us back beyond 600 B. C., although untold centuries of civilization extended far back into the unrecorded past.

The aboriginal Dravidian race that the Aryans found in the country is to-day the most primitive of the Indian type, for inasmuch as 3,000 or 4,000 years have elapsed since the first Indo-Europeans entered the Punjab, the distinctive type of these invaders became lost in time to a large extent through intermarriage with the indigenous inhabitants, but after a number of years they seem to have recognized the necessity of restricting marriage among their own mixed offspring, somewhat as the quadroons and octoroons of the Southern states, and this may have originated the caste system and which was subsequently developed to its most extravagant limits by the priests.

In view of the extravagant statements made at times relative to the indebtedness of Europe to the culture, and civilizing influence, of India, the following quotation from the eminent Sanskrit scholar, Dr. Lanman of Harvard University, may serve as a deterrent:

"Leaving out of account the extreme Orient, India has had no grand part in the history of world civilization. It is true the primitive Hindus are a branch of the same Aryan family to which we also by right of birth belong, but so far as their influence upon our life and thought, or ours upon them, is concerned, the Hindus might almost as well have lived on the planet of Jupiter as on the banks of the Indus or Ganges."

II

THE GOD JUGGERNAUT (JAGANNATH) AT PURI

IT has been the overmastering desire to see the god Juggernaut that has attracted many millions of devoted Hindus to Puri on the Bay of Bengal. For centuries this city has been a veritable Jerusalem, and continuous streams of pilgrims have come to its holy temple, that they might enter the innermost sanctuary and stand before the sacred shrine and gaze upon the thrice holy image of their Lord of the World. They come during all seasons of the year, during the intense heat and cold, in rain and sunshine. The greatest number in one year has been estimated at 200,000, although the average has been about 100,000, and the majority of these come for the great festival weeks in the month of July or the latter part of June.

The saddest feature of these pilgrimages is that about five-sixths of the pilgrims are women, and until within the last few years nearly all made the long journey on foot. There must have been powerful incentives brought to bear upon these people to induce them to make a pilgrimage that involved so many hardships and often at the cost of life. It was the controlling conviction that the sight of the god Juggernaut would secure for them remission of sin and deliverance of the otherwise countless rebirths in store for them, and gain a genuine passport at the close of this brief life to oneness with Brahma, or into heaven itself. With such vision of the glorious future they were willing to make some sacrifice and forego for a time their sad lot of drudgery at home, and which was without promise.

The women were most susceptible in mind, and they had the most to gain and the least to lose, and hence their sex furnished the vast majority of the marching hosts. Often many hundreds of miles must be traversed, and scores die by the way ; the deaths in a single year aggregating as many as 10,000. Lest any one should be deterred from attempting a pilgrimage attended by so many difficulties, and even with the uncertainty of ever reaching Puri, they are sustained by the assurance that the will will be taken for the deed in case they should fall by the wayside and not see the wonderful image, for then they shall behold the god Juggernaut himself, as their immediate entrance into heaven is guaranteed. The new recruits are secured by thousands of special agents sent out by the temple officials and as they are past masters of the art of persuasion a new contingent is enrolled each year. All sorts of questionable methods are employed by the unscrupulous travelling agents, and as there are no woman's rights nor equality in Hinduism it is not strange that these susceptible mortals should be persuaded to undertake any sacrifice for a few months since their destiny through all eternity is involved.

Any one acquainted with these perennial religious movements that through the centuries have exercised such a remarkable influence over the life of the Bengalese, and even the nations beyond, will agree that no intelligent traveller in India who is interested in the subject of comparative religions should fail to include a journey through Orissa to Puri. It will be worth far more than it costs and few places are so remunerative. I never lost the impression made upon my mind when a boy in seeing a picture of Juggernaut in the Bible Dictionary in our home, and this became deepened into an intense desire when travelling through India.

Whilst railroad travelling in India is by no means so comfortable and luxurious as at home, the earnest student will find little occasion for complaint, for the many objects of absorbing interest will engage his mind so completely as to make him unmindful of ordinary discomforts. Often we were shaken on the narrow gauge roads, and wished for relief but these were the exceptions. As there was but one express train every twenty-four hours we reached some cities at very inconvenient hours. Travelling by night is more comfortable over long distances than by day owing to the extreme heat, and in monotonous portions of the country there is no loss of scenery and a gain of time for places of interest.

The first class compartments have a wide and long leather cushioned seat on either side and two corresponding ones above, turned up vertically and strapped against the side of the car by day and let down and supported in a horizontal position at night to serve the purpose of two upper berths, so that four persons can sleep in each compartment; providing those in the berths overhead do not roll out, for there is absolutely no guard or projection of any kind in front, and the violent shaking at times, and especially on the narrow gauge roads would make them rather unsafe unless the unconscious sleeper could hold on to the straps by which the berth was suspended. There are a number of small sliding glass windows on either side, and of various colours so as to shut out the glaring light, and as a further protection there are Venetian blinds, and which may also be used for ventilation. There is a door on either side, and a third one at the end that leads to the small private lavatory. There are special apartments for ladies only. By paying the price of three tickets an entire apartment can be secured.

In the larger cities there are modest hotels, with the exception of the magnificent one that was just opened in Bombay. Where there were no hotels the railroad had made provision for sleeping apartments in a building connected with the station, and good meals were provided, although it was not a quiet place for sleeping. The government however provides the dak-bungalow in a more retired place and in a very commodious and quiet one we found quarters when visiting Puri. The furnishings were painfully plain and limited, for the traveller furnishes his own bedding; a doubly important precaution in this plague stricken and densely inhabited country.

We had travelled by railroad from Tuticorin on the south, stopping at the leading towns and cities and making dêtours to others of special interest that were away from the main line, but which every student to India should include in his itinerary. We had seen the great Dravidian temples in the various cities of Southern India, and had witnessed the Juggernaut car procession and the great annual festival at Madura that seemed to reach the climax and yet the greatest of all is the one to be seen at Puri.

The first unmistakable evidence that we had of this fact was when we reached Khurda Road, a station on the direct line from the south to Calcutta, where a branch extends east to the Bay of Bengal. As we stepped from the train we found ourselves surrounded by a swarm of excited pilgrims who were returning from Puri and anxious to board the train going to Calcutta. They rushed like a mob for the third class coaches until there was not so much as standing room, even for a thin half starved East Indian, and then the doors were closed and the disappointed ones were driven from the platform and without the station, either to await the next train or else like their ancestors of old to make the journey on foot.

We had secured our seats in a coach on the Orissa branch and there were several vacant places in our compartment, but the price of such a luxury was prohibitive for the ordinary poor pilgrim and they passed by. We had scarcely taken our seats before the gates were opened to the multitude of pilgrims who had been anxiously waiting and it seemed like bedlam let loose, as many with staff in hand and carrying a bundle with some extra rags and food for the way rushed pell-mell along the platform, and some with frenzied effort to crowd their way into a third-class car. Again I saw the disappointed ones and some almost with the look of despair, for many had come from a long distance and were hungry and weak and wearied from the journey, and necessity obliged them to ride the remainder of the way.

We saw the same drama of human disappointment and desperation enacted at all the leading stations. Never shall I forget the frantic efforts of some as they rushed for the train, for experience had taught them that the majority were doomed to disappointment. Such inadequate accommodations are open to criticism, for these poor people cannot secure either sitting or standing room in advance and with the desperate struggle of the many for a limited number of places the strong have a decided advantage over the weak, and there is no special deference shown to members of the gentler sex, but on the contrary the strong man elbows his way and crowds them out. Fortunately the third class transportation on this branch through Orissa to Puri is said to be the cheapest fare of any railroad in the world, but the accommodations are utterly inadequate to the demand, and during the weeks of the car festival the vast majority must walk, unless they have greatly increased their facilities for carrying passengers since the time of our visit.

We passed hundreds trudging along on foot, with all their temporary possessions tied together in a small bundle, with the addition of the indispensable bowl. Not one suffered any impediment from an excess of baggage, and never before did we see men and women travelling so far from home with so little to encumber them. There was not even an extra undergarment, for in India on such occasions they attend to their own laundry and wait while they stand and wash it. Poverty acquired a new meaning and such as we had not understood from the dictionary, for in our land of plenty it is only a relative term, but when we saw the dress or rather the lack of dress among many whose exposed slender forms showed every rib, then we saw poverty exemplified at its most deplorable stage.

Often we observed the poor during the cold hours between sunset and sunrise when they must have suffered from the inadequate clothing and food, for they had not sufficient of either. Their thin limbs were bare and the little clothing that they wore, with the exception of the loin cloth, was wrapped about their shoulders. The man of Bengal especially has thin legs of skin and bone, with scarcely any flesh, looking skeleton like, but having large "knocking knobs" for knees. Even his head is generally bare and his oiled black hair is the only protection against the terrible heat of the sun that the European dreads so much. During the colder weather he wears a thin white cotton dress, tucked up about his limbs for convenience in walking and working, as well as to distinguish it from the dress of a woman.

Among the many pilgrims that we saw on their homeward way were several strange groups in a nondescript dress, made up of odd portions of the occidental wearing apparel with the plain oriental, that made them look like a troupe of masqueraders as they hurried along the road. They were entirely ignorant of the European dress for they wore the clothing without any regard to the fitness of things so far as our ideas are concerned. Some with bare legs wore a pair of boots, and others wore trousers with the feet and the rest of the body bare. Some wore an English coat and over it a white shirt with the skirt outside the trousers. The coloured suspenders especially seemed to appeal to their pride as they invariably wore them on the outside, even over the black coat and they reminded us of the hoodlums seen in a circus-ring, or on some spectacular street parade. How they came in possession of this strange attire I know not. Possibly some English officials had abandoned them when returning home; or inasmuch as this class of pilgrims were hurrying along at an unusual pace for a native, there may have been a fortunate fire or some second-hand dealer may have been robbed.

Many of the returning pilgrims carried a stick or a small bundle with them, made of twigs and sold in Puri. Some used them as a cane and they were carried home as treasured souvenirs and in some cases as a sort of fetish; for when blessed by the priests or placed in the presence of the sacred images, they became invested with a potent charm. They recalled the Russian peasants whom we saw in the Church of the Holy Sepulchre in Jerusalem on the memorable day when they lighted the tapers from the Holy Fire, and then took them to their homes with a reverent belief in their meritorious character.

The province of Orissa, and especially the portion lying about Puri, is the Holy Land for these devoted pilgrims, for according to the Sanskrit the word Orissa means the "glorious country," and is so sacred and revered in the mind of ancient Hindu writers that they designate it as the "realm established by the gods, the land that takes away sin." In fact, one of their sages had most extravagant conceptions of the religious merit of this province for he wrote that "of all the regions of the earth, India is noblest, and of all the countries of India, Utkala (Orissa) bears the highest renown. Its fortunate inhabitants live *secure* of a reception into the world of spirits and even those who visit it and bathe in its sacred rivers obtain remission of their sins, though they may weigh like mountains. Who shall estimate the soul's gain from a sojourn in such a land? But what need for enlarging on the praises of a land in which the gods loved to dwell?"

Since the district for many scores of miles surrounding Puri is regarded as holy ground, in the minds of some, the merit accruing from a pilgrimage through it to the holy shrine is in direct ratio to the degree of self-abasement and physical suffering endured; hence there have been not a few who made that journey as difficult and as painful as possible when approaching the Holy City by prostrating themselves upon the earth and measuring the ground for miles with the length of their body, repeating the process time and again as they stretch their full length from head to foot and marking the point attained with the tips of their fingers or with an iron pin, and then rising and placing their toes at this mark, prostrating themselves again and again for weeks or more according to the distance to be traversed. One pilgrim made the extreme distance of seven hundred miles by this slow method during eight months.

We may call them fanatics but we cannot help but pity them as we contemplate their mental aberration and wasted energy in such a hopeless delusion that benefits no one, and yet the Hindu regards him not only as perfectly sane, but as a very superior and holy individual. It is difficult for us to overestimate the hardship endured by many of those devotees, yet the history of Christianity can furnish numerous examples of saints gone equally mad under the influence of some strange delusion.

It was a long time in making the forty-seven miles to the Puri station and when we arrived the pilgrims hurried out of the crowded cars and trudged along on foot for several miles to the city. The sun was sinking below the horizon and we lost no time in preparing for the remainder of our journey. With the assistance of the ever obliging station master we secured the only available vehicle, the forbidding bullock cart, without springs, and that jolted us from one side to the other over the rough road whenever the driver had his animal go faster than a walk. But there was no alternative except to grin and bear it.

We were to spend the night at the dak-bungalow and the distance seemed much greater owing to the late hour and the tedious drive. By the use of signs and money of the realm that always talks in every language, the bullock took on new energy ; but the accelerated speed only increased our agony and I was as ready to pay him to follow his accustomed pace. Far off in the distance on the right we saw the glimmer of a few lights that indicated human habitations, but we were not going in that direction.

In time we neared the Bay of Bengal and then we were cheered by the appearance of an unmistakable Christian edifice, a light gray stone chapel that was highly suggestive. Near by was the huge bungalow, and the bark of a dog and the call of our driver brought the caretaker from his humble dwellings. He had his appointment from the government and was held responsible for the faithful performance of his duty in providing good food and caring for native and foreign travellers, who before leaving wrote their impressions in the public book and in languages that he could not read. We arranged for our lodgings and gave the order for our dinner which was prepared in a very primitive manner, with all outdoors for a kitchen, and yet that caretaker was a born cook, and in a short time we were enjoying an excellent dinner consisting of soup, omelette, vegetables, chicken and dessert with

A FAKIR UPON A BED OF IRON SPIKES

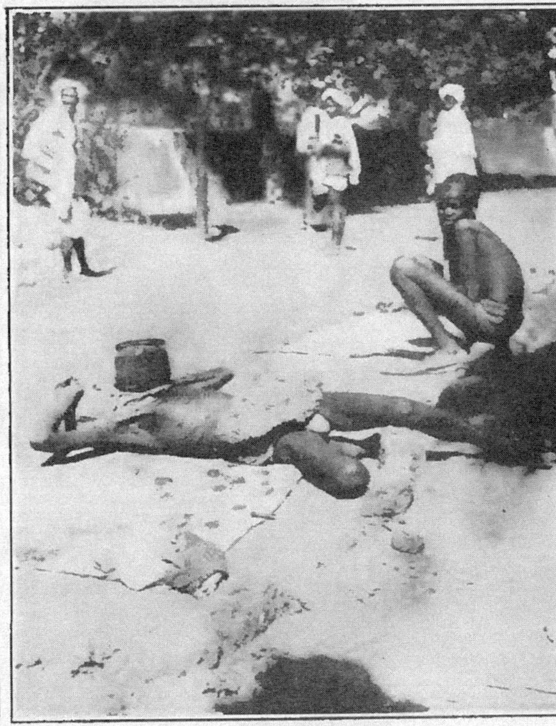

PILGRIMS AT PURI

tea. It was prepared within half an hour and it took less than that time to eat it, and we felt far better than when we arrived, for then a feeling of unusual loneliness and misgiving came over us.

It was a solitary place, away from Western civilization, and even the missionary had gone back to England and the church was closed. The language was a strange one and there was no interpreter, and we knew only sufficient words to order a meal. Surely it was no place to be sick, and in our reverie the suggestion came from my companion of travels for years: "Suppose something would happen?" With a smile I replied: "But nothing is going to happen."

I confess that never before did I feel so lonely, nor did I so keenly realize the actual situation, but I kept it to myself and I walked away to examine the bungalow and its surroundings, and I got a point of view that was glorious and all my feelings were changed and I hastened to communicate them to my companion. I said with enthusiasm: "Cheer up and come with me for I have just seen something that will inspire you, for we have seen it again and again at home." Of course she protested that I was only speaking for effect, but together we walked around the corner of that building in which we were to lodge for the night, and just across the bay, and some degrees above the surface of the water was that same old bright silver moon, and we laughed heartily as we looked into that familiar smiling face that we had witnessed so often at home, and we were comforted with the thought that God our heavenly Father was with us. After reflecting upon the magnificent view we realized our keen appetite and we relished our dinner without further anxiety.

Later the unexpected happened, for one of the Christian converts who spoke a working English appeared and through his kind assistance I arranged to have a two horse carriage call for us next morning so that we might visit the city and surroundings with some degree of comfort,—and we felt much relieved and grateful for this timely visitor. We were ready for a night's rest, and after making the plain rattan settees as comfortable as possible with our blankets and pillows, and seeing that all the doors and windows were secure, with a dim lamp in the adjoining room we lay down to sleep. All was still as a mute and we slept soundly until the rays of the sun lighted up our apartments. We relished an early breakfast and then anxiously awaited the promised carriage, which true to the traditions of the country was one-half hour later than the appointed time, but as we had made allowance for this oriental habit by ordering it one-half hour in advance of the time for starting we were not disappointed, but started on time. It was a heavy old carriage that had long been in service and no American city would tolerate it, for the outer and inner appearances were decidedly against it; but as it had springs and was much more comfortable than the cart of the preceding day we tried to enjoy it.

Whilst the great majority of the pilgrims were of middle age and even older most of them walked rapidly and showed no signs of fatigue, for no doubt their step was quickened by the thrill of enthusiasm that the goal was soon to be reached. It is true that some of the aged and infirm dragged themselves along slowly, but the vast majority appeared to be in splendid physical condition and their spirit was not lagging.

The numbers increased as we drove down the main street and approached the great temple. On either side were seated the saints or devotees who appealed to the passer-by for alms, and a small cup of rice or even as little as a tablespoonful was appreciated, for most of the pilgrims were poor themselves and could give but little. However there was a special incentive in addition to the inborn feeling of charity, for giving would secure a blessing, whilst withholding might involve a curse.

Sir William W. Hunter, that eminent authority on the history of India, has given us the following valuable graphic account of these pilgrimages to the sacred shrine at Puri: "The name of Jagannath still draws the faithful from a hundred provinces of India to the Puri sands. This longing after shrines forms a very important feature in the national character of the Hindus. Day and night throughout every month of the year, troops of devotees arrive at Puri, and for three hundred miles along the great Orissa road every village has its encampment. The party consists of from twenty to three hundred persons.

"At the time of the great festivals these bands follow so close as to touch each other; and a continuous train of pilgrims, many miles long, may often be seen on the Puri highroad. They march in orderly procession, each party under its spiritual leader. At least five-sixths, and often nine-tenths of them are females. Now a straggling band of slender, diminutive women, clothed in white muslin, and limping sadly along, announces a pilgrim company from Lower Bengal; then a joyous retinue with flowing garments of bright red or blue, trudging stoutly forward, their noses pierced with elaborate rings, their faces freely tattooed, and their hands encumbered with bundles of very dirty cloth, proclaims the stalwart female peasantry of Northern Hindustan. Ninety-five out of one hundred are on foot. Mixed with the throng are devotees of various sorts, some covered with ashes, some almost naked, some with matted, yellow stained hair, and almost all with their foreheads streaked with red or white, or strings of beads round their necks, and a stout staff in their hands.

"Every now and then, covered wagons, drawn by the high-humped bullocks of Upper India, or by the smaller breed of Bengal, according to the nationality of the owner, creak past on their wooden wheels. Those from the Northern provinces still bear traces of the licentious Mussulman rule, by being jealously shut up. The Bengali husband, on the other hand, keeps his women good tempered, and renders pilgrimage pleasant, by piercing holes in the wagon-hood, through which dark female eyes constantly peep out. Then a lady in coloured trousers, from some village near Delhi, ambles past on a tiny pony, her husband submissively walking by her side, and a female domestic, with a hamper of Ganges water and a bundle of dirty clothes, bringing up the rear. Next a great train of palankeens, carrying a Calcutta banker and his ladies, sweeps past. I met one consisting of forty palankeens, with three hundred and twenty bearers and about fifty luggage carriers whose monotonous chant made itself heard far off in the silent night.

"But the greatest spectacle is a north country raja with his caravan of elephants, camels, led horses, and swordsmen, looking resigned and very helpless in his sedan of state, followed by all the indescribable confusion, dirt, and noise of Indian royalty."

The pilgrims gazed with curiosity upon the many strange objects along the street, but they hastened on to the temple which is surrounded by a high wall and penetrated on each side by a guarded entrance through which streams of people and animals were passing from morning until night. The vast majority entered by the main and nearest gateway as the pilgrims approach the temple, and great crowds were congregated there to see the distinguished devotees or Saddhus which had their temporary quarters at this most conspicuous and favourable place for attracting the attention of every Hindu, for they were dependent upon the alms of the people. There they sat with that indescribable, inane expression—one which we can never forget; their faces whitened by the holy ashes rubbed over every bare spot of their body and even the long dishevelled hair that fell over their shoulders and breast. They wore but little clothing, scarcely as much as the law demands and not as much as decency requires for men who appear in public places.

Once some of these devotees arrogated to themselves such extravagant sanctity that the extremists denied that there was any obligation for them to wear any clothing whatever, as did one party of the ancient Jains, and they went about unadorned in nature's garb, as the primitive child of nature without a shred of covering. Even as late as the annual festival of 1887–1888 at Allahabad, on one of the chief days four hundred naked ascetics went in procession to the river for ablutions, and thousands of men and women stood by in admiration, and some of the overzealous superstitious women bowed and prostrated themselves in reverence before this shameful and disgusting spectacle of religious fanaticism gone mad. The government officials however were more critical in their discriminations, for they saw the fictitious character of the preposterous claims of these religious mendicants as to supermundane sanctity, and they prohibited similar exhibitions of public indecent exposures, although the clout, called a girdle, is at times so small as to be a disgrace to Hinduism.

The great temple and one hundred smaller ones within the sacred enclosure are surrounded by a quadrangular wall twenty-two feet high and about six hundred and fifty feet on either side, each one pierced by a large gateway. The main entrance faces the east, and is called the Lion gate from the colossal stone lions crouching on either side as if guarding it against all intrusion. Directly in front stands the monolithic pillar noted for its age and beautiful carvings at the base. With the death of the last ruler of the Lion line of monarchs the worship of Siva became supplanted by that of Vishnu, and the present temple was built within fifty years from the rise of the new monarchy in 1324, and dedicated to the god Juggernaut who is one of the incarnations of Vishnu. The temple has an endowment that provides an annual income of about $150,-000 and an equal amount is supposed to be derived from all the other sources, for in addition to the modest contribution of the overzealous pilgrims the rich give large sums in hope of special merit.

In the midst of the numerous smaller temples, rises to the height of nearly two hundred feet the conspicuous conical pagoda, overtowering all the other buildings and surmounted by the mystic wheel and flag of Vishnu.

We are indebted to Dr. Mitra, a Hindu, for the following reliable information regarding the holy precincts into which Hindus alone are admitted: "Within the enclosure or compound, and to the right of the flight of steps leading up to the great temple are the buildings for the sale of the sacred food (Mahaprasad) and beyond the large kitchen where the food is prepared. Another inner wall encloses the temple and other buildings, including the famous Buddhist bo-tree and which is supposed to possess marvellous virtues, for the Kapila Sanhita says: 'Whoever stands under the shadow of this tree immediately clears himself from sin of killing Brahmans. Of him who walks round the tree and then worships it, Hari remits all the sins committed in the course of one hundred generations.' Close by is an open pillared choultry or hall of salvation, where pundits daily assemble to expound the Shastras. There are in addition about fifty small shrines of gods and goddesses, as different incarnations from Vishnu, Lakshmi, Siva, Hanuman, Ganesa, etc.

"The great temple includes four distinct buildings opening one into the other. In the first and opposite the Lion gate the food prepared by the temple cooks is presented before the idol, after which it is sold as holy. The next is the dancing hall for the musicians and the dancing girls to amuse the god. Beyond is the audience chamber where the pilgrims are allowed to look through the door into the shrine beyond and see the god. A bar of sandal wood prevents entrance, but persons paying largely are allowed to cross the bar and enter the shrine. Those having special permits, which cost from 500 rupees to 5,000, enter by the sacred gate, and have the right of entering the sanctum or holy place. The sanctum is so dark that without the aid of a lamp nothing is visible."

No doubt this adds to the mystery and the "priests of the temple persuade the pilgrims that it is on account of their sins that they cannot see the divinity. When they remain in the sanctum for a little time sin is destroyed by devotion and the divinity becomes visible." However it is owing to the fact that they have suddenly entered from the glaring sun and time is necessary for the dilated pupils to expand.

The three sacred images are made of the close grained Nim wood and their preservation during the centuries is owing to the peculiar bitterness that protects it against all insects. The rude images are made of a solid block, and are hideous caricatures of the human figure, without hands or legs. The images of Juggernaut and his brother are each about six feet high and the former is painted black and the latter white. The statue of the sister is but four and one-half feet and the colour is golden. Together they occupy a place on a long platform throughout the year until they are taken out during the car festival season. Each one is provided with an extensive and varied wardrobe and their dress is frequently changed, and these rude images are greatly improved by having the most of their imperfections covered.

The chief place of distinction among all the attendants is that of the sweeper, who strange to say is the raja of Khurda, for this office is hereditary with the royal house of Orissa, although the social position of sweepers elsewhere in India as a class is a low and despised one. However, the great god Juggernaut changes all customs at Puri. There we find what is unique in Hinduism and which is in contradiction to what is taught and practiced throughout the country, namely, the disregard of all caste. The explanation is that Juggernaut makes the place so pure that no low caste nor outcaste can make the place ceremonially impure, and the food placed before the image is rendered so holy that no Brahman can be contaminated by eating it with the low caste, not merely with the respectable Sudra, but with the despised Panchama. There can be no taint although cooks from the lowest castes prepared it in the culinary department, for the goddess Lakshmi superintended its preparation and even tasted it, and hence no mortal need hesitate to eat, and it is sold indiscriminately to all classes and they suffer from no law of caste though they partake of it with the outcastes.

Inasmuch as several thousand at least are connected with the maintenance of this elaborate temple establishment, including priests, cooks, attendants and travelling agents, a large revenue is necessary. But they have great treasures of wealth contributed by rich patrons in addition to the receipts from ordinary pilgrims.

Had not the purposes of Ranjit Singh miscarried, this temple would contain the richest single gem in the world for he bequeathed the famous Kohinoor diamond to the shrine of Juggernaut with the hope of obtaining untold meritorious blessings, though his life was far from blameless and at Lahore we saw the celebrated monument of this once noted maharajah of the Sikhs, commemorating himself as well as his numerous wives and concubines who ascended his funeral pyre and suffered self-immolation. Fortunately this priceless diamond was diverted from its intended mission and it found its way into the English Crown, a far more appropriate and magnificent setting than the hideous image of Juggernaut. In the Tower of London in the midst of other historic treasures it is not only securely guarded, but it may be seen to the best advantage in a well-lighted place and by all men and women irrespective of race, rank or religion, for all are freely admitted regardless of social standing, although the line of exclusion would be drawn against the favoured animals that have the right of way at Puri.

In order that we may the more clearly appreciate the character of the Juggernaut we need to remember his position among the gods. Vishnu as the Preserver is one of the most popular gods in the Hindu Triad and is generally represented as a black being with four arms, for it is common to add a number of extra arms to the deities to symbolize their potency. Of the nine incarnations of Vishnu, Krishna was the eighth, a preeminently popular divinity among the people of India to-day, and one of his manifestations is that of Juggernaut, who has the supreme place in the minds and hearts of many millions. According to the account of some, Puri owes its origin to legendary claims connected with the fatal arrow that killed Krishna and whose bones were allowed to remain for some time exposed under the tree where he fell, until a pious monk discovered them and gave them a worthy resting-place. Later the king Indradhumna, who sought to propitiate Vishnu, was told to make an image and place the bones inside of it, and he would be richly rewarded for his labours, and he secured the architect of the gods to make the image.

Certain legends of their sacred writings state that one of their holy men as a pilgrim had seen "an inimitable image of Vishnu in sapphire" at Puri and he reported it to Indradhumna who hastened thither to pay his devotions to the wonderful image. On his arrival he was greatly disappointed to learn that it had mysteriously disappeared beneath the sandy shore. However he was encouraged by the assurance that if he should offer a great sacrifice other images of equal merit would be given him. He was directed to a floating log of Nim wood, and "a very aged man much afflicted with elephantiasis" finally prevailed upon the king to be permitted to fashion the log into the promised images, and on condition that no one should be permitted to enter nor peep into his room for twenty-one days. That was too much for the raja's patience and especially for his wife's curiosity, and becoming impatient with the delay and unable to withstand the constant jeerings of his wife, he broke into the workshop on the fifteenth day, when he discovered the three rude and unfinished wood images but their divine sculptor had suddenly vanished. The raja bitterly regretted his intrusion and suffered great remorse for he was convinced that the aged man was none other than the god Visvakarma, and hence these rude images are so greatly revered.

It is true that any ordinary sculptor without superhuman aid could have produced superior images and in less time, but the raja's faith was not disturbed by such a trifling fact and he began at once to build a suitable temple, and with the marvellous revelation made in connection with the making of the images, henceforth Puri became a holy place and the most sacred shrine for pilgrimages.

The learned Vishnuite scholar, Dr. Mitra, who made a special study of the temple, believes that the car festival of Juggernaut is a relic of a Buddhist procession. Undoubtedly Puri owes much of its religious sanctity to its earlier association with Buddhism, for it was once one of its chief centres, and according to a legend a magnificent temple was erected here by a king in which to place the revered tooth that had been rescued from the funeral pyre of Buddha by one of his devoted followers, and from that circumstance the city was called Dantapura, "the city of the tooth."

Some centuries later, or about 300 A. D., when the kingdom was threatened by war and the king being anxious for the sacred relic of Buddha that up to this time had been securely treasured in the temple, delivered it to his daughter who concealed it in her hair and hastened with it to the Isle of Ceylon for safe preservation, and where for a long time it has been kept as a most sacred treasure in the richest jewelled casket on earth.

A brief digression to Kandy will not be inappropriate because of the transferrence of the holy relic, inasmuch as for centuries it was not only inseparably connected with the sacred shrine at Puri when Buddhism was the dominant religion in India, but it was the most potent if not the sole object that attracted the countless number of pilgrims because of the untold merit that was in store for all who might gaze upon the priceless relic, for the fabulous stories of its wonder-working power almost rivalled those of Aladdin's lamp. We can easily imagine the wild enthusiasm of the pilgrims at Puri, for we witnessed a wonderful exhibition of Buddhist devotion to that tooth in the temple at Kandy.

It was an unusual occasion and many notable persons from that stronghold of Buddha in Burma had made the pilgrimage, including many women of equal rank. Their coming had been heralded and great preparations had been made and thousands of the Singalese had been attracted from the country and all the available space in the open square about the temple was crowded with an expectant multitude, whose privilege was limited by merely seeing the favoured few who were permitted to enter on the memorable day. They had to content themselves with a look at a facsimile under a glass case in the town museum. Our anxiety was intense for we had been promised admission and we occupied our reserved place for some time before the few dignitaries came and whom we were to follow into the most holy shrine. It was not merely to satisfy a prurient curiosity to look upon the fictitious tooth, but it was the history, devotion, wealth of consecration and the unmeasured influence connected with that object throughout the Far East that appealed to us and stimulated our desire to enter the sanctum sanctorum of Buddhism, and in imagination we had visions of past centuries as the countless millions of pilgrims passed in review.

We experienced a peculiar sensation as we were led through the narrow passageway and then entered the small chambers—a very holy of holies to the Buddhist believer. There was not a sound from the outer world and the stillness was profound, for no one spoke and the prolonged silence became oppressive because of its significant uncertainty. In the centre of this inner sanctuary stood a unique golden ornament, wrought by some skillful designer of the once famous ancient Singalese art. It was conical in form, about thirty inches in height and probably twelve inches in diameter and enclosed the sacred relic, but no key was produced and not one of the priests approached to unlock the treasure. The silence became ominous and we appealed to the most commanding person present, the keeper of the shrine and the master of ceremonies, for our only hope was in him. There he stood like a giant Saul, towering head and shoulders over the priests, wearing a singularly unique uniform and bearing an enormous staff as the symbol of authority. He must win the attending priests to a man, for each one held a key that alone could unlock a particular golden cover and which must be removed in order before the next one could be reached and the tooth finally exposed to view.

The Oriental is never in a hurry and the usual preliminaries were necessary to adjust the amount to be paid for the rare privilege accorded us, and then all smiled approval and one after another advanced to the altar and with key in hand slowly unlocked the outer covering. The enthusiasm increased as each cover was removed, for they improved in quality, and the two inner ones were of solid gold, and closely studded with the costliest precious stones,—emeralds, rubies and diamonds. There was a breathless suspense when the last golden conical cover was lifted and we gazed intently upon the small piece of ivory, standing upright from the base of a golden receptacle, with a narrow rim and which may have been suggestive of the lotus, but not resembling it. I mention this in detail for whilst the tooth in the museum is a facsimile it is held in a horizontal position by a wire fastened in the lotus, but the original rises from the bottom of the small golden vessel and stands in a vertical position.

The pictures that I have seen have evidently been made from the copy in the museum, for I saw the original in a clear light and scrutinized it carefully and could not be mistaken. I am also persuaded that it is not a genuine tooth from Buddha for it is much too large, and civilized men have not been found with a tooth of that size and shape. Evidently it was not grown in the jaw of any mortal but taken from some animal and most likely from the hippopotamus.

Returning to the Juggernaut car procession at Puri it is important to correct a very common erroneous impression, and which we hear frequently repeated respecting the alleged self-immolation as a prominent feature of the festival and which is said to be encouraged by the priests. Inasmuch as the god Juggernaut is of another form of Vishnu who was not only the Preserver of men but one of the gentlest of all the gods, it is an unauthorized misrepresentation to characterize Juggernaut as the Moloch of India, and that beneath the wheels of his ponderous car the lives of many of his devotees have been crushed out. Had this charge been made against Siva, the Destroyer, or his blood-thirsting wife Kali, then there might have been a semblance of excuse, but there is none for making the god Juggernaut and his car a synonym or figure of speech for the most cruel slaughter of human beings, and intelligent people repeat it with a feeling of shocking abhorrence. The slander is not deliberate but only due to false impression of the old and oft repeated story, for so sacred is the life of an ordinary animal to the god Vishnu, that his followers condemn the sacrifice of the goats that are made to Kali, and how infinitely more abhorrent it would be to sacrifice human beings!

Undoubtedly accidents have occurred during the car procession when as many as 100,000 pilgrims come together, just as lives have been sacrificed by attending automobile races, but the lives lost were accidental and it would be unjust to charge us with religious self-immolation, although at times guilty of culpable neglect. In like manner accidents must at times occur at the car processions at Puri, owing to the vast number, and uncontrolled enthusiasm of several thousand tugging at the ropes to draw the ponderous car, which goes by fits and starts, and no wonder if some deaths at times occur through carelessness or when overcome by weakness or sunstroke. India is a hot country and during the festival season the heat is intense and it would not be strange if the minds of some fanatics would become affected and occasionally a suicide might result, as in our country, but we must not charge it up to the account of Juggernaut as encouraging it. We have an appalling number of suicides, even among the intelligent and well-to-do class. The fact is that Sir William Hunter, who spent many years in India, made a most careful examination of all the available records on the subject since the fourteenth century, and they prove that whilst such suicides rarely occurred they were not inspired by the religion of Juggernaut.

Whilst the pilgrims in their early enthusiasm seek an opportunity to assist in drawing the car, owing to feelings of devotion and the expected merit for such an action, there is a special reserve of several thousand for any emergency, and who are to complete the procession. Many hours are required as well as strength to drag the enormous car which rests upon sixteen heavy wheels of solid wood, seven feet in diameter. The distance to be made is less than a mile but that broad and crowded street through which the procession moves is not a brick or asphalt pavement, and if it were a macadam road the progress would not be so slow and difficult, but it is often through the deep sand into which the wheels sink and it is with the greatest difficulty at times that they are able to move the car.

At such a time the 4,000 men reserved for the purpose pull at the ropes with their united strength. Beset with such difficulties, several days may elapse during the procession to the Garden House at the end of the avenue. But there is too much variety for monotony in the barbaric splendour of the festival, for they strive to give spectacular effect and to captivate the minds of the pilgrims who crowd the great thoroughfare. Many prostrate themselves and with the wildest fanaticism shout the name of their god Juggernaut as they behold the image borne on the car. The priests are the masters of ceremony and they see that the excitement is kept up by the beating of drums and clashing of cymbals. Even the women at times tug at the ropes, and where there are so many old fanatics the wonder is that the deaths are not more frequent.

In former years the sufferings and mortality at Puri were much greater, owing to the utter disregard of the laws of sanitation, the lack of proper food, lodgings, hospitals and medical attendance. These evils have been remedied to some extent at Puri and at places on the roads traversed by the pilgrims, and yet with all the improved conditions, the overcrowding during the festival seasons means much hardship for the poverty stricken class and the mortality is great.

It may be well in passing to correct the extravagant reports respecting the great antiquity of the records contained in the temple. Certain advocates claim that they have old manuscripts that give an unbroken list of the kings of Orissa from the beginning of the Kali age in 3102 B. C. to A. D. 1871, with much detail. These palm leaf archives are treasured in the temple but a critical examination of them by scholars has shown them to be utterly unreliable anterior to 1100 A. D. The temple was built during the latter part of the eleventh century and the early portion of the twelfth. With all the strange history and religious devotion associated with the holy temple at Puri and the image of the god Juggernaut that is housed within the sacred precincts, it is not strange that we should have had an ardent desire to approach the mystic shrine and look upon the effigy of the great Lord of the World who for centuries had wielded such a mighty attractive power over his millions of adherents, who with unfaltering faith are annually drawn from every part of Bengal and from distant quarters of the empire.

With few exceptions we had been freely admitted to the temples throughout the Far East, for the Jains and Mohammedans had certain reservations, and the Parsees not only practice the absolute exclusive act but so construct a wall in front of their temple that you cannot obtain so much as a glance through the portal. We did not anticipate any difficulty at Puri, where caste distinctions are practically ignored, and the very scum of humanity, including the lowest of the Panchama, are admitted, and the poorest elbow their way among the surging crowd, and even bulls, cows and monkeys have the right of way and pass through the gateway without interruption, although moved by no religious motive. Hence as we observed the motley crowd of the animal kingdom entering without any protest from the temple officials, we never imagined that they would make the invidious distinction when we attempted to enter. In fact we took it for granted that we were among the eligibles as we followed the nondescript crowd towards the Lion's gate, for all men, women and beasts had been freely admitted.

There are times, as the traveller has learned from experience, when it is policy to presume upon one's ignorance and take it for granted that you are not debarred, for whilst it inspires you with confidence to gain admission, it disarms the objector who is too much embarrassed to turn out the courteous and well meaning traveller in search of knowledge. However, in this instance I had presumed too much upon the native courtesy and apathy in the local requirements of the observance of their ancient custom, for we did not escape those lynx-eyed masters of the caste system who easily discerned our foreign pedigree, and several of them stopped us when within twenty feet of the portal, for at that distance the presence of a foreigner was supposed to be safe, but nearer would mean pollution.

These sticklers for such religious proprieties have developed a keen scent for discriminating between the clean and the unclean, the elect and the outcaste and the exact distance at which the presence of the latter would cause ceremonial pollution to their exclusive set, and temple set apart for their own benefit, whilst all the rest of the world of humanity must be excluded. I reasoned with them and they listened with all that patience and courtesy that for centuries has characterized the Hindus, but to all my earnest appeals the master of ceremonies answered with that one ominous word: "Impossible!" although he expressed himself as very sorry, but custom had so decreed it. I assured him that we were entitled to enter, for I was not only his brother man, but a high caste Brahman, being a lineal descendant of his Aryan ancestors and that it was an unjust and invidious distinction to admit every native regardless of caste, social distinction or moral character, and even the descendants of the aboriginal Dravidian races were not excluded. This argument had no weight whatever, for keen as the mind of the educated Brahman is for metaphysical speculation, he has little knowledge of history, and hence he could not appreciate my claim to relationship, and I abandoned all hope of entering at the Lion's gate.

I was encouraged by an attendant to go to one of the minor gateways where entrance might be obtained and no questions asked. I rewarded him for the valuable information, and we followed the street around the enclosure that is safeguarded from all profane intrusion of the unclean by a massive wall about twenty feet in height. The first gate that we approached was closed and we hastened to the one on the side opposite the Lion's gate. Fortunately we met the treasurer of the temple at this entrance, a fine looking and well proportioned specimen of humanity—well dressed, and with an unusually large emerald in his ring. He spoke English perfectly and so did the officials and some of the priests about him. He received us most courteously, and among these select Hindus and away from the rabble of pilgrims, we felt encouraged. I presented my card and passport as my credentials and told him of my interest in his country, and that when a boy I had seen pictures of the image of Juggernaut and had come the long distance that we might visit the sacred shrine. He was a man of feeling and susceptibilities and his close attention and sympathetic expression left no suggestions for doubt, for he declared himself as much honoured by our visit and was anxious to favour us in every way possible.

After making due allowance for the oriental custom in offering to share so generously with us, I could scarcely suppress my impatience with the delay of further formalities and asked him to admit us at once. But he reassured us that there was no occasion for haste, for he like all the Hindus was in no hurry even though he saw that we were. And why should he be? For he had not merely a lifetime before him, but millions more in the countless rebirths that he must yet pass through on earth, and what he could not do in this brief life he could complete in the next or succeeding ones, for practically all eternity was before him, and before his earthly careers would come to an end. His religion did not seem to weigh heavily upon him, for he had a genial countenance and by his unusual avoirdupois and dress it was evident that he had never suffered from fasting and had not practiced the self-denial of the ascetic, but belonged to the most prosperous class who thought that life was worth living and enjoying.

It was a warm day, and as my time in India was more limited than his I could scarcely maintain my composure, and the effort made my temperature rise, and I pressed my claim. He had acted his part so naturally that I was astonished when he assured me that he was very sorry but their unchanging custom made it impossible for a foreigner to enter. I reasoned with him but in vain, and in order to convince me of his sincerity he related an incident of a disguised European who obtained entrance by this dishonourable strategy, and that it cost them three hundred rupees, or one hundred dollars, to purify the temple. He appealed to the officials standing by and they all corroborated his statement.

Whilst I could not dispute the fact, I protested that whilst I did not know the polluting character of the particular European in question I was confident that in my case it certainly would not cost them one-half of the three hundred rupees to purify it from any possible ceremonial defilement, for I had been in the greatest temples on earth and in not a single instance was any defilement entailed, nor was subsequent purification necessary. They were too courteous and adroit to make the matter so personal, and that I might be right, but they could not incur the responsibility.

Then I pressed the question: "Is this the only reason that you cannot allow us to enter?" They frankly assured me that it was, not suspecting the purpose of my question, for at once I offered the three hundred rupees, and insisted that we be allowed to enter, since the only condition that barred our entrance, according to their own assurance, had been met. They were not prepared for this and they showed their em-

THE GOD JUGGERNAUT AT PURI

barrassment whilst I insisted upon the logical conclusion, but they shook their head.

I tried to reason with them that there was one God and Father of us all, and hence all people were His children and we were brethren, having descended from the same ancient Indo-European stock. I reminded them that America had proved her interest in the welfare of their people by doing so much for them, pouring millions of dollars every year into their country, as well as ship-loads of provision during famine and the scourge of the bubonic plague; that we had sent them many hundreds of noble men and women to labour for their social and moral as well as religious betterment; that we had given them schools and teachers to educate their children and fit them for positions of usefulness; that we had founded and equipped hospitals for healing the sick; even without money and without price when too poor to pay; but led to do all this through the constraining love of Christ. They admitted it although they did not show any of that enthusiasm that a sense of gratitude would inspire.

I reminded them that we made no such invidious distinctions, for in all India there was not a Christian church that would exclude any of them, and that if they should come to America we would welcome them into our most magnificent churches and give them a choice seat. Then the treasurer of the temple conferred with the priests and my hopes revived, but imagine my amazement when he assured us that he would like to grant our request, but should I enter, the gods would kill me. I replied: "You do not mean to say that those gods would kill me if I should appear before them?" I was assured that it would be fatal and as proof, though not convincing, they stated that a European who entered the temple some years ago fell dead when he approached the shrine. Of course I wanted to convince them that their wooden gods were harmless and that an American would be perfectly safe in their presence, and I wanted to make the test as I moved towards the gateway. But they crossed my path and protested so decisively that I abandoned all further attempt to enter.

Fortunately there are many excellent copies of these images. I secured a good sized one of the famous Juggernaut and which is authoritatively stated to be a faithful reproduction of the original. This in a measure compensates for our disappointment, for I can see and study it in a clear light and which is denied to those who gain entrance to the shrine of the temple and stand before the sacred image that can be only faintly discerned owing to the dim light.

There was another compensation in our disappointment, for as we reflected we received vivid impressions of the thrilling experience that the Apostle Paul encountered on that memorable day in Jerusalem when the devout and fanatical Jews suspected him of having taken Trophimus of Ephesus with him into the temple, thereby defiling it by the presence of a Gentile or foreigner, and they became an infuriated mob as they rushed upon him and dragged him out of the sanctuary and would have torn him limb from limb had not the vigilant Roman guard rushed into the outer court and rescued him. We had realistic visions of all this as we stood face to face with these overscrupulous custodians of the holy temple of Juggernaut at Puri and who would not allow us to cross the threshold.

III

THE ASCETICS AND RELIGIOUS MENDICANTS

WHILE other nations and religions have had their ascetics, in no land has asceticism flourished to such a baneful extent as in India, and no religion has produced such a countless host of devotees as Hinduism. The evil has spread like an indigenous contagion and found many recruits among the Mohammedans who imitate the dominant religion in not a few things. The Moslem ascetics are distinguished from the similar class of Hindus by being designated as fakirs. Deussen in his "Philosophy of the Upanishads" says: "It is a tribute to the high metaphysical capacity of the Indian people that the phenomenon of asceticism made its appearance among them earlier and occupied a larger place than among any other known people." He refers to "Rig Veda," page 136, which "portrays the inspired *Muni* as with long hair, in dirty yellow robes, and girt only with the wind he roams on the desert paths." Since then it has found a favourable soil for its development into many most extravagant forms, and if we include all the religious mendicants in this class of unproductive humanity the aggregate numbers at least five millions.

Every observing traveller must become interested in the study of this unique and ubiquitous class, for we find them everywhere on the frequented roads or sitting in groups in some secluded place about the villages and sacred places, and especially in front of prominent temples where the multitude pass, for they do not earn a rupee and are dependent upon the charity of an indulgent people. They are easily recognized by their conventional appearance and many by their distinctive attire or lack of dress. Their ranks are filled by men and women who come from the various social strata, for they are not such sticklers about the rules of caste, but high and low, and even the outcaste who join the ascetics may live or exist together, although each one eats exclusively from his own bowl. They have abandoned all their duties to the family, society and state and become wanderers, eking out a miserable and worthless existence. They suffer from exposure and exist upon the scanty food doled out to them, but they give nothing in return for their self-pauperized and unproductive life of a social parasite.

Many of the Saddhus or holy men excite our deepest sympathy because of the severe austerities that they practice. Some of the devices with which they afflict themselves are so ingeneous that they seem to crave whatever may make their life most miserable and painful. There has been some mitigation of the worst features of torture during recent years, for the British government placed a limit to certain barbaric practices of their revolting fanaticism. No doubt many of these pitiable deluded mortals are sincere in acting this morbid drama of life, but the vast majority may be safely classed as immoral parasites and who are productive of a brood of evils.

The self-imposed tortures that some have endured almost challenge our belief, for there have been some who stood for years, and never once slept, and the tortures of such an existence are hardly conceivable.

Whatever hallucination had mastered the mind, there was the element of will power in its supreme control, for in spite of the rope suspended from the tree to arrest the body of the Saddhu, if dropping forward when momentarily overcome by being deprived of sleep for years, at once he would recover himself and continue sustaining the worn-out body that must have been terribly exhausted from prolonged fatigue. Did the tyranny of religion ever surpass this? A saint run mad is mad indeed.

Huxley says that "No more thorough mortification of the flesh has ever been attempted than that achieved by the Indian ascetic anchorite; no later monachism has so nearly succeeded in reducing the human mind to that condition of impassive quasi-somnambulism, which, but for its acknowledged holiness, might run the risk of being confounded with idiocy. Their aim is to abandon or suppress every natural trait in man until all that remained of a man was the impassive, extenuated, mendicant monk, self-hypnotized into cataleptic trances, which the deluded mystic took for foretastes of the final union with Brahma."

According to the rules of particular cults the dress was to be as limited as the food for whilst certain ones were accorded the distinction of wearing the conspicuous saffron coloured robe others were limited to the ordinary loin cloth, but another sect had risen to such an ethereal plane that they discarded all material vestments and they went forth as primitive man in Eden, clothed in space. The observer in India sees many whose only adornment consists of the necklace of rosaries made from the sacred tulasi or from the lotus seed. The long matted black hair falls over their shoulders and breast and affords them frequently more covering than the clout for a girdle.

These so-called saints or Saddhus constitute a large and interesting class for psychological study in connection with comparative religions. Some of the noted Saddhus of India were at Puri and as they sat just outside the wall that surrounds the temple and near the main entrance they attracted the attention of all and we studied them with much interest.

They were willing to be photographed and like ordinary mortals they wanted to appear to the best advantage in their pictures by assuming a proper pose. One even stood erect, drew back his shoulders and arranged his long beard so that the picture might do him justice, for with all his repression and elimination of self it was evident that the inherent vanity remained and it may require a number of future reincarnations to eradicate it. Others appeared to be completely absorbed in their dreamy state and with averted faces showed their stolid indifference to the pride of being immortalized by means of a kodak, although they picked up the coins that I placed by their side in the vain hope of attracting their attention for a moment. These were supposed to have so completely overcome the flesh and the devil that even vanity of self had been suppressed. Their abundant locks of matted hair partly concealed the ashen face of the usual weird and ghostly appearance. The peculiar inane expression is said to be due to their excessive use of opium and hemp, and, I may add, to their lack of vigorous thinking. No one would ever mistake that face as the product of profound intellectual exercise, for it is the expression of mental imbecility, and not of hard and sustained thinking.

There is nothing attractive about the situation of Puri for the low, desolate, sandy coast at this place is monotonous except during certain seasons when the rolling waves make the approach of boats impossible. Even the unprotected roadstead which is some distance from the shore is only accessible for boats during the favourable months owing to the violent surf between March and September. Many of the pilgrims were bathing and on the shore were a number of fires that were reducing to ashes the bodies of those who had made the pilgrimage but who were destined not to return, and their ashes were thrown into the bay as has been the fate of thousands.

The sand along the street of the town to the beach was so deep that we were finally obliged to leave the carriage and walk, but we saw many unique sights as we passed a number of devotees who seemed bent upon surpassing all others in their efforts to afflict their body as much as possible, although they believed it to be a highly meritorious act and which would certainly greatly lessen if not wholly remove the countless reincarnations charged up to their account. I can only describe a few of the many, and I recall one who made desperate efforts to make himself as uncomfortable as possible by lying on the ground and supporting two heavy weights, the one upon his chest and the other upon his abdomen. It made breathing difficult and deep breathing impossible, and he appeared sickly looking and panting for a good breath. It was not conducive to physical development, but we must remember that he was not engaged in this uncomfortable exercise for the sake of his health, but sustained in his martyrdom by a very different motive. He was perfectly willing to become immortalized by being photographed, and I was instinctively seized by an impulse to reciprocate his favour by removing the oppressive burdens from his chest and abdomen so that he might rise and stand upon his feet like a man ; but against this he sincerely protested and we passed on and saw him later in the same position.

Another Saddhu, who attracted unusual attention because of his personality and the nature of his self-inflicted suffering, occupied a most conspicuous place by the main thoroughfare so that he might be seen of men, for every pilgrim to Puri had to pass his way. He sat tailor-like, squatting upon the bare ground between four fires with the burning sun overhead and which was credited as the fifth to his merit account. He sat motionless in this position which he had occupied with brief intervals for four months. He was to receive great merit in accordance with a teaching in the Sacred Books. The scorching rays of the Indian sun combined to make the hottest of the five fires for he had no protection, though we found it necessary to use the sunshade and pith helmet as a safeguard against sunstroke. He had remarkable self-control and an interesting face of the conventional ascetic type.

Two others that we witnessed had reached the climax of self-torture, and so self-conscious were they of the fact that they acted as if they were on public exhibition. They were quite naked, with the exception of a small rag, and were lying upon a bed of iron spikes, the one bed being suspended by ropes from the branch of a tree and which he used as a swing for diversion and apparently for our entertainment, inasmuch as he ceased the swinging immediately after we left him, for the motion must have increased his discomfort. The other bed of iron spikes upon which the naked Saddhu lay rested upon four wheels and the man was stretched out full length upon these iron points that were several inches in length.

They found no fault with our presence and encouraged us to photograph them, doubtless with the expectancy of a gratuity. They paid little attention to our interest and curiosity in examining the spikes to test their material and to see how sharp the points were, and the ascetic even turned over so that I could see whether they had anywhere penetrated the skin of his back. In fact the skin of his back was almost as callous as the hide of a rhino, and the blunt nails could not penetrate it. It would have been very different with ordinary mortals untrained for this torture, and yet it must have been a most uncomfortable bed even for this East Indian saint, inured to hardship, and he did not select it for its comfort but for its excessive merit, and which was greatly multiplied by being practiced in the holy city of Puri.

The supreme motive for practicing these grievous austerities is the hope of thereby cutting short the ceaseless round of reincarnations, and the greater the severity of the ascetic the greater is the merit; far better endure even the most excruciating pain for a single lifetime, if necessary, than to run the terrible gauntlet of the multiplied woes that are incident upon an unlimited number of rebirths with their successive hells of limited duration.

Inasmuch as this institution of asceticism has the sanction and encouragement of religion it is not strange that India has been such a fertile field, and numbers as many as five millions in its vast army of worse than worthless unproductive religious mendicants. They are the human parasites that prey upon the body politic for their support. They contribute nothing to the nation, but exert an immoral and degrading influence upon the people, and if all were to follow their pernicious example the race would become extinct. They affect utter indifference to everything that has contributed to the elevation of mankind and which have been the chief elements in the civilization of the greatest nations on earth.

The Saddhu, as the Hindu ascetic has been designated, has but little of this world's goods to encumber him, for his indispensable outfit is generally limited to the begging bowl, made from the cocoanut, gourd, wood or clay, for the brass bowl is not so common among them. They wear the rosary or string of beads about the neck and which they count when wishing to repeat a given number of times the name of their favourite deity. A water pot and staff complete the assets of the majority of these beggars.

The Mohammedan fakirs are also numbered among the ascetics of India, for in this respect as well as touching the principle of caste they have been influenced by their Hindu neighbours and on a certain occasion we saw one of those who was literally weighed down with a load of chains, but as the conditions were unfavourable for a good picture I have introduced one made from a photograph that was taken of a fakir in Bombay in 1894. He had gradually added one chain after another until he became so weighed down with this self-imposed burden that he was unable to walk, and the railroad officials refused to admit him into the passenger coach with the unpaid additional freight of eight hundred and fifty pounds of heavy iron chains that had been attached to an iron ring that had been forged about his neck, and which rested heavily about his shoulders. He was on his way to Mecca and was regarded as a very saintly man by the Mohammedans who carried him into the freight car, after having been weighed; he was then shipped on his religious pilgrimage as so much live freight.

W. Crook in "Popular Religious Folk-Lore of North India" records a most remarkable story of one of the past saints, a Baba Farrid, who for the last thirty years of his life took no material food into his body, but "supported himself by merely holding to his stomach wooden cakes and fruits whenever he felt hungry." As far as we know that was a most unique example of carrying the law of suggestion to the limit and in attaining practical results for the living. Christian Science has not yet attained to such marvellous powers of mental assimilations, and cannot hope to surpass it.

It is a standing challenge to Hinduism to furnish some tangible form of proof that their theory of Maya (that all is delusion) is based upon a truth that has been proved by an unmistakable ocular demonstration. It is a very simple process to the Hindu mind to solve the mystery by a subtle metaphysical formula, but unfortunately it is so theoretical that all practical tests prove that it utterly fails as a working hypothesis. Our senses assert themselves and the gnawings of hunger, the agony of pain and suffering, and the bitter disappointments and sorrows of life, with its manifold ills, are so real and universal that no mere verbal panacea, however ethereal, can so hypnotize our senses and reason into believing that there is no reality corresponding with these, but that all is Maya—illusion.

As an illustration, I am reminded of the ancient Egyptians who were greatly concerned for the preservation of the body after death, and in order that they might not suffer from hunger and thirst in the next world, they took extra precaution by placing food and drink in the tomb with the mummified body. In addition to this expedient, and in order to provide against all possible failure of the necessary supply, they resorted to the unique device of substituting the law of suggestion for the genuine articles. Hence they placed with the deceased mere outward forms or representations of the necessary provision, and instead of the roast goose, bread, water, beer and other numerous articles of diet which were liable to perish, they substituted the mere symbols of the elaborate menu, but made from the enduring material of alabaster or wood, whilst the accompanying wooden statuettes, or models of servants and cooking utensils, would serve to provide the meals that were supposed to have the magical effect of satisfying any hunger that might possibly afflict the deceased. Whilst such substitutes might answer for all the practical needs of the departed in transit to the next world, the living have such real wants that the hunger can only be satisfied by assimilating substantial food.

But what is the sociological effect of the vast horde of religious mendicants—many of them moral degenerates—who swarm over the country of India like a plague of locusts? They have abandoned the highest ideals of life, turned beggar, and have become indifferent to all personal opportunities and responsibilities of service. The unmitigated evil is great in a country like India with its vast and underfed population, where there is so much of human misery, suffering and want; and such a lack of food produced on the native soil that no less than forty millions do not have their hunger satisfied, although there is sufficient uncultivated arable land that might easily be made sufficiently productive to feed many millions if these worthless parasites of able-bodied men and women would devote their energies to the cultivation of the soil. Then they would be able to feed others, as well as relieve the poor of the necessity of feeding them from their own scanty store. As it is they are productive of evil only and are sufficient to bankrupt a people.

Whilst we condemn them unsparingly we must not forget that even Christians at times were deluded into believing that God is pleased to see us suffering pain and misery, and that the life of the anchorite practicing the severest austerities was particularly pleasing to Him. Along the valley of the Nile, mummies were cast out of the ancient tombs and their places filled by useless living bodies of so-called saints. In the famous Monastery of Troitsa, the Loretto of Russia, but a few hours by rail from Moscow, we visited the dark and damp subterranean cells in which deluded Christian monks once immured themselves for years or until death released them of their melancholy existence. Such subjects of mental aberrations were not only sanctioned by the Church but they received special commendation and honours from the ecclesiastical authorities.

It was a humane Russian Czar who was wise and

Christian enough to suppress this horrible delusion that had been fostered by the Greek Catholic Church and he emptied the cells, liberated the fanatics, and henceforth forbade the inhuman practice. Should any civilized government to-day treat any of its prison criminals with such barbaric cruelty it would be denounced in unmeasured terms by the leading nations on earth. Hence we must not be too severe with the ascetics of India, for even Christians have at times copied their pilgrimages, and sat in sackcloth and ashes, and the stylites and flagellants courted as much suffering as they could inflict upon themselves, whilst labouring under the gross hallucination that Christ and their heavenly Father were greatly pleased with such a bloody human sacrifice. Many of these unchristian abuses were but the recrudescence of Eastern paganism under the name and guise of Christian sanction.

Joly in his "Psychology of the Saints" gives a remarkable statement of St. Theresa: "Suffering alone can make life tolerable to me. My greatest desire is to suffer. Often and often I cry out to God from the depths of my soul; either to suffer or to die is all that I ask of Thee." That state of mind was due to a morbid emotional nature stimulated by an utter misconception of the spirit and teaching of Christ, and she became mastered by the habit of her terrible infatuation. It was the mental confusion of her thoughts for those of a tender and all loving Saviour.

In connection with the ascetics of India the mind naturally reverts to the extravagant stories heard respecting the wonderful deeds of the yogis, for they belong to a special class of the devotees and receive distinguished esteem from the common people. Those who have become adepts in their art are supposed to have passed beyond the limitations and ills to which ordinary mortals are heir, and I had heard startling stories concerning their marvellous wonder-working powers.

During my college days I became interested in the clever tricks of magicians, and Hermann and Kellar deserved much credit for the entertainment that they gave to their large audiences. We had witnessed the surprising skill displayed by some of the magicians of Egypt that recalled the marvels of their famous ancestors in that land of wonders, and hence we were prepared to pass judgment upon what we were to see in India. We had been assured by those who repeated the stereotyped stories that the yogis of India wrought marvels that easily eclipsed the traditional wonders of the magicians of ancient Egypt. As examples, the yogi would sit for hours high in the air, with no other support than that of an iron rod which he held by his right hand. He would plant a mango seed and cause it to sprout and grow into a plant several feet high in your presence, and you had to wait but a few minutes to behold this phenomenon enacted before your eyes so that there could be no gainsaying it.

But this did not exhaust the list of wonders, for a real Indian yogi, with flesh and blood, but seemingly hovering between the terrestrial and supermundane world, would gaze intently into space and then suddenly throwing a long rope into the air would climb up the same rope with the swiftness of the wind and like it disappear out of sight, whilst the startled beholders looked in vain for his return.

Such examples increased the mystery and were regarded as sufficient to confound the most skeptical, but the limit had not been reached. The most staggering demonstration had been reserved for the last, and as a climax a celebrated yogi would allow himself to be decently buried in the earth for a number of days and even weeks, and at the appointed time for the grave to be opened, the dead yogi would come to life again with a smile.

No wonder that with such inexplicable mysteries my college enthusiasm for clever tricks revived and I determined to make as thorough an investigation as possible as to the merits and reliability of these extravagant stories. In every town and city I made diligent inquiry from every available and reliable source, and with an inquiring mind ever alert for the unexpected to appear, especially in India, that land of surprises. In short we saw the most clever tricks, for such they were, throughout Ceylon and India, but all of which could be easily duplicated, and have been excelled by our noted magicians at home. I speak with confidence, for in every instance I paid the so-called magician or yogi in Ceylon and India to show me in private the secret of all the tricks that he had performed in public. Of course the novelty and interest disappeared when mystery was revealed just as conundrums do not sustain our wonder when once we know them.

I want to assure the reader that the often-repeated story about making the mango tree or plant grow in your presence from a seed, and while you wait, is an utter contradiction of terms, for at its best it is rather a bungling trick, and these Indian performers would be driven out of the business if they were compelled to compete with some of the noted prestidigitators of our own country. Of course no man ever sat unsupported in the air, but the fanaticism and superstition of the ignorant crowd never presumed to investigate the claim or they would have discovered that the fakir was supported by a concealed ring that extended from the iron rod that he grasped. The story of climbing up the rope thrown into the air is too absurd to be repeated in seriousness, although some have been so unscrupulous as to refer to it as eye-witnesses. There have been standing offers of one thousand rupees for many years, by well-known men of India, and which have been offered to any man who would furnish reliable evidence that such a phenomenon was ever witnessed in that country.

In that poverty-stricken land where there are so many millions who need money, and who would walk across the empire for less than one hundred rupees, no doubt the challenge would have been accepted and the information would have been furnished long ago had there been a scintilla of truth in the story itself. It was a mere oriental fabrication and the nearest approach to the verification of the genuineness was furnished by an ignorant ascetic who had heard that his grandfather was supposed to have heard such a story told him when a boy, that a yogi living in an unfrequented part of India had made such an unverified claim. No court in any civilized country would accept such testimony as valid.

Unquestionably some of the yogis through many years of most rigid discipline have done strange things with themselves and which would have been impossible and fatal for the uninitiated. Some of the strange stories told about their suspended animation of life for a number of days have not been fully nor satisfactorily explained, for after making due allowance for all extravagant speech there is still a residuum of mystery in the strange power of certain yogis that we cannot account for. However this is not offered as an apology for the very general and uncritical statements that are so frequently heard, and which even appear in the journals without any interrogation mark as to their credibility.

As an illustration of such exaggeration, Bishop Thoburn quotes the following from the *New York Mail and Express:* "Much has been written of late about the capacity of frogs to live for years in rocks. Of much greater interest, however, is the fact that human beings can also lie for months buried under ground and then be brought to life again. Such phenomenal beings are not of course found on this continent or in Europe, but in India, that veritable realm of wonder working. A German writer has recently written a very interesting essay on the capacity often proved of Indian fakirs to let themselves be buried for longer or shorter periods, and to come to life again smiling after the ordeal."

Whilst the noted bishop missionary of many years in India had heard similar stories he could never learn of a well-attested case, for they were always confused rumours about some yogis hundreds of miles away and of whom he could obtain no reliable evidence, although he made special efforts for years.

The most notable instance of the suspended powers of animation heard of in India was that of Hari Das, who according to the statement of Dr. Honiberger "threw himself into a hypnotic or unconscious state and was wrapped in the linen on which he was sitting; the seal of Ranjit Singh was stamped thereon, and it was placed in a chest on which the maharajah put a strong lock. The chest was buried in a garden outside the city, belonging to the minister; barley was sown on the ground, and the space enclosed with a wall and surrounded by sentinels. On the fortieth day, which was the time fixed for his exhumation, a great number of persons from the durbar, with General Ventura and several Englishmen of the vicinity, went to the enclosure. The chest was brought up and opened, and the fakir was found in the same position as they had left him, cold and stiff. They endeavoured to bring him to life by applying warmth to the head, injecting air into his ears and mouth and rubbing the whole of his body to promote circulation. On the day of his burial he ordered his beard to be shaved, and at his exhumation his chin was as smooth as on the day of his interment, thus furnishing complete proof of the powers of vitality having been suspended during that period."

Whilst the integrity of Dr. Honiberger is not called in question, we must remember that he is not giving a statement from his personal observation for he was not an eye-witness, but received his information later from an officer of Ranjit Singh, and for certain detail we must make due allowance for the universal tendency to hyperbole among the Orientals and the lack of critical investigation. Bishop Thoburn in referring to the above admits that "there is nothing incredible in the statement that the fakir threw himself into a state which resembled death, for that can be done by many men, both in India and elsewhere. Nor is it incredible that he was buried in the presence of Ranjit Singh.

There however the admission must cease. It is perfectly credible that the body was removed from the grave almost immediately after the guard had been set, for it is also stated that the man Hari Das had a bad reputation and that his moral character was of the worst description."

We may well be skeptical about receiving the story of this forty days' burial at its full face value because of the general reputation of this yogi as being nothing but a disreputable juggler. Our confidence is also shaken by the fact that the English residents of the province in which it occurred questioned its genuineness, and that the yogi refused to repeat the experiment under similar conditions, but with English safeguards against any possible fraud or collusion with friends to relieve the body. The generous reward offered was refused because they insisted that no opportunity should be given for fraud by the intervention of the friends of the so-called yogi. Moreover this problematical case took place some seventy years ago and since then many intelligent men have made the most careful search throughout the entire country of India for a similar authenticated example, but not one has been found, and hence even in the far-off land of wonders such delusions and marvels are not so common as the newspaper referred to would have its readers believe.

IV

BENARES

THIS holy city is the Mecca and Jerusalem of Hinduism, and hundreds of thousands of pilgrims, not only of the common herd, but many distinguished Hindus are included among the countless hosts who through the centuries make the pilgrimage to this far famed city of their holy religion. Never has the most devout sandalled Moslem made his pilgrimage to Mecca with profounder faith and greater religious expectations than those that stir the soul of the barefoot Hindu as for days and weeks he trudges along beneath a burning sun, but sustained by an unfaltering faith or intense desire to find the goal of his quest at Benares.

Continued streams of humanity from all parts of India converge here, for it is the centre and the stronghold of Hinduism. The most divergent forms of Hinduism pour into this common centre, although not losing their distinctive character whilst commingling with this heterogeneous influx of diverse religions; for whilst they elbow their way through crowds of pilgrims with whom they have nothing in common, and pay their devotions at the same sacred shrines, and march down the same ghats and bathe indiscriminately in the Ganges, they maintain their peculiar belief and customs, and return to distant homes to continue as their fathers lived generations before.

Because of the special religious merit in store for all

who come to Benares, and inasmuch as the poor pilgrims have no monopoly of religion, it is not strange that many of the rich and distinguished men of India, including princes and rajas, as well as wealthy bankers have made this holy city their favourite retreat during certain seasons of the year for religious retirement from world or business affairs. Their commodious and attractive houses amid shrubs and shade trees are suggestive of their princely estates and that their life is worth living, but there is a tremendous chasm between these favoured lords and the multitudes that we see on the streets in the bazaars and at the bathing ghats, and the contrast is appalling.

However, a pilgrimage to this holy city is so meritorious that millions covet this devoutly wished for privilege of visiting the sacred shrines and bathing in the sin-washing-clean waters of the Ganges, and are so mastered by this thought that I do not presume that they entertain any thought of envy as they pass these princely homes of wealth and comfort, for it is the deeper wants of the soul that they seek to have satisfied. Inasmuch as the god Siva who presides here is supposed to take special delight in human suffering, as some others once thought of their God, certain devout ones make their coming as miserable as possible by afflicting their famished body as well as their soul; and hence they complete the last miles in the most deplorable manner of measuring their length upon the ground, and with such repeated prostrations as described in the chapter on Puri.

It seems almost incredible that in Benares, a city of 200,000 population, there should be as many as 2,000 temples, besides innumerable shrines. With its one-

THE GHATS AT BENARES

half million of idols it surpasses what the Apostle Paul beheld in Athens where he saw the city full of idols. The manufacturers of idols do a thriving business, for all the pilgrims will carry one home with them at least, and no doubt these makers of idols would as bitterly oppose an interference with their trade as did the Ephesian makers of the image of Diana, should a mighty apostle of Christianity denounce and interfere with their traffic.

We hastened to the river early in the morning, for the Hindus are early risers, and the wonderful spectacle of the bathers in the Ganges attains its climax at an early hour in a country where the extreme heat causes the streets and places of business to be abandoned during the middle of the day, for the scorching rays of the sun would almost blister the bathers at these hours. The city was crowded, and there was the greatest variety of people, scenes and objects of interest. The familiar street scenes were such as confront us in all the cities of India, the weavers, barbers, cobblers and hawkers of articles of food, with a full contingent of beggars, but which became greatly multiplied as we approached the sacred places, for they knew where the multitudes came.

The pilgrims were not attracted by our presence for they came to Benares with a supreme purpose which was ever in their mind as they sought out every temple so as not to pass by any possible merit that the city contained. But the beggars had a different mission for they were professionals, and no foreigner escaped their gaze and plaintive appeal. We observed many of the devoted pilgrims as they sought out the chief shrines and gave their humble offerings and occasionally bestowed a garland of flowers, but which was later sold and resold for the same purpose to as many unsuspecting pilgrims as could be induced to make the same meritorious offering. Some sprinkled the Ganges' water upon the ubiquitous linga and then bought some smaller ones to be treasured at home.

Lest I should give a false impression in speaking of the interest of the scenes witnessed in Benares I would state that it was confined to a study of the objects themselves and the people in connection with them, for the attraction did not consist of any beauty and magnificent splendour, for there was too much of poverty and a decayed civilization. There was such an utter disregard of sanitation among the thronging multitudes through which, in the crowded holy places, we elbowed our way, that few cities are more favourable for a plague than Benares.

The city stands on a slight elevation, crowning the west bank of the Ganges, facing the rising sun, and extends for nearly four miles along this cliff which is crowned with palaces, temples and mosques, and the picturesque view from the boats on the river is unrivalled by any city in India. We reach the river by the ghats or flights of stone steps of gigantic proportions. There are fifty of these ghats that descend to the water's edge and some of them extend far into the river. One of them is said to contain three hundred stone steps, and they have platforms, at certain intervals, occupied by sacred shrines and their attendants. They are marked by the conspicuous mammoth palm leaf umbrella and which looks like a gigantic toadstool.

Here are found the teachers and priests, a sort of

bureau of information for the unsophisticated pilgrim who is making his first pilgrimage and who must be confused by the bewildering conflict of religious claimants, and the babel of voices competing for his patronage; for here also where the vast multitudes congregate, are located the agents for the various gods and who put forth the most extravagant claims for the merit of their special divinity, and some stood half dazed, with the uncertainty of a lottery.

I felt that I was in the midst of pandemonium, and it was a most extraordinary place for the psychological study of the phenomena of men and women carried away with a religious frenzy that lacked all the reason of intellectual ballast. No wonder that many of the poor pilgrims looked dazed, for the rivalry between the agents for their respective deities recalled the bedlam witnessed in the Board of Trade when men act like madmen in the effort to recover their financial interests. Poor deluded mortals, they were in a dilemma at their best, and they took their choice and paid the money, only to be assured at once by an unscrupulous competitor that his god had the supreme merit and he persuades the hesitating one, but only to filch him out of some of the money which he will yet need before reaching his distant home.

These are the false shepherds that fleece the flock by promising them a stock of merit in case they contribute to another god. Numerous beggars are sitting about with the alms bowl, and that emaciated form and that beseeching look are far more eloquent than their unknown language of words, and the smallest gratuity is most gratefully acknowledged.

We descend to the river by flights of stone steps

of gigantic proportions, but which were crowded by pilgrims. It was a motley crowd in appearance and also representing the greatest social extremes of humanity, for the haughty Brahman stood there, so self-centred that he would not stir to give room for an outcaste to pass, and would not deign to let so much as his eyes to rest for a moment in sympathy upon the depressed Panchama, but spurned the degraded Pariah class as he would a dog. Here however he could not escape the inevitable, for here the streams of a common humanity brought the rich and the poor, the prince and the pauper, the proud caste Brahman and those of the lowest scale of ignorant and superstitious human beings together, but for a moment, for they had nothing more of sympathy and love for one another than the dry leaves of the forest blown together by a passing breeze.

Some of the Sannyasi strode by with their vacant look, but arrogant manner, as if hypnotized with the thought of their superiority over the common herd that surged about them. These picturesque, saffron-robed, self-centred zealots were the very Pharisees of Benares for they did not practice their religion in the closet where no eye could see them, but out in the open, in the most public place in order to be seen of men. Modesty was not one of their virtues, and vanity was most conspicuous.

Strange sights are witnessed among the various religious fanatics that congregate at Benares, and some of the ascetics are disgusting. These devotees often excite our wonder if not our admiration for it is amazing to what extremes some carry their craze. Some are specially proud of their long hair, as though the glory of a man were in the length of his hair, for in some cases it reached almost to the ground and they exhibited it in a manner that indicated this as one of their chief aims in life, to grow their hair to an extraordinary length. As a rule they had a profusion of hair that was grown carelessly and hung in matted locks about their shoulders.

The Ganges, which is so sacred to the Hindu, is a great and remarkable river, having its source in the Himalayas at an elevation of 13,800 feet above sea level, and then begins its winding descent for 1,557 miles until it empties into the Bay of Bengal, and where its daily discharge far exceeds the quantity of water that our famed Mississippi pours into the Gulf of Mexico.

Daily bathing is an inseparable part of the religious life and ceremony of every Hindu, and no stream is so sacred as the Ganges, and at Benares the merit of its waters is particularly efficacious. In fact the future of every man is assured who comes to bathe in the river at this holy city, however wayward his past may have been. With such extraordinary inducements many of the wasting wrecks of humanity in the last stages of disease and the weakness of old age are brought hither to enjoy the supreme advantages of dying where an immediate transfer to heaven is made, without the necessity of any transmigration of souls. Hence the mortality at Benares is exceeding great and beyond all comparison with other cities in proportion to the population, for many are brought hither in a dying state.

We saw many pathetic examples of the infirm and aged who were unable to walk but were supported and borne by their friends to the sacred place so that they might at least touch the life-giving waters. Many had come a long distance, and it seemed a cruel wrong to bring the aged, sick and dying ones in a bullock cart, without springs, and jolted over rough roads instead of being allowed to lie quiet in their homes, and attended by loved ones. They suffered great hardship from exposure in their weak condition whilst travelling as much as one hundred miles and even more. They suffer from heat or cold according to the season, and I saw the emaciated aged forms shivering from cold as they were brought up from the Ganges. No doubt the death of many is hastened by hardship imposed by Hinduism, but the unfortunate one has a countless number in store for him.

In no country have we seen such pitiable specimens of humanity, and we were deeply impressed by the deplorable condition of the many aged and sick ones who were poor in the things of this world, and with an irrepressible desire to improve their future and escape the otherwise inevitable evils, they had made the greatest possible sacrifice in having abandoned their humble home, and trudged along for days, weary, hungry, footsore and faint, in only a scanty muslin loin cloth to protect them from cold. No wonder that so many perish by the way.

We saw some emaciated forms that seemed nigh unto death lying in the open by day, exposed to the sun, for that kept them warm, and the dome of heaven even at night was their only covering. But they murmured not, for all that they seemed to covet was the privilege of bathing in the saving waters of the Ganges, and dying at the holy city of Benares. My indictment against Hinduism is that it should attribute such transcendent merit to these waters at the holy city, but which can only be secured here, and hence the inhuman discomforts entailed. The poor, suffering ones are induced to forego all personal considerations of present comfort and endure any amount of hardships in order that they may die by the Ganges or at least that their ashes may be cast into the sacred river, for the Garuda-purana teaches that "Whatever sins a man may have committed during life, if his bones are cast into the Ganges he must certainly go to heaven." Hence many carry the calcined bones of relatives long distances to throw them into these marvellously regenerating waters, for the most astounding claims have been declared as to their virtues.

As proof of their boundless transforming power the same Purana cites this remarkable illustration: Many years ago a tiger killed a hunter who had been the terror of the province because of his notorious crimes, and his lacerated body lay unobserved for years and gradually wasted away, leaving only the skeleton remains, whilst the disembodied evil spirit freed from the carcass wandered about as a devil and as wicked as the original prototype when dwelling in the body, and causing all manner of mischief. But the unexpected came to pass, and here was the marvel. One day a crow spied the bleaching bones, and seized by some strange impulse this raven, with inscrutable instinct, picked up the bones, one after another, until all had been transferred to the Ganges, and at once its marvellous waters transformed the spirit of the dreaded demon into a saint—too holy for this world—and he passed in a celestial chariot into heaven. With such high authority from their sacred writings as to the merit of these waters it is not strange that millions have made the pilgrimage to the Ganges.

A modern anecdote from one of their magistrates

will illustrate their present faith in this river. On a tour of inspection he overtook a poor old woman who could barely trudge along, and to his question whither she was going, she replied: "To the Ganges with my husband." He looked about for her old man whom he supposed was following her but he was mistaken, for she had all the mortal remains of her husband calcined into the most concrete state and done up in a handkerchief that she carried on her shoulder, and which she carefully opened for his inspection. There was the dust and some bones and teeth that had not been reduced to ashes on the funeral pyre—all of which she was carrying a long distance with a wife's devotion to deposit in the Ganges so that it might be well with him in the next life.

At the common ghats at Benares the Hindus and Mohammedans bathe indiscriminately, but this is the exception to the rule for the Hindus generally have places reserved for their exclusive use, and there are likewise several large ghats that belong to the Mohammedans and no Hindus bathe there. There are also ghats that are used exclusively by the Brahman class, the men taking the one side and the women the other. Bathing there has none of the disgusting exposure that I witnessed among the Russian peasants at the Jordan, during their Easter festival, for both men and women retain such clothing as not to offend our sense of decency. The women carry an extra garment with them into the stream, or, strictly speaking, an uncut strip of a half dozen yards of muslin, and after their ablutions, put it in the place of the one previously worn and which is modestly drawn off into the water and then washed before coming ashore.

Naturally the poorer outcastes, and they are legion, are not always so fastidious about washing their garments, for their supply or change of dress is limited, and they want the soul effect of the waters. Some bring vessels from the culinary department and wash them also, and many even carry some of the sacred waters with them into their homes to drink. Some engage in elaborate religious ceremonies in connection with their prolonged ablutions, such as repeating the mantras to the sun, counting the rosary, taking handfuls of the water and then with outstretched arms allowing it to trickle through their fingers.

I often gazed with earnest thought upon some of the representative class as they stood in this reverent attitude facing the rising sun and gazing intently at the blazing orb for so long a time that it seemed sufficient to blister their eyeballs, whilst their lips muttered their morning prayer to the sun: "Let us meditate on the excellent glory of the Divine Vivifier: may he enlighten our understanding." As the early religion of animism or the deified phenomenon of nature prevailed, we can easily understand how the sun with its unrivalled potency received a full share of adoration, and the Sun God was once prominent in the Vedic system because of its transcendent splendour and power as the golden-deity, and still receives universal adoration from the Hindus every morning of the year.

All who went into the Ganges did not take their religion so seriously, after having attended to the prescribed ceremony, for there were some lively scenes of sport, and some enjoyed swimming and diving, leaping up and down, and splashing the water, as well as indulging in the religious bathing. We were shocked to see certain evidences of the utter disregard of sanitation, for whilst the Ganges is a most sacred river to the Hindus, its waters cannot be very savoury and sanitary at Benares, owing to the enormous quantity of foul sewage poured into it.

Imagine the bathers standing within ten feet of the mouth of great sewers that empty the filthy abominations of a large city into the Ganges. The devoted pilgrims have no scruples about such an incongruity, for they have never even heard of a germ theory, and as there is no accounting for taste, some who are most zealous in their efforts to get all the virtue, that they can out of the Ganges will even take handfuls of the filthy water and sip it, and thus literally purifying themselves within as well as without. However, their motive is not only to bathe the entire body with the salutary water but to receive its inner cleansing power also.

I was disgusted with the view and I thought of the microbes and pestilence inherent in the sewage, and how it would poison their internal organism and hasten their death; but I was assured that, on the contrary, these salubrious waters were an antidote for intestinal troubles, and the secretary of the maharajah made the statement that according to a chemical analysis they are the purest waters in all the world. We may well question the truth of his statement and suspect that it was only a metaphysical or religious analysis, for some of the ingredients that find their way into it cannot conduce to its purity, for not only is all the sewerage of the city emptied into it, but they also cast into it their dead cats and dogs, and the dead bodies of the small children and also holy men who need not be cremated.

The burning ghats or the places where the funeral pyres are located introduce us to a gruesome spectacle which characterizes India's method of disposing of her dead, and it is far superior to sepulture for this warm and thickly populated country. Inasmuch as the bubonic plague was raging in many places we witnessed numerous examples of the funeral pyre, and on some occasions when prudence might have kept us away, but our intense desire to see and get impressions saved us from all fear, if not danger.

In one enclosure the place looked like a great number of bonfires, for they were cremating scores of the dead and several victims of the plague were brought in whilst we walked about the funeral pyres, and the air was thick with the offensive odour of burning human flesh. To prevent the spread of the disease the bodies were brought here soon after life became extinct, and the public was excluded from this place of horrors, but through the influence of an official I obtained the permission. Of course we had witnessed many individual examples at the ordinary public places of burning in other cities, but at this time the terrible death rate from the bubonic plague in Bombay was so appalling that special precaution was taken by cremating all such in a special inclosure from which the public was excluded, but to which we gained admission.

I shall attempt a description of a remarkable cremation that we witnessed one morning at the Manikaranka Ghat, the most sacred of all the ghats at Benares and one of the five famous places of interest for all pilgrims and visitors to this city. We were in a boat on the river so that we could see whatever was transpiring on shore. We were suddenly attracted by an unusual noise, and then we saw a great crowd following a funeral procession.

It was an occasion of rare interest for the deceased was the late distinguished General Jeet Jung Bahadur Rana, second son of the famous Maharajah Sir Jung Bahadur, commander-in-chief of the army of Nepal. In addition to the numerous friends and retinue of officials, there followed a host of howling beggars according to the custom of that country when some notable one is borne to his funeral pyre, for this is their hope of receiving a generous distribution of alms. They filled the air with their shouts of lamentation, appealing for mercy in the form of alms.

Like an unruly mob they crowded the procession and never have I witnessed such a confusion at a passing funeral. The procession moved at a rapid pace and often the two sons turned about and threw a handful of coins into the air for the clamouring horde that scrambled for the money as it descended to the ground. Some of the beggars came with large baskets, frames of canvas and inverted umbrellas that they held up to catch the shower of coins. The family of the deceased seemed to be wholly at the mercy of this persistent rabble that forced them to follow a lively pace along the bank of the river, but as the funeral procession neared the place of burning the beggar mob dispersed.

We hurried ashore so as to witness the cremation ceremony. The two sons sat on one of the steps of the ghat whilst the barbers shaved their heads, and the face of the older one who had a full black beard, and who wore the European dress. Then they went to the Ganges where they exchanged their accustomed dress for the winding sheet, and after their ablutions came up the steps with only the thin wet cotton sheet that clung to their body. The younger brother was shivering from the cold for he had less flesh and blood than the elder one. The latter brought the lighted torch from the low caste Domra who enjoys this rich hereditary monopoly of providing the necessary firebrands to light the funeral pyre.

Thrice they walked round it and then each one applied his lighted torch, and soon the funeral pyre that resembled a catafalque, with its white decorations of silk and its tinsel of gold and silver, was enveloped in flame, and the body that had been concealed became partly exposed. The wood and body burned freely because of the abundance of ghee that had been poured upon them, and the mixed spices gave a more savoury odour to the burning flesh. The two sons stood by until all but a few bones had been reduced to ashes for there was an abundance of fuel. The older one occupied a prominent position in the government and spoke English perfectly.

We conversed freely together and he was quite willing that I should take the snap shots during the cremation, and at his request I sent him several pictures and which he courteously acknowledged and thanked me for my letter of sympathy. I realized as I stood and talked with him the power of the truth contained in the words that "One touch of nature makes the whole world kin," for I felt that I was his brother man, and I have never ceased to feel profoundly for his welfare.

I had a vivid vision of the past century as I witnessed the cremation of this distinguished Hindu general who had died the day preceding, for all about were many stone monuments that had been erected to the glorious memory of the worthy wives who proved their loyalty to their husbands by yielding to the persuasions of the priests, and who immolated themselves upon the funeral pyre of their husbands.

Some of these enduring monuments had been sculptured with the picture of the husband and wife, and with these objective surroundings of silent but eloquent monumental witnesses, and with the background of history, and aided by the imagination, I was enabled to reconstruct the past and in imagination at least become an eye-witness of the appalling scenes that were often witnessed at Benares and elsewhere, and to the fact of which these monuments testified. It was a scene too horrible for civilized people to behold and yet it was supported by the religious leaders of Hinduism and who bitterly opposed the reform measures when proposed for its suppression. Had it not been for the power of the Anglo-Indian government, influenced by Christian thought and civilization there, I might have beheld the shocking spectacle of the wives of the deceased general, bound and made living torches, to be consumed with the dead body of their husband.

Up in the city of Lahore is the noted mausoleum of the Ranjit Singh's Samadh. In the centre, on an elevated platform, are twelve marble lotus flowers, the central one covering the ashes of the Ranjit, and the others the mortal remains of his four wives and seven concubines, all of whom immolated themselves on his funeral pyre. That holocaust of the polygamous wives and concubines that composed his harem was an awful indictment of the religion that contended for the continuance of this most barbaric practice. When the prime minister of Nepal died some thirty years ago, four of his widows were burned alive with his body, for Nepal as a feudatory or independent state did not at once acknowledge the law enacted in 1829 for the suppression of the infamous suttee rite.

The Hon. Mr. Justice Sankaran Nair in the *Contemporary Review* for August, 1911, says: "It is a matter of common observation that almost all the rules of Hindu law in favour of progress were laid by English judges against the protest of Hindu judges of great eminence. That English judges have not yet succeeded in stopping the consecration of young girls to prostitution in temples, and that they hesitate to enforce the provisions of the Penal Code and root out the institution of dancing girls by treating their usages as immoral, is perhaps one of the latest concessions to Indian judicial opinion."

"Burning a widow alive on the death of her husband was declared a crime about 1830, despite the indignant protest of orthodoxy." "It seems inconceivable to a person who has come under the influence of Western civilization to imagine that anybody was ever found to advocate as a religious duty the burning of a widow alive on the death of her husband, and one would think that if certain diseased minds ever carried out that theory in practice, it had only to be denounced to be put an end to; yet when the great Indian reformer, Rammohun Roy, denounced that practice, he met with stout opposition; and this was the more remarkable because in Bengal, where he began his agitation, sati was carried out in a revolting manner. There the practice was to bind down the widow with the corpse of her husband, and then pile upon her such a quantity of wood that she could not rise; and when the fire was applied to the pile she was forcibly held down with bamboos."

The judge quotes some passages that the Brahman priests employed in order to persuade widows to ascend the funeral pile for self-immolation, and who were responsible for this barbaric practice in the name of the Hindu religion. "That woman who on the death of her husband ascends the burning pile with him is exalted to heaven, an equal to Arundhati. She who follows her husband to another world shall dwell in a region of joy for so many years as there are hairs in the human body, or thirty-five millions." "The woman who follows her husband expiates the sins of three races: her father's line, her mother's line, and the family of his to whom she was given a virgin." "There is no other way known for a virtuous woman except ascending the pile of her husband. It should be understood that there is no duty whatever after the death of her husband."

"There can be no doubt that in the face of these extracts it is impossible to deny that the abolition of sati was opposed to the modern Hindu sacred law; and they are here referred to to show that an exegesis which can supply so many sacred authorities for this horrible practice cannot be in want of similar holy injunctions to support almost any detestable superstition."

It is not easy to account for such a barbarous practice among a civilized people and under the sanction and encouragement of religion. It ought to have been especially abhorrent to the Hindus, among whom all life is held so sacred, even of the most insignificant creatures and including the deadly cobra, and yet, strange and shocking as it must seem to us, they appeared to lapse into the savage state when they encouraged the burning of widows on the funeral pyre of the dead husband.

We saw some repulsive features in connection with the many cremations that we witnessed, especially among the poor who could barely provide fuel enough to reduce the body, and often the skull and large bones and joints remained among the dying embers and which were collected together and cast into the river. The undertakers differ greatly from ours for there is no hearse nor casket and flowers; but the undertaker engages to cremate the body, and he provides the quantity of wood paid for, and the torch to light it after it has been arranged in a funeral pyre for the body.

The space at the different ghats is limited so that only a few cremations can take place at the same time, and the other bodies that are borne thither are laid by the edge of the river, with their feet in the sacred waters that confer merit even upon the dead; and the fact that these corpses are filled with the innumerable germs of various deadly diseases do not act as a deterrent upon the living fanatics who sip the same waters a few rods away, for they experience no qualms from such indiscretions, for these sacred waters sanctify all things whether living or dead.

Whilst we had been occupied with these gruesome scenes our attention was suddenly called to a far more agreeable and festive one. There were a number of pleasure boats on the river with brilliant decorations and all the occupants were dressed in their best costume, for they were celebrating the festivities of a wedding. It was a unique ceremony, for the ends of two bales of cloth were fastened to the shore by a boatman, on either side of the boat that bore the happy couple, and as they rowed across the river the cloth was gradually unrolled and taken up in festoons by those in the boats that followed, until the opposite side was reached. Then they returned and rolled up the cloth again.

We witnessed several of these joyful occasions and they formed a striking contrast with the sombre and mournful scenes that we beheld at the ghats. The contrast was emphasized by the proximity, but neither seemed to be in the least affected by the other, for they appeared to be as indifferent to the ways of the others as though they had absolutely nothing in common. To begin the journey of life as husband and wife by crossing the Ganges ensured blessings for the future, for even their pleasures are not without a religious significance.

Among all the holy places in Benares the Golden Temple has the preëminence; not because of any magnificent proportions or architectural splendour, for it is lacking in these features, and none of the hundreds of temples in this city can be compared with the many vast and magnificent ones in Southern India. It has a picturesque exterior with its five domes, the largest one in the centre rising above the others, and all said to be covered with the precious plate of thinly beaten gold. The transcendent sacredness of this place is due to the famous Well of Knowledge situated in the centre of a quadrangular courtyard that separates the Golden Temple from a mosque, for the god Siva has his abode there and this is sufficient attraction for his millions of votaries.

I wished the well had overflowed and flushed the place just before our visit for the immediate surroundings were exceedingly filthy, owing to the presence of several bulls and cows that defiled the place and even the platform that covered the well. In the bottom they tell us lies the celebrated idol of Siva dropped by the chief priest to preserve it from the profane invaders when the old temple was destroyed. No one questions the evidence nor doubts the sanctifying and enlightening presence of that wonderful but invisible image, and for centuries the thirsty pilgrims drink its filthy waters which the attendant pours from a ladle into their hands, or bowl. There are openings in the platform through which the rice and offerings of flowers are thrown, and all the filth from men and beasts that is washed down into the well, to be drawn up again and drank, is sufficient to increase the specific gravity and indefinable flavour, as well as to render it unfit to drink. In the West we speak of the Well of Knowledge as being pure and undefiled, but this cannot be said of the Hindu Well of Knowledge at Benares.

The roof is supported by forty columns but the many bulls and cows give it the appearance of a stable. The Brahman who poured out the water would have made a successful auctioneer, for he proclaimed the virtues of the waters with a loud voice and did a driving business. The rush equalled that for the entrance to a circus and there was a continual din from gongs and the cries of men and women, coming and going, but amid all the confusion, mad rush, crowding and scolding and bullying, they never once came to blows.

In all the motley jostling crowd, the conspicuous ones that never lost composure, but maintained a dignified reserve, were the lordly bulls that had advanced to the very centre of interest, evidently attracted by their thirst for the water drawn from the Well of Knowledge, and one of the finest specimens of the bovine herd stood on the platform and directly in front of the Brahman priest. He was familiar with the place and was utterly indifferent to his surroundings for he was undisturbed by the accustomed noise and crowding, and no one was impatient with his occupying the coveted place, for his presence would greatly add to the merit and sanctity of the place.

It was a rare place for reflection upon the vagaries of Hinduism run mad, and the bulls and cows appeared to be the most normal of all the creatures gathered there. Religious fanaticism, ignorance and superstition had reached their limit of excess. The atmosphere was warm and foul and it was only the excessive interest that held us so long, for here the very frenzy of religious fanaticism reaches its climax. Many of the devotees drank the water from their hands or snatched the bowl with frantic haste ; and others bathed their faces with it and then rushed through the crowd with the look of despair, as they hastened away to some other holy place and in the hope that they might find peace for the soul. No sacrifice was too great if they could only satisfy that longing. That was the object of their quest in making the long pilgrimage and enduring great hardships in order to reach the holy Benares and pay their devotions at its holy places. Did they find the goal of that search ?

As I looked upon the frenzied faces of some of the pilgrims who hurriedly drank the bowl of water as though it were a salutary drink, I thought that whatever virtues it may lack, it was not insipid, and I thought that the elderly Scotch lady could not have found the objection to this water that she did when the new supply of water was brought into her city, for when the committee asked her how she liked it, she replied: "Oh, there is no taste to it." There must be a positive taste to the water from this Well of Knowledge.

As a matter of fact the sacred animals mentioned have the right of way about all holy places in Benares, and there was not one from which they were prohibited, but everywhere unrestricted freedom was accorded them. We were surprised to see them at the ghats, and in temples from which foreigners were excluded, and they wandered at liberty through the streets and by the stands loaded with fruits and vegetables and where they helped themselves without ceremony, and without money and without price. Their sacred character exempted them from censure, or chastisement, although any man, woman or child who would have committed such highway robbery would have been severely dealt with, but to strike with a blow these favoured lords from the quadruped kingdom would have been an unpardonable sin.

On the contrary these superstitious merchants rather coveted the meritorious presence of these animals although they must often have annoyed them by their provoking manner of overturning a table of fruit upon the ground. The Western women often felt timid when crowded through narrow places by the bovine species, but we were assured that they were quite inoffensive, for whilst they were not human they approached the divine. To appreciate this fact we must understand that they teach that these animals are so sacred that this sanctity adheres to the minutest particle, even to a single hair, and none are to be thrown away; and these animals being so excessively sacred within as well as without, nothing that proceeds from them can defile, but only sanctifies the place and everything with which it comes in contact, and even the ashes of the cow-dung is so potent in its ceremonial efficacy as to transform the Hindu sinner into a saint merely by sprinkling it over his body.

Not only is the worship of the bull and cow preeminent among all the animals in the Hindu pantheon, but the bull has the marked distinction of being dedicated to the great god Siva, and is inseparably associated with him in his special function, and his images may be seen at the linga shrines. It is a coveted privilege on the part of the men of wealth to turn one of these sleek animals loose to wander at will about the temples, shrines and bazaars as the distinguished representative of the chief god of Benares, for it ensures great merit, and no wonder that we are jostled by so many of them in the crowded places.

I saw countless numbers of emaciated and half-fed men, women and children who were on the verge of starvation, some looking like living skeletons, but I never saw a bull or cow so underfed as to remind me of the lean kine that Pharaoh saw in his dream. I saw mothers with their starving babes in the crowded bazaars and no man gave to them, but the bulls were allowed to eat freely from the stands, and the poor Hindu women did not clamour at such inhuman injustice and invidious distinctions, for they were held by the grip of their religious customs.

TWO SONS BURYING THEIR FATHER AT BENARES

EMACIATED HOLY MAN AND HIS IDOL

Christianity following the Gospel teaches that human beings are created in God's image and worth far more than an ox, but Hinduism teaches that a cow or a bull is far superior to a woman, and hence that animal is allowed rare privileges and grows fat, whilst woman is degraded and impoverished. The cow in virtue of her abundant utility, if not necessity to the life of mankind in India, won for her even in the early history of the country a prominent and secure place of distinction among the sacred beings that often rivalled the honours paid to the multitudinous gods.

In those remote times when with confused ideas they failed in their discrimination between gods and men, the cow became exalted to a divine station that woman had not reached, and, in the sacred literature of the Atharveda, was placed among the beings to whom worship was given, without stint or qualification. There has been no revision of this animal deification in Hinduism to this day, for bulls and cows have the right of way, though college professors were excluded from many of the temples to which these irrational animals had access. Not far away there is a temple wholly dedicated to the special use of the cows, and from which all but the elect are excluded. I wanted a photograph of the interior that housed the sacred animals, but even the coin of the realm only secured for me a place in the portal for I was not allowed to cross the threshold lest the place should suffer pollution, and the passing women counted themselves fortunate in being able to catch a glimpse of the holy interior, for their presence would defile the sanctity of the temple reserved for the exclusive use of those exalted creatures.

I frequently saw men seriously engaged in the particularly meritorious act of stroking the side and back of the cow, but some seemed to have reached the extreme limit of the cow cult when they crawled humbly and reverently towards the passive demigod, and taking hold of the tail held it firmly for the transferrence of a current of virtue from the divine source into their degraded self. Then they pressed it to their lips with a smack of satisfaction for this bovine fellowship.

I met an American on a steamer from Bombay to Suez who had been utterly misled by this strange attachment to the cow, and was extravagant in his praise of Hinduism because of the affection that the people show to the animals, for he said that he had seen many men caressing the cow. I assured him that he was very much mistaken, and that the men whom he saw stroking the back of the cow were not caressing it as an expression of their fond affection for the cow, but because of their supreme concern for themselves, for the "Institutes of Vishnu," Chapter XXIII, page 60, says: "Scratching the back of a cow destroys all guilt." Hence the man, instead of being interested in caressing the cow, was only stroking the back of that animal for his own sake, to rub out the debit account of his guilt, and if such an easy process were effective many men in America, who are reaping what they have sown, would invest in a cow or two to escape the suffering of misdeeds.

We first saw the Saddhus, ghost-like in appearance from their ashen covering, sitting outside the gateway to the great temple in Madura, gently stroking the favourite animal. I would not say that no Hindu ever caressed a cow, for some in their confused thought and feeling as to the extreme belief in the sacred character of the cow might be inspired with a feeling of love from a sense of gratitude to give expression to that gratitude by caressing the animal, but that is not the design as clearly stated in the "Institutes of Vishnu," no more than our afflicted ones gave their blood to the leech out of love to that worm-like creature but solely to get rid of their own ailment. It was for self and not for the sake of the leech.

There is one unique and most attractive place for all the sick and infirm who come to Benares and that is the sacred Well of Healing, the celebrated Manikarnika, a quadrangular stone basin or tank thirty-five feet square with about three feet of water and which is reached by steps on the four sides. The name means a jewel for the ear, and was given to this well according to an interesting legend that the god Vishnu excavated this basin with his discus and perspired so freely during the exercise that it became filled with the perspiration from his body instead of water. But whilst this remarkable event was transpiring the god Siva appeared on the scene and he became so exhilarated by the flattering compliment that the other great god Vishnu paid him, that he was almost convulsed with laughter and one of his earrings was shaken off and dropped into the well, thereby increasing its sanctity and efficiency.

Whilst it is held as most sacred, its appearances and disgusting odours are against it, owing to the variety of offerings of milk, sweetmeats and flowers thrown into it since the legendary earring fell to the bottom, and which cannot neutralize the offensive odours arising from the decaying matter. Besides, thousands of pilgrims who suffer from all manner of diseases, and cutaneous ones as well, partly bathe in these healing waters. Many were so sick and infirm that they were carried by their friends, and their emaciated skeleton forms were laid upon the hard stone steps so that their hands or feet at least might touch the salutary waters. They lay on no rug or cushion, and the only protection or covering was the scant loin cloth, a sad picture of the despair of Hinduism.

The priests and attendants were loud in proclaiming the virtues of this well and in collecting the fees. I saw them urging the people to pay for garlands of flowers that they hung about their neck for a moment and then cast to the god in the well, and later I saw them fish out of the same filthy pool garlands that had lost all their fragrance and purity, if not their virtue, and which were made to do service for other pilgrims who wore them for a few moments and then threw them into the well as an offering to Siva. Time and again I went to this well to contemplate the scene and get impressions of Hinduism in the very centre of its stronghold, and see it at work, without hindrance, and witness its unadulterated works. These fruits were its own condemnation.

After Macbeth had committed the foul murder of King Duncan, conscience smote him, as he looked upon his blood-stained hand, and Shakespeare makes him startle and exclaim: "Will all great Neptune's ocean wash this blood clean from my hand? No: this my hand will rather the multitudinous seas incarnadine, making the green one red."

Had he been a devout Brahman priest he might have substituted for his wail of despair the advice to go to

Benares and bathe in that far-famed sacred well of Manikarnika, and which would wash away the stain of sin committed, even that of foul murder.

In the southern suburbs of the city is located the *Durga* or *Monkey Temple* as it is familiarly called and which has been especially dedicated to these nondescript creatures, but who are not regarded by the Hindus as our ancestors but as the descendants of divine ones. Notwithstanding such lordly ancestors they are a nuisance to the community, for they utterly disregard proprieties and the rights of others. We often saw them running about, with tail curled over the back and chattering their unintelligible speech. They climbed the trees and would suspend themselves by the long tail, swinging back and forward and then spring to a distant branch, or drop to the ground. They recognize no law against trespassing, but entered the houses, went up-stairs, and out on the verandas and terraces and across the roofs and entered rooms, eating whatever they could find, and they are destructive, for there are great numbers of them, and none are molested, owing to the quasi-divine character attributed to them because of their association with Hanuman, the famous monkey god whom they have enthroned in the pantheon of Hinduism.

Whilst poor children and their mothers suffer from want, and millions go hungry and lack the barest necessities of life, and drag out a miserable existence, without sufficient food to properly nourish the body, never did I see a starving monkey. They were always well fed and frisky and no one would have them go hungry, but would rather regard it as a distinction and favour to have these interesting quadrupeds sneak into the kitchen and help themselves with whatever they might find in the larder to satisfy their cravings. Hence they scamper about with the utmost license and do not have to labour nor worry about obtaining a livelihood, for it would be a grievous wrong to deny them the necessities of life.

Inasmuch as Durga is another form of Kali, the great goddess of modern Hinduism, her blood-thirsty propensity is sought to be gratified by the slaughter of animals, and the tender kid is particularly acceptable. Her special abode is at the famous Kali ghat in the suburbs of Calcutta, and she has millions of followers. Since she is one of the wives of Siva it is not strange that she has a temple at Benares where Siva is the chief god.

Because ceremonies connected with the Kali ghat are of unusual interest I shall introduce a description of what we witnessed there instead of making reference to the minor temple of Benares, and which cannot be compared with the one at Calcutta. Whilst this mighty goddess is revolting in appearance she exerts a vast influence over her followers. She is represented under different forms and names, first as Parvati, but it is as Durga that she displayed her invincible power and acquired the unrivalled influence among the people, for she overcame the dreaded giant-demon who was also known by the name of Durga.

Among the legends, we learn from Dr. Duff that this marvellous giant brought such disaster upon gods and men that the overthrow of the world was threatened, for he not only became irresistible among human beings but he had dethroned all the multitudinous gods except the sacred Triad, and the helpless underling gods appealed to Siva for deliverance in their misfortunes. His heart was touched and he requested his wife Parvati to destroy the giant destroyer. Durga was not dismayed but marshalled a host of 30,000 giants of such enormous size that they covered the face of the earth besides having ten millions of swift footed horses, ten millions of chariots, and 120,000,000 of elephants, and soldiers as numberless as the leaves of the forest, and he was prepared for a great victory as he moved forward to the encounter of his presumptuous enemy.

But he knew not the mighty powers of his unconquerable foe, and Parvati awaited the shock of battle without fear. The vast army darkened the heavens with arrows that were discharged at her, and the great giants tore up trees and rocks and hurled them at her, but the goddess turned them all away from their course, and she sent forth from her body millions of strange beings that destroyed the entire army, and the great Durga alone was spared. In rage he hurled flaming darts at her but in vain, and finally he broke off a peak of the mountain and hurled it towards her, but she cleft it in seven pieces by her spear.

Then he assumed the form of an elephant, mountain in size, and rushed at his antagonist, but was utterly destroyed in the conflict. The strain of the intense excitement during this battle and the signal success threw the victorious goddess into an uncontrollable state of exultation that became so violent as to shake and threaten the destruction of the universe, but all the earnest appeals to stop her dancing that had rocked heaven and earth were unavailing. Then men besought the great god Siva to intercede in their behalf, but she heeded not his appeals. Finally in a fit of desperation he threw himself at her feet, and when she discovered that she was dancing upon the prostrate body of her husband she thrust out her long red tongue and laughed, and the threatened disaster of the universe was averted.

It reads like a story from the "Arabian Nights," and if the common people ascribe such marvellous powers to Kali, no wonder that she continues to attract them to her chief shrine at Calcutta. Monier Williams states that "at least one thousand distinct appellations are assigned to Parvati, some expressive of her benignant, some of her ferocious character," of which Kali is one, and who is "black in colour, fierce and irascible in character," and potential to a degree that appeals to millions, especially of the women; and hence this local digression.

It is about a one-half hour drive from the central portion of the city to this suburban part of Calcutta, and we passed many ghats along the river—where we saw the unattractive habitations of the poor who lived in sheds that could not be dignified with the name of houses. Their rags and squalor showed their depressed social condition. As we approached the temple of Kali we found the narrow street crowded with zealous pilgrims and it was with difficulty that we succeeded in elbowing our way through the excited multitude that swarmed about the entrance. There was nothing beautiful in its low situation nor attractive in the surroundings, nor even in the architecture of the sacred buildings, but that scene of humanity was one of absorbing interest, for it was a rapidly moving picture of religious devotion to their mother Kali.

The fact that it was a high day of unusual interest in their calendar was a fortunate coincidence for us, inasmuch as there was an unusual number of pilgrims present and the animals sacrificed on the occasion exceeded the number slaughtered on ordinary days and there was a more elaborate ceremonial. There were two points of special interest that attracted us most: the one was the place of bloody sacrifice and the other was the holy shrine that enclosed the sacred image of the goddess. In the former place there was much excitement and the women were greatly in excess of the men, and some had come from afar, for they had heard of the marvellous powers of Kali and the wonderful blessings that some had received through the sacrifice that they had made at this far-famed temple. It is enclosed by a high brick wall to exclude the rabble, and a small fee is collected from all who enter. The courtyard had the appearance and odour of a slaughter house, for many animals had been slain and the ground was soaked with blood.

There was a surging crowd and the vast majority were poor in this world's goods, but out of the abundance of their intense heartfelt desires they had practiced stern self-denial that meant poverty, and for a long time, in order to lay aside a small portion of their scanty earnings, to make possible the pilgrimage that was so full of expectation. There were some features that recalled the Jewish Passover, but not to be compared with that sacrifice as we witnessed it in all its vivid realism on Mt. Gerizim.

Whilst the pilgrims come to the Kali ghat to offer their bloody sacrifice to the black goddess, we must not misconstrue the significance of these offerings and confound them with the Old Testament sacrifices that were offered for the expiation of sin, for there is no thought of atonement connected with the animals sacrificed near Calcutta, as though the offerer sought forgiveness of sin. After the pilgrim had procured the kid he paid a small fee of about fifteen cents to the attending priest for the services of having the animals slain, as well as for the special privilege of offering the sacrifice at this favoured shrine.

We studied the interesting faces of the men and women who came with this living sacrifice; and I recall an exceedingly anxious expression of a modest woman who brought her own kid, and in her devotion kissed it fervently after it had been purified by the water, and then turned it over to the executioner who placed the neck in a "V" shaped wooden fork fixed in the ground and then lowering a lever across the neck of the victim so as to hold it firmly, with one blow from a cleaver the head was severed from the body, and the former was laid before the shrine in the presence of the sacred image, and where the offerer later appeared to mutter a few words and then disappear among the crowd.

The open platform near the place of slaughter was a moving mass of humanity with the exception of a few well centred Brahmen who were engaged in reading the mantras, and apparently oblivious to all their surroundings. Among the motley crowd I saw several marked representatives of the Saddhus; the one was literally loaded down or clothed with chains, in lieu of the ordinary clothing worn in the country, for he was practicing severe austerities so as to increase his merit account, for the cruel Kali is supposed to be pleased with such tortures of the body.

Another member of the same class was even more conspicuous for he towered head and shoulders above the others, and he stalked about with the freedom of an animal, for he rushed about, pushing everything before him like a giant, and no one questioned his right of way, but made room as though he were a superior being. He moved about with the freedom of an athlete through the surging throng, and apparently aimless, mastered only by the one supreme thought of his matchless superiority. I never saw such a haughty mortal before, and he strode about unincumbered by any unnecessary clothing, for he wore but a small patch, not as much as decency required, for his only adornment consisted in the plain iron chains. He was tall and commanding in appearance as he moved like a Hindu god among the obsequious pilgrims who bowed him reverence, although he pushed them aside with as little consideration as would one of the temple bulls. The lesser satellites of the ascetics gazed upon him with jealous amazement, for he was easily the most bizarre personage at the Kali ghat, and I was anxious to add him to my collection of photographs. Unfortunately he rushed hither and thither through the crowd that jostled me on every side, that I had to take my chances as to focus or lose my opportunity in getting a snap shot of this interesting specimen of objective Hindu fanaticism, and in the despair of my photographic effort I lost his head, but the partial success illustrates certain distinctive characteristics of the Saddhu class, although I failed to get his portrait.

Within the temple proper is a small narrow chamber or shrine that contains the sacred image of Kali, but the hideous features are somewhat relieved by the dim religious light. In the grotesque image there was not the remotest suggestion of sympathy, love and mercy, but rather the blood-curdling stories of the Thugs who claimed the special protection and favour of Kali, and under whose sanction this dreaded fraternity of highwaymen robbed and murdered in accordance with the religious rites of their patron goddess.

What Canon Liddon said of the Divine cannot be said of this famous goddess of Hinduism: "The idea of God kindles in the soul the sense of beauty, and beauty that meets the eye suggests the immaterial beauty of the invisible King. No religion can afford in the long run to neglect this instinct in the soul of men." This was true of the gods of ancient Greece and Rome but there are some remarkable exceptions in the Hindu pantheon, and the grotesque elephantine head of Genesa, the hideous image of Juggernaut and the repulsive one of Kali are remarkable exceptions, and they still exercise their sway over the many millions of followers. This black goddess is represented with four arms and in one of her right hands she holds the scimetar with which she struck off the head of her enemy, and her dress and ornamentation consist of a girdle of human hands and a necklace of human skulls, and with frenzied look she protrudes her tongue.

However the distinguished Hindu Jogendra Nath Battacharya, president of the College of Pundits, in his authoritative work on "Hindu Castes and Sects," puts a much worse interpretation upon the goddess, for on page 408 he says: "As a matter of fact, the image of Kali, that Mr. Murdock of the Madras Mission has attempted to hold up to ridicule, is a thing far worse than he has taken it to be. What its real meaning is cannot possibly be explained here. Those inclined to dive into such filth must study the ritual for Kali worship."

No doubt this eminent scholar knows what he is writing about, and as a native Hindu would not slander the goddess of his own country, and hence we may well ask: What moral and spiritual help and comfort can the people get from worshipping such a discredited being whose character cannot be translated into English? As the door to the sacred shrine was opened for a few moments whilst they were permitted to get a glance of the hideous image of the goddess, what conceptions did it convey to them and what impressions did they receive?

The people are supposed to come either in the hope of obtaining some much desired future blessing, or else to present an offering for some particular blessing already received, and hence it is either a sacrifice in fulfillment of a vow or a pledge of some offering in return for a blessing not yet materialized. Hence they suspend from the branches of the trees near the temple small stones or lumps of clay, similar to the rags that some hang on the trees in Syria, but as pledges that they will redeem with the sacrifice of a goat whenever the prayers have been answered. With such reservation the petitioner is perfectly safe in withholding his gift until Kali has bestowed the coveted blessing.

As I contemplated the simplicity and earnest manner of several of the pilgrims who suspended their rude votive offerings from the boughs of the sacred trees near by the temple, with a prayer and fond hope that their cherished desire might some day be realized, through the favoured offices of the goddess Kali, I had vivid impressions of a thrilling experience through which I had passed years ago when spending some months in Palestine.

It was towards the close of a long day's ride, and when we were still some miles from our camp, that we came to one of the most interesting of the many shrines scattered over the mountainous parts of Syria. The plain whitewashed tomb, with its regulation dome, had been decorated for a special occasion, and there was an unusual number of burning tapers, and the reverent manner of the Mohammedans was an evidence of the sanctity of that shrine and the hallowed place that the departed weli or saint had in their hearts, for they regarded him as a sort of local divinity, possessing superhuman power, and whilst they feared to offend him by any acts of omission or commission, they sought just as scrupulously to gain his favour. Inasmuch as his spirit was supposed to dwell there, the place itself was sacred and not to be violated by the profane intrusion of any outcaste. Because of the special occasion that had drawn them together for this annual ceremony, they were unusually fanatical and not only manifested their displeasure at our presence but ordered the dragoman to leave with us at once. Their angry looks, threatening signs, and harsh mutterings were a language that we could not mistake, and we were ready to leave without ceremony or protest.

In the midst of excitement and hurry the unfortunate thing happened, for in leaving the tomb we passed by the sacred tree only a few yards away. It was a large oak or terebinth with wide spreading branches, and the lower ones almost reached the ground. To these hundreds of small strips of rags had been attached at various times by anxious souls, and for secret purposes as diverse as the different bits of cloth, for they were as variegated as Joseph's famous coat of many colours. But each piece suspended there, whether white, red, blue, yellow or green, represented a votive offering that was inseparable from some humble vow or prayer made by the Moslem who had tied it securely to the bough with the hope that the abiding spirit of that saint or local divinity might be moved to intercede in their behalf. Whilst these innumerable bits of variously coloured cloth did not add to the beauty of that tree, neither did they conceal its verdant attractions from the poorly fed animal on which I rode, for he saw the passing opportunity, and yielding to the impulse of his insatiable instinct, he suddenly raised his head and snatched a tempting branch of the sacred tree with the votive rags attached, and these he began greedily to devour.

It was a shocking case of sacrilege and in holy horror at what might happen the men threw up their hands in dread of the direful consequences, for the spirit of the departed saint was in some way connected with that sacred bough, whilst the hopes and prayers of the petitioner had been breathed into that bit of cloth, and now they were grossly profaned by being devoured by a horse, and however confused their ideas may have been as to the possible results great confusion followed, and I had become the abhorred but innocent victim of circumstances. In short my animal had unwittingly exposed me to their violent outburst of religious frenzy, and their horrible execrations equalled those that once fell upon the ears of the Apostle Paul when the frenzied mob at Jerusalem shouted their murderous anger: "Away with such a fellow from the earth, for it is not fit that he should live."

Several of the infuriated Mohammedans rushed upon

me like madmen. They grabbed the head of the impious beast and pulled from its jaws all that remained of the abstracted branch and rags. I was in no way responsible for the unfortunate occurrence that I greatly regretted, for my attention had been directed to the threatening attitude of the men who had driven us from the shrine, and I had no thought of my horse but they seemed determined to wreak their vengeance upon me, and a stalwart fellow, showing his teeth in anger, and with clenched fist began to pound me unmercifully, and as my thigh was not an anvil I could not endure many such blows, and my only hope was in flight, and pressing the spurs hard into my animal he darted forward and I escaped the enraged and unreasonable fanatics.

After some experience I am convinced that there is no such thing as "horse sense" so far as the unrestrained and unsatisfied propensity of that animal for indiscriminate eating and gnawing is concerned. You may take him from a well provided stall, but if a few minutes later you stop in front of a neighbour's home, that horse will at once begin to stretch his neck full length for anything within reach, from the short grass along the curb, to the flowers and shrubbery, and overhanging branches of the tree, or the bark of the trunk, and if possible he will even gnaw the corner of the house as well as the wooden or even iron post to which you may have tethered him. Hence, let the traveller guard well against these morbid tendencies when riding near sacred trees in the Orient, and not in Syria alone but in India also, for you would not escape with impunity should your horse attempt to feed upon a branch of a sacred tree at the Kali ghat where may be seen many striking examples of religious fanaticism run mad.

As I reflected upon some of the extravagant and irreconcilable contradictions witnessed at the latter place, I could not but wonder at the marked inconsistency that prevails among the leaders of the Hindus, for it is strange that Brahman priests who so scrupulously hold all life as sacred, with the once notable exception of widows, should make this remarkable exception by officiating at the temple of Kali where great numbers of goats and buffaloes have been sacrificed in the name of religion, and which holocaust is unrivalled by any other city in the world. This peculiar rite and exception to Hinduism has been explained to be due to an event during the destructive wars of the goddess, for on a certain day when, faint from lack of nourishment and finding nothing else, she drank the blood of her enemies, and hence the people still offer up the blood sacrifices in the belief that blood is still pleasing to her and in return she will grant their desired favours.

With this brief consideration of the great goddess of Hinduism at her chief shrine in Calcutta we return to Benares to consider her husband Siva, the Maha-deva or great god who holds the supreme place in this holy city of Hinduism. This position he enjoys, not to the exclusion of the many other favourite divinities and godlings, for every pilgrim has the right to cling to his own peculiar cult and worship the local god of his ancestral village without any interference so long as he strictly conforms to the rules of caste. To Siva have been dedicated many magnificent temples in South India, but he is seldom represented in any of them by any image of himself, and his only symbol in Benares is that of the linga, generally in the form of a plain conical stone. This symbol is most sacred in the eyes of the pilgrims and attracts the multitudes who stop to pour over it the water which they have brought in their bowl from the Ganges, and some bestow their offerings of grain, rice, ghee, flowers or money, all of which are received and properly cared for by the attending priests.

Whilst phallic worship has long existed in India it is generally without any impure or immoral character, and the object is often a roughly shaped stone, but a conspicuous object from being stained or painted in the vermilion, or covered with leaves of the bilva tree and kept wet from the profusion of water poured upon it by the followers of Siva, who in that symbol recognize their god. Near the Well of Knowledge is the large image of the Nandi bull, Siva's sacred beast, and which is connected with the same idea as the linga, and is one of the universal objects seen wherever Siva is worshipped. The great temples in Southern India are dedicated to him, and perhaps the most magnificent is the one at Tanjore, with the famous colossal Nandi, carved from black granite and in a recumbent position, nearly thirteen feet in height, and a superb specimen of Indian sculpture.

Within the vast quadrangle of this temple, on two sides, are low arcades, in which are ranged one hundred and eight large linga, carved from black granite, one for each of the one hundred and eight principal names of Siva, by far the largest number that we ever saw grouped together. There is a low wall extending round the court to prevent any intrusion among the sacred symbols. This conventional form is absolutely free from any impure suggestion, and as the symbol of their god they adore it as such. In most instances this symbol is practically formless, and I agree with Barth respecting its general character when he states that "The phallic ideas and rites, and worship of the phallus with the Yoni which symbolizes Devi that there is nothing indecent in the form of these figures. In appearance they are pure symbols, etc., and of all the representations of the deity which India has imagined these are perhaps the least offensive to look at."

Whilst this is true of the vast majority that are only symbols, and at times very remote ones, there are some shockingly obscene exceptions, and where the symbolism has been transformed into the most indecent realism of figures imaginable, far surpassing the most vulgarly obscene figures discovered in Pompeii. These striking examples of phallic worship I have seen on the temples and sacred cars in certain cities of India, and they should make every Hindu with a moral sense of refinement blush because these disgraceful representations are retained by their religion, and in defiance of every sense and standard of decency in our modern civilization. There can be no justification for the continuance of these shameful public representations of vulgar sensuality in the name of religion, for they must exert a low and demoralizing influence upon the young and middle class. Such lascivious exhibitions cannot have a moral tendency for good, but are productive of evil only.

I hesitate to introduce this phase of Hinduism, but I am constrained to do so because of the misconceptions and misrepresentations pertaining to it, and which I would correct. In this I am guided wholly by what I have seen and photographed of the iniquitous and unspeakable evil which exists in many cities of India, away from the beaten tracks of tourist travel.

I am aware that among some noted scholars who never visited India and who are dependent upon others for their information, there are also travellers and tourists who claim that they never saw anything to offend the most refined sensibilities, for what they had heard and seen was the conventional linga, and which is so absolutely remote from any realism that no one would recognize its symbolic character unless he had been told of it. But unfortunately these writers have obtained their information and impressions from the same general source and hence they agree in their conclusions. The time and extent of the observations of the tourists are limited, as they follow the beaten track at the rapid scheduled rate, and there is no opportunity for personal inquiry and research among some of the most remarkable places off the main line of travel.

In these towns and cities, unfrequented by foreigners, there has been but little "housecleaning" for the sake of strangers and in them you see Hinduism in its bald and repellent forms, in the old edition, and not revised and improved by the growing influence of Christianity. English rule has compelled them to remove the vulgar indecencies referred to from the centres of travel, with the exception of the out-of-the-way Nipalese temple in Benares that has the grossly indecent carvings around the building, and which should be removed.

Just because some eminent professors, who never varied their travels from the tourists' itinerary that follows the line of least resistance, failed to see these things, we must not conclude that they do not exist. As a student in search of knowledge and anxious to investigate the facts respecting controverted and contradictory reports, I determined to visit the cities and temples in question, and see things as they are and not as writers have thought they were. I did this in the interest of truth and knowledge, for Swamis have denied that these shameful representations exist on their temples, and they have spoken of them as their holy symbols just as we do of the cross. This comparison of the cross with their lewd figures is as misleading as it is odious and the Swamis know it, but the unsuspecting people who have been charmed by their sophistry should know the actual facts. Many others have been left in doubt because of the misrepresentations and hence I present this information. Such vulgar realism I did not anticipate, and had a missionary reported what I saw, most men would have discredited him as being biased, for it is inconceivable to our civilization that such a shocking monumental disgrace to Hinduism should be perpetuated in the name of religion.

I took photographs that I have never shown to any one, but which I will submit in evidence to a court of inquiry should any Swami deny my statements. Such pictures are prohibited even in India, for Section 292 of the Penal Code states: "Whosoever sells or distributes, imports or prints for sale or hire, or willfully exhibits to public view, any obscene book, pamphlet or paper, drawing, painting or representation or figure, or attempts or offers so to do, shall be punished with imprisonment of either description for a term which may extend to three months, or with fine, or with both. This section does not extend to any representation sculptured, engraved, painted or otherwise represented on, or in any temple, or on any car used for the conveyance of idols, or kept, or used for any religious purpose."

This foul blot upon modern Hinduism and for which she alone is responsible should be removed, for there is nothing to justify its demoralizing continuance. I would refer the reader to the notorious temple garden house at Puri, within a walled enclosure, and where the Juggernaut car is brought with its deities for a rest after the tedious procession. The obscene figures are too shocking even for the temporary abode of these gods, but we can imagine their degrading influence upon the promiscuous crowds that gather there. There can be no moral and spiritual uplift among the pilgrims who gaze upon such lascivious figures, but moral defilement only.

We saw the worst possible scenes that a vile imagination could design in the relief figures on the gopura of the temple in the centre of Cocanada. They were too shameful for a foreigner to photograph, and yet there they have been exposed in all their shocking lewdness to the public gaze to corrupt men, women and children. In the suburbs of the same city there is another temple so holy that no American or European is allowed to approach within fifty feet, and only a respectable caste Hindu is accounted ceremonially pure enough to enter its sacred precincts, but no amount of its extreme sanctity can purify the abominably vulgar indecencies of the figures that surround the gopura of the temple, and the common herd of humanity could approach no farther than this portal with its filthy abominations. I said to the priest that in the name of

COCANADA TEMPLE

morality and common public decency he should remove these vile erotic exposures, but he amazed me with his indifference and replied that if they were removed that huge tower would fall in ruins. Although he spoke English it lacked common sense.

Conjeverim is one of the sacred places in India, the Benares of the South, and in front of the great temple of Siva there towers a gopura nearly two hundred feet in height. Less than two miles away is Little 'onjeverim, with a magnificent temple, and near by was a handsomely sculptured pavilion of modern construction. It had some remarkable carvings of the deities but one reached the extreme limit of the obscene in realism, and debasing influence upon the young who stood about was plainly evident in their sinister looks.

One day after visiting some rock hewn temples, we went to Mangalgeri, where we were astonished to find the most indecent figures imaginable in the wood carvings around the base of a modern car that stood in front of the temple, but from which all but the elect were excluded, and hence we confined our observations to a study of the car; and if such things were tolerated in public, we can hardly discredit some of the things said to transpire within the temple itself, but which are too unsavoury for even a reference.

An apologist for the sins of Hinduism states in terms that may be intelligible to him in his Western study: "Indian art is essentially religious and aims at the imitation of Divinity," and "it expresses in concrete imagery ideas that belong to the transcendental and mystic aspects of religion," and that "nature is a veil and not a revelation," and that "religion for India is much more a metaphysic than a dogma." Such mental gymnastics in the jugglery of words do not change the indecent character of the realistic figures, and which the government recognizes to such a degree that they are only tolerated for religious purposes at the temples, and to expose photographs of them is a penal offense. The subjects are so immoral that the government will not permit photographs to be sent through the mails.

In our age and civilization, culture and refinement have fixed certain inherent ethical standards that are inviolable, and the moral consciousness will not tolerate evils that were permitted among primitive races. The privacy of the nursery and the home is not exposed to the public gaze of the street, for things permissible and necessary in the home would shock our sense of propriety if made public, and our common laws of decency forbid it.

The academic writer, who draws upon his imagination for his data and evolves his idealized theory from his inner consciousness, informs us that all this sex-symbolism is only a veil, and that the Western mind is too materialistic to grasp and interpret the idealism of divinity expressed in this profound psychological mystery. Unfortunately for their ethereal speculations they have not seen with their eyes and hence they have gone wide of the mark, for it is not the idealism, but the vulgar indecencies of the unmentionable realism that we condemn. These may be seen on their temples and sacred cars in their real stark and obscene nakedness, and without any mask, or even so much as a modest veil.

V

HINDUISM IN INDIA

IT is Hinduism as it has been taught, believed and lived in India for many centuries that I wish to discuss, and not as it has been presented at times in a highly idealized form in our country by special advocates of certain phases of this multifarious religion. With Christian thought and phrases read into it many are attracted by the beauty and spiritual character, but in this form it has become so Christianized that the original teachings are scarcely recognizable. This is especially true of many of the Vedantists, and who frequently employ the form and seemingly the content of the Christian religion, but it is due to the infiltrations or appropriations from Christianity that the Swamis are able to charm their hearers.

It is impossible to define Hinduism owing to the bewildering diversity of beliefs and practices among the multiplicity of sects, for they are frequently contradictory as well as irreconcilable. The Hindu mind possesses a wonderful elastic faculty for religious adaptation, as well as a marvellous capacity for assimilating the most astounding differences. Hinduism is preeminently the religion of India, for there are more than two hundred millions of Hindus, and more than two-thirds of the entire population. With all their difference of race, language, belief and social standing, there are certain marked characteristics of faith and practice that may be regarded as essentials. In brief, they may be said to recognize the Brahmanical supremacy and the rigid observance of the laws respecting caste, and they also believe in Karma and the transmigration of souls, and pay a proper worship to their respective gods. Their household god is worshipped daily by libations of water and floral offerings, but there is no weekly worship in the temples corresponding with that which is observed in the Christian churches, but only an occasional religious observance at the temples during the great festivals, when offerings are made to the idols and alms bestowed on priests and mendicants.

Whilst they have many gods, and abound in superstition, it is the opinion of many scholars who have spent years among them that the great majority of the Hindus have a firm belief in One Supreme God, and that this faith "involved a clear idea of a single personal God, and is not limited to the more intelligent, but is also distinctly characteristic of Hindus as a whole.

This does not prevent their belief in other divinities; the *Devata* or godlings as distinguished from the *Deva* or Gods, and in the minds of the people who believe in them there is no more conflict than there is between an official and his orderlies. They hold that their Supreme God is "responsible for the existence of everybody and everything, but is too exalted to be troubled about ordinary, every-day affairs," and which are committed to the countless tutelar gods or godlings. "The code of morality of the ordinary Hindu is much the same as that of most civilized nations, although almost any moral law may be broken to save the life of either a Brahman or a cow" (Burns in "Census Report").

The sects like their gods are legion, owing to racial differences, and there are abundant traces of animistic usages in Hinduism. These are the survivals of the infiltrations from the Dravidian races as well as from the Vedic Aryans. In the gradual development from the confused spirit of animism to anthropomorphic gods there was a great advance, even though their functions may not always have been clearly defined, and their ethical character at times may have been questionable. In some cases the gods were personified abstractions of certain well recognized virtues that later became embodied in the person of gods and goddesses, just as we have many monumental or objective examples of the divine beings upon the ancient coinage of Greece and Rome. As spirits were supposed to make the grain grow these " vaguely envisaged spirits " became gods of the corn or other grains, and as such are frequently represented upon the medallic monuments.

Many of the religious cults in India had their counterpart in ancient Greece where the people worshipped unhewn stones and anointed them with oil for the sake of the spirit or *numen* that was supposed to be resident in it. In India such stones exist everywhere, whether hewn or in formless state and they are generally conspicuous by being covered with the sacred vermilion, and the tulsi plant; and the pilgrim performs his act of devotion by pouring over it a bowl of water, and if it has been obtained from the Ganges the merit is greatly increased.

Ancestor worship has played an important part in the religious history of India, for the extensive pantheon has been largely recruited from the common ranks of human beings, and some of them displayed propensities that were inhuman, though invested with superhuman powers. It was a comparatively easy process to transform heroic men into gods and elevate them to seats among the mighty in those primitive times of superstition when the people lacked scientific knowledge, and that historical and critical faculty for investigating facts, but possessed a remarkable capacity for assimilating whatever seemed marvellous.

Even to-day demonphobia characterizes the mental state and feelings of a large proportion of the people of India, especially of the southern portion of the country, who believe that they are surrounded by malignant spirits who afflict them with all the misfortunes of life. Though invisible, they are no less real and aggressive in their diabolical methods to bring disease, especially fevers, cholera, smallpox, and the common bodily afflictions to which they are heir ; and these demons destroy the cattle and crops, and thwart their daily efforts. Hence they implore the aid and worship the local guardian deities of the particular village, for whilst the demons have superhuman power, the gods are endowed with superior might and are more than a match for the malicious spirits that dwell in lonely places, in trees and by the riverside. Inasmuch as these demons cause all the manifold ills of life they are of far greater concern to the people than the gods, and they must be propitiated or placated by sacrifices to buy them off so as to escape the dreaded calamities that they would otherwise inflict upon them.

I am aware that these statements are not in harmony with the glowing accounts of the Swamis from India who tell of an idealized Hinduism and such a religious consummation as they may greatly desire for their people, but which unfortunately does not exist in their country, and we must speak of the Hinduism that has been taught and practiced in India for many centuries and as it prevails to-day. The idealized and transcendental religion that some of the representatives of the recent cults have brought to the attention of those who have become interested in theosophy and the Vedantic philosophy would not be recognized in India among the rank and file of the priests and the tens of millions of the Hindus. In confirmation of this I would quote from that authoritative work, the "Census of India."

The writer, after describing the varied beliefs that belong to Hinduism, adds: "Between these extremes of practical magic at the one end and transcendental metaphysics at the other, there is room for every form of belief and practice that is possible for the human imagination to conceive. Worship of elements, of natural features and forces, of deified men, ascetics, animals, of powers of life, organs of sex, weapons, primitive implements, modern machinery; sects which enjoin the sternest forms of asceticism; sects which revel in promiscuous debauchery; sects which devote themselves to hypnotic meditation; sects which practice the most revolting form of cannibalism—all of these are included in Hinduism and each finds some order of intellect or sentiment to which it appeals. And through all this bewildering variety of creeds there is traceable the influence of a pervading pessimism, of the conviction that life, and more especially the prospect of a series of lives, is the heaviest of all burdens that can be laid upon man. The one ideal is to obtain release from the ever-turning wheel of conscious existence and sink individuality in the impersonal spirit of the world."[1]

We frequently saw evidences of the prevailing influence of magic among the people of India, especially in the southern portion. Some of the extravagant public exhibitions were very startling and no doubt the spectators were wrought up to such a mental state of expectancy that they were easily deceived by appearances, just as the devoted believer who goes to the famous cathedral in Naples to see that professed marvel of the liquefaction of the blood of St. Januarius never inquires whether deception has been practiced, for such unbelief would be a sin.

In like manner the unsophisticated Hindus do strange things in their credulity that look like child's play to us, and on elevated places and upon the top of buildings they station formidable-looking warriors, mounted on their spirited steeds, made of various material, and who are supposed to aid mightily in riding down all visible and invisible enemies, and to guard the family against the malignant spirits of earth and air. All that is necessary for the magician is to have an effigy of the enemy, however rude or incomplete, and to pierce it with a real or imaginary dagger, or to destroy that doublet and the dreaded enemy will perish.

Whilst we condemn magic as irreligious and irrational, it still exerts a remarkable influence over the minds of millions of the ignorant and superstitious people. Certain psychological phenomena may still remain unaccounted for, but magnetism, hypnotism, telepathy or the law of suggestion may account for some of the unexplained mysteries of the skilled en-

[1] Page 360.

chanter's wand. It may well seem strange to us that any people at this late day should be found so lacking in the rudiments of ordinary intelligence as to believe in the absurdities involved in magic as practiced in India, but it cannot be compared with the most extravagant magical rites of ancient Egypt, for the potent spell which they exerted challenges the powers of the gods.

We can appreciate the marvels wrought by the magicians of the Pharaoh in the days of Moses when they duplicated the wonders that he performed through the command of the Lord. No wonder, for even some of the gods of Egypt were numbered among the famous magicians, and they exerted tremendous power over the destinies of men,—even life and death were subject to them, and all nature yielded to their behests. They have left a record of their startling powers and from their ancient books we learn of their astounding claims to have power to divide the water of a river, to cut off the head of a man and put it on again without harm.

Such wonderful results of their enchantments were wholly dependent upon knowing and using aright the potential formula. One of these from the book of the god Thot shows the supernatural powers that were exerted by reciting the formula, and which rivalled the startling wonders credited to the magicians of Pharaoh: "If thou recitest the first of these formulæ, thou wilt charm heaven, earth, night, mountains, water; thou wilt understand what the birds and reptiles say, thou wilt see the fishes of the abyss, for a divine power will bring them to the surface of the water" (as St. Anthony did by preaching to them). "If thou recitest the second formula, though thou be in thy grave, thou shalt assume anew the form thou hadst on earth." It is hardly necessary to add that those who practice magic in India have no such clearly defined system of formulæ, nor have they been so successful in producing startling results.

Whilst the pantheon of Hinduism includes more than three hundred millions of greater and lesser divinities, many of the more intelligent Hindus would explain these innumerable so-called deities as being so many different manifestations of the One Supreme Being, and this is the growing tendency not only among the learned class but even the less cultured ones are imbibing this thought, though with confused ideas. Monier Williams described the indefinable and amorphous state of Hinduism as bristling with "contradictions, inconsistencies and surprises."

However, we must endeavour to put ourselves in their place, for frequently as much depends upon the point of view as the character of the thing itself that we are looking at; whether we view a landscape from a plain or from some lofty elevation, whether we see the mountain from the base or from the slope or summit, the man as a warrior on the battle-field or as a father in his home. Hence we must endeavour, as far as possible, to get the point of view of the Hindu worshipper, and his conception of the image before him and the invisible being he is worshipping, for that material image is not his god, nor the one that he sees in his mind, but at most only the idol in which the divinity is envisaged and may dwell for the time. In itself it is merely a symbol that aids the illiterate one in concentrating his confused thought and making his deity more real and vivid to his mind, for that invisible being is always personal and not inanimate, however imperfect and befogged his religious conceptions may be: just as when the most ignorant Christian peon in Mexico bows and prays before the images, for they are not his gods; and the cross is only the symbol of Christ, and through it he sees though dimly the personalization of his divine Saviour.

The countless idols among the Hindus are regarded as idols and not as gods, for they know that the image of stone or wood or mud fashioned by hand is not a divinity; and yet, after a priest has consecrated that image by a special ceremonial, the spirit of the divinity is supposed to become inherent or resident in that image, and hence the priest in presenting the offerings of the family to their particular god treats the image in a sense as though it were really a living thing; but it is owing to the indwelling divine essence with which the consecration invested it, and with the ignorant class it becomes a fetish. However we may hold that the most degraded and illiterate idolater who reverently bows before the rude image of clay is convinced that the gross material form is not a divinity but only the symbol or at most the embodiment of the god that dwells in it at the time, for after the prayer of the worshipper it may be thrown into the river.

Images in the Christian Church have been held most sacred and worshippers have bowed before them and repeated prayers, and I cannot think that the most ignorant of mankind ever worshipped stone or image as such, but that fetish as the medium of superhuman power. As Lyall states: "Queer idols and grotesque are to be seen everywhere in India," but the worshipper may have some "profound meaning underlying the irrational and superficial observance."

Farnell in his discussion of the religion of Greece shows the importance of getting the correct point of view in our interpretation of the belief of others, for similar terms may have conveyed a very different meaning to them. "The word worship is used very loosely by the ancients as well as by certain cotemporary writers, and by its value and indiscriminate employment an effort is made to convince us that the pre-Hellenic and proto-Hellenic world worshipped the lion, the ox, the horse, the ass, the stag, the wolf, the pig, the bird, especially the dove, the eagle, and lastly even the cock. We should have to deal with a savage religion rioting in theriolatry," and such was not the cultured Hellenic race. We must not confound merely outward appearances and ceremonies with their real motives and religious convictions in offering the sacrifices, for they knew that those animals were not actually their gods; and they did not pray to them and worship them as we worship the One Supreme Being.

Rammohan Roy, the distinguished Hindu reformer, returning to Bengal in 1820, wrote that "Debased and despicable as is the belief of the Hindus with three hundred and thirty millions of gods, the learned pretend to reconcile this persuasion with the doctrine of the Unity of God, alleging that the three hundred and thirty millions of gods are subordinate agents assuming various offices and preserving the harmony of the universe under one Godhead as innumerable rays issue from one sun."

To-day many eminent scholars and missionaries are convinced that in spite of all the gross superstition, polytheism and pantheism that pervades Hinduism there is among the people a more general recognition of a Supreme Being than was once supposed. The many local divinities may be but subordinate messengers to whom minor duties have been delegated by the Supreme One, somewhat as has been conceived of angels, although there may be much confusion of ideas in the mind of the illiterate.

Grierson claims to find traces of monotheism in the Vedas but which was later supplanted by a form of pantheism, and he contends that Bhagavatism is the religion of the masses of India, with belief in One God, and to the Hindu mind there is no inconsistency in believing also in polytheism which affords a sphere for the subordinate gods or godlings in the performance of their special duties, and as messengers of the One Supreme Being, who cannot be personally concerned for the daily needs of all the material world. No doubt there is much vagueness in the minds of many as to the exact functions of the subordinate divinities, and yet they need not trouble themselves about defining and attempting to explain the obscure, no more than most people are disturbed as to the particular function of the angels.

Hinduism was born in a country of diverse peoples and cults, and it sought to accommodate itself to the different beliefs by assimilating from all the creeds, even from the aboriginal as well as from the cotemporary and hence the amorphous and anomalous system of this heterogeneous system of religion, with its many absurd practices. As Monier Williams states: "It has not scrupled to encourage the adoration of the fish, the boar, the serpent, trees, plants, stones and devils: it has permitted a descent to the most degrading cults of the Dravidian races, while at the same time it has ventured to rise from the most grovelling practices to the loftiest heights of philosophical speculation; it has not hesitated to drink in thoughts from the very fountain of Truth, and it owes not a little to Christianity itself. Strangest of all, it has dissipated the formidable organization which for a long period confronted Brahmanism, and introduced doctrines subversive of sacerdotalism. It has artfully appropriated Buddhism, and gradually superseded that competing system by drawing its adherents within the pale of its own communion."

Whilst few temples exist to the worship of the sun god he still continues to be the object of universal adoration, for every Hindu, high or low, and to whatever sect he may belong, on the return of every morning pays reverential homage to the rising sun, as he turns about facing the East and then gazing upon the blazing orb repeats from the "Rig Veda" the Gayatri prayer: "Let us meditate on the excellent glory of the divine Vivifying Sun." They see things in the sun, moon and stars, animals and plants that we do not see, and I am persuaded that their religious perception is often very much out of focus. I have heard of people in America who could see a man in the moon, but in India they behold gods in the moon and cherish it with reverent devotion; but the sun is supreme, and they gaze upon it until blinded by its blazing splendour.

Unfortunately as the people interpret Hinduism they do not have their eyes directed towards the future but they turn about and face the past when seeking to solve present day problems, for they must consult the customs that prevailed in remote generations. That finding is finality, the supreme tribunal of their religion, and from which no appeal can be taken. The priest and people may freely admit that it is neither just nor reasonable, nor for the highest welfare of all concerned, but they deeply regret that they cannot do otherwise for it is according to custom. This is the common excuse that one hears when they apologize for some most absurd customs of to-day.

They often reminded me of the old Scotch lady who said that whenever she took the train she always rode with her back facing the engine, for the Hindus of to-day as well as for many centuries seem to have been going into the future backwards. They always faced the past, and strictly conformed to the ways of their remote ancestors for no god nor religious belief exercises greater power over their minds and lives than custom. They suffer many evils, misery and wrongs by conforming to primitive and unjust laws promulgated several thousand years ago when conditions were different. Their religious requirements and customs stand in the way of progress and modern civilization, and impose upon them their many unnecessary grievous burdens. Their patient endurance challenges our sympathy and admiration, but their apathetic state of indifference to their self-imposed burdens, and their persistence in continuing to bear them, excite our commiseration, for it is next to impossible to modernize them, and many generations will come and go before the dream of some enthusiasts will be realized. Kipling's familiar lines suggest the situation:

> "It is not good for the Christian race
> To worry the Aryan brown;
> For the white man riles,
> And the brown man smiles,
> And it weareth the Christian down,

And the end of the fight
Is a tombstone white
With the name of the late deceased,
And the epitaph clear :—
A fool lies here,
Who tried to hustle the East."

Illiteracy and bondage to custom, in connection with the universal dominion of caste, constitute a well-nigh irresistible barrier to human progress and modern civilization.

It seems phenomenal how Hinduism has flourished for so many centuries, and continues its sway in spite of the lack of any organized and centralized authoritative ecclesiastical head. There have been no great and ecumenical councils to operate through subordinate councils, and there have been no popes nor patriarchs with unlimited delegated powers. There has been no thorough system of organization that extended its ramifications throughout every city and village of India, and which made every priest amenable to his superior, and he in turn to the one above him, until the pope himself was reached. There is no such system of authority that controls Hinduism, and yet there are certain inherent and dominant elements that prevail for the enforcement of certain essentials in that religion, and which sways the destiny of the two hundred millions of Hindus. The reason for this remarkable sway has been due to the supreme character of the Vedas, the Brahmanical supremacy and the rigid adherence to the system of caste.

Their Sacred Scriptures exercise a tremendous influence over their lives and whilst the Vedas, and certain writings that were once of supreme authority among the people of India, are now seldom referred to, there are others that control the minds of the countless millions, the most popular of which are the famous epics, Ramayana, and the Mahabharata, the favourite portion of the latter being the Bhagavid Gita. As these are widely circulated in English, Europeans and Americans are familiar with their contents, and we are ready to acknowledge all that is beautiful and ennobling in them, and which have done so much for the betterment of their followers, but many have exaggerated views of their contents.

There are many public readers of the Ramayana, Mahabharata and the Puranas. These may go from door to door at times and often they have many hearers, hundreds and even thousands, and they may read for hours at a time. Wealthy men to secure merit often send out readers for the people, and hence this is another way for receiving religious instruction. These books also contain promises to those who hear them. A mere academic study of the contents of these religious books—at wide range in our library at home—may be misleading. We will get very different impressions if after having read them we then visit the country itself where these religions have held undisputed sway for several thousand years over the minds and destinies of the people, and borne their legitimate fruit. We must see the kind of men and women that they have produced, and what they have done for the social, intellectual and spiritual welfare of these teeming millions in far-away India, who believed and practiced these teachings.

To gain this practical point of view we must go to India and become eye-witnesses, and test Hinduism by its fruits, for after all that is the infallible test by which the real and practical value of a religion is to be judged. It is easy to magnify and idealize Hinduism, and to read into it some of the deepest spiritual truths of our own religion but which were utterly foreign to the minds of the writers of the Sacred Books of the East. There can be no misunderstanding of the fruits, for every religion brings forth according to its own kind, and India has had ample time for abundant fruitage, and the practices and its effect upon the people are unmistakable.

It is greatly to be regretted that Max Müller, the eminent Sanskirt scholar, did not visit India, for he would have discovered the difference between the real and the ideal from a study of the ancient Vedas. Dr. Moncure Conway was profoundly impressed with this important fact when from personal observation he wrote: "When I went to the great cities of India the contrast between the real and the ideal was heartbreaking. In all these teeming myriads of worshippers, not one man, not even one woman, seemed to entertain the shadow of a conception of anything ideal or spiritual or religious in their ancient creed. To all of them the great false god which they worshipped appeared to be the presentiment of some terrible demon or invisible power, who would treat them cruelly if they did not give him some melted butter. Of religion in a spiritual sense there is none." This is a crushing indictment and not from a source blinded by the merits of Christianity, but he gives the irresistible convictions that were made upon him from a personal observation.

Hume, who for years has been regarded as one of the able missionaries, declares that popular Hinduism is doomed. "Its features are superstition, degrading ceremonialism, polytheism, idolatry, and all the undescribable characteristics of caste." "The first mark of greatness in the higher Hinduism is the acuteness and consistency of its thought. Probably no religion in the world equals Hinduism in intellectual keenness. Notice that I do not say that Hindu thought excels in correctness, but only that it excels in keenness and in consistency from assumed premises. In intellectual vigour, Hinduism is a great religion."

Maurice Bloomfield writes that "there has been and is still too much so-called religion in India: Brahmanical hierarchy, sacerdotalism, asceticism, caste, infinitely diversified polytheism and idolatry, cruel religious practices and bottomless superstition." In thus summing up the religious character of present day Hinduism, he might have added that it has been directly responsible for some of the worst evils that have afflicted the millions of its followers through the many centuries. It may rightly be charged with having originated and fostered the system of caste that has cursed and degraded the social condition of the people, whilst it introduced and perpetuated that barbaric and inhuman rite of the suttee or burning alive of widows upon the funeral pyre of their dead husbands. It is also responsible for child marriage and the evils resulting from forbidding widows to marry. Hinduism is also responsible for that unproductive army of human parasites that constitutes the five millions of religious mendicants and ascetics, who debase society by their vicious influence.

No one who is familiar with the supreme influence of woman in the history of Christian civilization can fail to recognize one of the secrets of the weakness of Hinduism and its failure to keep abreast of modern methods in reform and social betterment. This religion has prevented woman from attaining to her fullest and highest intellectual development as a power for good in society and in the state. How can Hinduism be great, elevating and progressive when woman is debased and restricted in her far-reaching influence? Hinduism has been tried for several thousand years and found wanting.

One of the Hindu lecturers in our country attempted to perpetrate a joke, and even provoked laughter among the thoughtless ones in the audience, by informing them that there were no old maids in India but that a husband was provided for every young woman. There would have been no laughter had he told them the whole truth by informing them that there were twenty-six millions of unfortunate widows in India because their religion forbade them to remarry, but compelled them to suffer many disabilities, severe hardships, and which led to the enforced ruin and shame of millions of lives because of this outrageous wrong in the name of religion. They insist upon the most punctilious observance of this law that is productive of so much evil as well as that of caste, although they do not always have the most rigid scruples about some moral shortcomings. Should a Brahman marry a widow he is persecuted and loses caste, but should he keep a Mohammedan mistress he suffers no religious censure nor social ostracism.

Dr. John P. Jones, who writes with authority, gives the following trenchant challenge to the theosophists of America who have been won by Hindu thought as presented in the form of theosophy: "What is theosophy, but the stupefying philosophy and the benumbing metaphysics of the East, clothed in its own garb of oriental mysticism and senseless, spurious occultism? It is a sad reflection upon our Western life that so many people who fail to find rest in the divinely inspired teachings of Christ sink into the depths of a credulity which will accept the inanities of Mrs. Blavitsky. Let these people go out to India and live there for years to see how Hindu thought and teachings have, for three millenniums, worked out their legitimate results in the life of the teeming millions of that land. Let them observe the debasing immorality, the hollow ceremonialism, the all-pervasive ignorance and superstition which rest, like a mighty pall, upon that people and which make life mean and render noble manhood impossible. . . . Whatever one may say about Hindu thought and philosophy as a basis of conduct, that people have been living for many centuries in the dense fog of ignorance, superstition and ceremonialism; and their life has been unworthy and debased because it rested upon nothing."

The Jains of India are a distinct sect and number about one and one-third million. Their pantheon is composed of a number of worthless beggar saints and these deified mortals hold the life even of the lowest creatures so sacred that when they go forth they sweep before them lest they should crush out some living thing, and they carry a fan or wear a gauze screen over the mouth lest a gnat should lose its life by flying down their throat. They carry quite a settlement of vermin in their filthy garments, and no matter how much these insects may trouble them they do not dare to indulge the luxury of scratching themselves lest in so doing they should destroy the precious life of these little creatures. For this reason the Jains cannot cultivate the ground for in so doing they might crush a worm or spider and that would be a grievous sin. I saw some honey that they dared not eat, for the minute red ants had taken possession of it.

The Jains are preëminently the Pharisees of India, for whilst they strain out the gnat they swallow far greater evils. Although their country swarms with human beings who are starving, suffering from disease and wronged, they have no serious concern for them; they have provided no hospitals for the aged and infirm men and women, but they have such places for animals and vermin. They justify themselves by appealing to the doctrine of metempsychosis, and they include all living creatures as members of the one great family, whether they be gods, demons, men or lower creatures, for the gradation is merely temporal, and their ancestors may have made their descent to the grovelling worm, and in treading upon it they might destroy their own grandmother. They are logical at least, but what deluded and worthless fanatics they are. They must be continually annoyed by the foreign population that fills their wardrobe and grazes upon their filthy bodies. No wonder that Hopkins says of them that "of all the sects, the Jains are the most colourless and the most insipid. They have no literature worthy of the name. A religion in which the chief points insisted upon are that one should deny God, worship man, and nourish vermin has no right to exist nor has it had as a system much influence on the history of thought."

A HOLY MENDICANT

VI

KARMA AND TRANSMIGRATION

THE climax of the pessimistic philosophy of Hinduism is reached in the doctrine of Karma and the transmigration of souls. According to the teaching of Hinduism all suffering is penal and the consequence of wrong-doing in a previous existence; and the limit of the possible series of such reincarnations or rebirths has been fixed at 8,400,000 or practically infinity. Whilst this latter dogma may be losing its hold upon many of the people, especially among the educated class, all recognize the inflexible and relentless law of Karma from which there is no escape, but each one must reap what he has sown, and neither God nor demon can interpose to prevent or mitigate the full measure of the penalty imposed in accordance with the deeds committed in the body, for there is no All-Loving God—the heavenly Father—to pity and come to their relief, and no Christ—the Saviour—to save them.

All that men now enjoy or suffer are the results of former deeds in a previous existence, and the character of those particular deeds is the cause of our present happiness or misery. The apparent inconsistency for the sufferings endured by the virtuous man is explained by saying that he is now suffering the penalty for sins committed in a former life, whilst the notoriously wicked man who is enjoying prosperity is merely receiving the reward for the good done in a previous life and which was carefully credited to his account; for in this infallible system of bookkeeping all credits and debits are correctly given, and no erasures nor fraudulent entries can be made, but each one receives his full portion in due season, and with unmistakable certainty. The loathsome leper is abhorred because he bears the mark of Cain as proof that in a former life he committed one of the greatest crimes and hence this curse came upon him. With such convictions the people would naturally have little or no sympathy for lepers, however deplorable their condition may be, but shun them, for they are the once dreaded criminals.

According to the sacred book of Hinduism the soul survives the death of the body, and in accordance with its previous deeds, it passes into heaven, or into hell for a number of years, and then returns for reincarnation in a higher or lower being according to the character of its preponderating credit or debit account. The revolting description of the horrible hell is given in the Vishnu Purana, and the torments are limited to one thousand years, but this may be repeated with the infinity of reincarnations. Hence the Vishnu Purana referring to the condition of those even in heaven says: "Not in hell alone do the souls of the deceased undergo pain; there is no cessation even in heaven, for its temporary inhabitant is ever tormented with the prospect of descending again to earth, and again must he die. Whatever is produced that is most acceptable to man becomes a seed whence springs the tree of sorrow." There is no such note of fatalism and despair in the Gospel of Christ who taught that "God so loved the world that He gave His only begotten Son that whosoever believeth in Him should not perish, but have everlasting life."

The practical workings of the fatalism of this philosophy is often seen in the apathy and patient endurance of the people in meekly submitting to evils and sufferings with a spirit of indifference, instead of inquiring into the causes, and seeking for a possible remedy so as to escape them. They have practically disregarded the remedial agencies for the prevention of smallpox, the bubonic plague, and for the relief of the blind and the many lepers, for their misdeeds have fated them to suffer the misfortunes that have come upon them, and from which there is no escape.

As an illustration of the working of the deep ingrained belief of this doctrine in the minds of the lower classes, the story is told of a judge who sentenced a cartman for a certain crime of which he claimed to be innocent. However, he received the sentence with stolid indifference, and then said to the judge that he did not care, for in the next life the tables would be turned and then he would get even with him; for the judge would be reincarnated as a bullock for the wrong, and as the cartman driving that unjust judge, he would drive him over the highest precipice to his destruction, and he found satisfaction in that hope of revenge.

We had a most practical illustration of their firm belief in the doctrine of Karma when visiting Poona. We had seen the plague-stricken cities and visited the places of burning, and witnessed the appalling ravages of this deadly disease, but we were surprised at the condition that prevailed in this city, for there was no segregation of the people from the quarters doomed by the malignant disease.

I suggested to a resident physician who accompanied us that it looked like criminal negligence on the part of the government officials. He assured me that they had done their best to prevent the spread of the disease and to rescue all who had not as yet contracted it, and we drove out to the suburbs where he showed us the many temporary buildings that had been erected for the care of the people, so that they might not be exposed to the pestilence. Strange to say the buildings were unoccupied, for the people would not abandon the plague-stricken district and when men were sent to compel them, a bloody riot followed, and they were obliged to abandon the Hindus to their fate, for they claimed that England was invading their legal rights by interfering with their religious liberty that has been guaranteed to them, as well as to all the creeds of India.

In accordance with their religious belief the bubonic plague was only a punishment for sins committed, and that it could not have been prevented, and neither was there any possible escape from it on the part of those who had been doomed to suffer it. They never inquired into the possible natural causes, and the utter disregard of sanitation that prevailed, for Karma had mastered their minds.

No doubt this pessimistic philosophy of fatalism has been a most potent agency in developing and spreading the plagues that have cost the lives of millions of unfortunates in India. This fact was vividly impressed upon me on an occasion when speaking to a leper. There are several hundred thousands at least of this horribly afflicted class of humanity who suffer from the loathsome disease that is often worse than death. No hospitals are provided for them by the Hindus, and they receive scant sympathy from a people who believe that these grievously afflicted ones are only suffering the bitter fruits of their own misdoings.

One day I was attracted by a leper whose face was covered by deep lines in which was written much of the story of his life of bitter suffering. That pathetic expression appealed to me in an unusual degree, even in that land where we are surrounded by the unfortunates, and I asked him how long he had been afflicted and he informed me that all his life he had suffered from the leprosy. I expressed my sympathy and spoke some kind words, when to my surprise a big boy who had gathered with the crowd laughed and said: "Don't pity him; it is all his own fault that he has the leprosy." I replied that it was not his own fault for he had told me that he was a leper from a little child, and had not done anything to bring such an affliction upon him. But he answered me: "Oh, he was born that way because of the great crimes that he committed in a former life." He only uttered what I have since read in one of the Sacred Books, that for the greatest crime that a man can commit he will be born a leper in the next life; and hence the very man whom I was profoundly pitying had been a great criminal and was now only suffering his just desert, and was deserving of no sympathy according to the doctrine of the Hindus, and he received no kind consideration from them.

The doctrine of the transmigration of souls is an attempt to account for the existence of evil and the sufferings of the innocent, as well as for the unjust inequalities of life; but the bitter fruits endured by its followers show that it is an unsatisfactory solution, for this cheerless and fatalistic creed has paralyzed ambition and the spirit of progress and self-betterment. There is no ray of hope or inspiration in the belief that my birth and present life have been irrevocably fixed by a previous existence of which I have no knowledge, and for deeds committed of which I have no consciousness. This countless series of existences into which every one is destined to be reborn for a brief sojourn, and then have an intermission in heaven or in hell before plunging into another reincarnation on earth, is sufficient to drive them to desperation. Fortunately the people are sometimes wiser than their philosophy and they escape some of its logical sequences, for there are grave difficulties in the way.

Who in such a system can keep a clear record of their genealogical tree; and who can explain how identity is possible in an intelligent being who becomes degraded from being a philosopher through a process of transmigration and appears in the new rôle of a chattering monkey, a dog or perchance a cobra? Such a confounding and compounding of conceptions and beings that are separated by an impassable chasm is contrary to Western thinking. It is impossible that man should become an ape or some four footed beast, for this is contrary to all that science teaches in reference to the law of evolution, the lower to the higher, but Hinduism reverses the order an infinite number of times by abruptly arresting man in his ascending scale and hurling him down again to become one of the lower creatures. I cannot understand by what intellectual or moral forces the ascent to man could be attained after such reverses. The effect of such a belief upon the people is expressed in one of the folk-songs of South India:

> "How many births are past, I cannot tell,
> How many yet to come, no man can say.
> But this alone I know, and know full well,
> That pain and grief embitter all the way."

Sir Alfred Lyall mentions a case that illustrates how the people believe that at death man's spirit must be provided with some temporary tenement, whether animate or inanimate. "Some fifty years ago a very high English official died in a fortress in a place that is one of the centres of Brahmanic orthodoxy, and at the moment when the news of his death reached the Sepoy guard at the main gate, a black cat rushed out of it. The guard presented arms to the cat as a salute to the flying spirit of the powerful Englishman; and the coincidence took so firm a hold on the locality that up to a few years ago neither exhortation nor orders could prevent a Hindu sentry at the gate from presenting arms at any cat that passed out of the fort at night."

Dr. Wilkins who spent many years among the people mentions an instance that forcibly illustrates their belief in transmigration of souls: "When Gulab Singh, the father of the late maharajah, died, the Brahmans and Pundits declared that he had passed by the process of the metempsychosis into the body of a fish. Now the lakes of Cashmere, as well as the rivers and the canals, are full of fish, and owing to this belief no one was allowed to catch them, lest the maharajah might be taken and eaten." Dr. Wilkins quotes directly from the account published at the time that the death occurred.

Owing to belief in this doctrine, the future is involved in great uncertainty and startling surprises may be experienced in the successive reincarnations as they are made to assume the character of higher or lower beings, as the following story will illustrate. "There was a great and good king who being tired of life presented himself at the gate of heaven with a dog that had been his companion and friend of many years. On being told that his good deeds entitled him to enter heaven he was also informed that his dog could not be permitted to accompany him. Then said the king, 'I will go to hell.' To hell he went, and when taken before Yama (the judge), the king told the story of his not being admitted to heaven. 'Oh,' said Yama, 'this was simply to try your constancy: that dog is your father, and as you have proved yourself worthy, you and he can now enter upon the enjoyment of heavenly bliss.' Then the dog resumed the human form of the father, who then with his son entered heaven together."

Colonel Sleeman, in "Rambles and Recollections," cites a true and remarkable instance of this firm belief in connection with the sati rite. "In this case it was not the wife of the deceased man who voluntarily burned herself, but the wife of a man then living, she believing that in three previous births she had been his wife, and that in her present birth she had been separated from him as a punishment for sin committed in her last previous birth. It is easy for us to laugh at such superstitions, and it is difficult to understand how people can be enslaved by them; but there is no doubt that they have had and still have a firm grasp of the minds of millions."

Colonel Sleeman obtained the information from a

relative of the deceased and the story that he related is as follows: "When my eldest brother, who was so long a native collector in this district under you, died about twenty years ago at Sehora, a Lodhee woman, who resided two miles distant in the village of Khittolee, which had been held by your family for several generations, declared that she would burn herself with him on the funeral pile; that she had been his wife in three previous births, had already burnt herself with him three times, and had to burn with him four times more. She was then sixty years of age, and had a husband living about the same age. We were all astonished when she came forward with this story and we told her it must be a mistake, as we were Brahmans while she was a Lodhee. She said there was no mistake in the matter; that she in her last birth, residing with my brother in the sacred city of Benares, one day gave a holy man, who asked for charity, salt by mistake for sugar with his food; that in consequence he told her that in her next birth she should be separated from her husband, and be from inferior caste, but that if she did her duty well in that state, she should be reunited to him in the following birth. We told her that all this must be a dream, and the widow of my brother insisted that if she were not allowed to burn herself, the other should not be allowed to take her place. We prevented the widow from ascending the pile and she died at a good old age two years ago at Sehora. My brother's body was burnt at Sehora, and the poor Lodhee woman came and stole a handful of the ashes which she placed in her bosom, and took back with her to Khittolee. There she prevailed upon her husband and brother to assist her in her return to her former husband and caste as a Brahman. No soul else would assist them, as we got the native chief to prevent it, and these three persons brought on their own heads the pile on which she seated herself with the ashes in her bosom. The husband and his brother set fire to the pile and she was burned. After this the members of the family firmly believed the woman's story, and the father of the man whose wife she declared she had been in previous births bore all the funeral expenses, and a tomb marks the site where the sati took place."

In the doctrine of Karma there is no place for an almighty, all loving and merciful God, who pities as a father and comforts as a mother, and who has taught us to come to Him with all our sins and sorrows, and receive that peace of God that passeth all understanding. The relentless law of Karma sends man adrift upon a sea of trouble without chart or anchorage or any help from a Supreme Being, but thrown entirely upon his own resources. Where is the justice in Karma that punishes a man for hypothetical evils charged against him, but of which he has no knowledge whatever? What is the moral and remedial effect of a doctrine that punishes a man for theoretical crimes of which he is not guilty and of which he has no moral consciousness? How can he reform when innocent of the guilt charged against him? Why should he suffer the grievous misfortunes when there is no conviction nor remembrance of the sins imputed to him? We can imagine the deadening influence in paralyzing the conscience when subject to such a lying oracle that would persuade the innocent that they are guilty.

Dr. John P. Jones, a conservative scholar, speaking

from many years of observation of its moral effect upon the people states: "The prevalence of this doctrine in India is one of the saddest facts connected with its life. It is sombre and depressing in the extreme and robs the mind of a good portion of the small comfort which the idea of absorption might otherwise bring to it, for it has exercised a mighty influence over high and low. Nor does it appear how this process, as a method of discipline, can achieve what is expected of it.

"It is maintained that ultimately all the myriads of separate souls will cross over this terrible stream of human existence and reach the further shore of emancipation. But by what aptitude or efficiency there can be in metempsychosis itself to reach this end is not apparent. Some claim that its highest merit is that it is a powerful deterrent from sin and incentive to virtue, but the all-sufficient refutation to such a statement is the present condition of the Hindu race itself. If any people on earth, more than others, sin with 'fatal facility,' and seem perfectly oblivious to the character and consequences of their deeds, they are the descendants of the rishis of old. To judge this doctrine by its results in India is to pronounce it an error and a curse."

Whence came this teaching of metempsychosis that for so many centuries has pervaded the Hindu mind? Paul Deussen in his "Philosophy of the Upanishads" states: "In no Vedic text earlier than the Upanishads can the doctrine of the soul's transmigration be certainly traced; but from the Upanishad times down to the present it has held a foremost position in Indian thought, and exercises still the greatest practical influence."

Maurice Bloomfield states that "the germs of belief in transmigration are very likely to have filtered into the Brahmanical consciousness from below, from popular sources, possibly from some of the aboriginal, non-Aryan tribes of India. Like a will-of-the-wisp the belief in transmigration flares up in many parts of the world,—traces among the Egyptians, Celts and Greeks. As far as India is concerned one thing is certain: real metempsychosis does not enter into the higher thought of India, or at least is not stated unmistakably until we come to the Upanishads. When, however, this belief has finally taken shape, we find in it the following established items of faith. Every living creature is reborn in some organic shape, every living creature had a previous existence, and every living creature is again and again the prey of death, until in some life all desire and all activity as the outcome of desire shall have been laid aside. This is the Hindu salvation, viz., absolute resignation of the finite, futile, illusory world; cessation of the will to live, and the act of living. This of itself produces union with Brahma." "There is in all Hindu thought no expression of hope for the race, no theory of betterment all along the line."

VII

CASTE

THE caste system in India is the unique social-religious feature of Hinduism and it is enforced by an inexorable law, for however heterodox the Hindus may be in doctrinal beliefs, they are most scrupulously orthodox and exacting in the observance of caste. There is no social institution in any other country with which we may compare it, for it is characteristic alone of Hinduism, which owes its strength as well as its weakness largely to the persistency of the system of caste.

The vast population of more than two hundred millions of Hindus has been subdivided by this artificial social cleavage into countless numbers of groups of mutually exclusive aggregates, though often separated by the most superficial standards of superiority or inferiority. Whilst they tolerate the greatest laxity of beliefs they are most intolerant in regard to any violation of the inflexible law of caste, for the most heretical and contradictory religious ideas are overlooked; but any insubordination, for conscience' or convenience' sake, to the established rules of caste subjects the offender to the severe penalties that make his life a burden, and even his relatives may be involved in the disabilities imposed for such infractions of an unjust social system. In extreme cases the entire family has been denied the use of water from the common village well.

The extravagant claims made by the Brahmans for the divine origin, immutable and inviolable character, of caste seem incredible to us. They have inflicted outrageous wrongs upon the lower and outcaste population. They have not only denied them all the benefits of education and the opportunity for improving their deplorable condition so that they might rise in the scale of humanity from generation to generation, but they have degraded them to the depths of the depressed classes, with whom they have nothing in common, and not even recognizing them as their brother-man, and the One Supreme God as the Father of all.

On the contrary, strange as it may seem, they are even denied the inalienable rights of religion; for according to the "Laws of Manu" the Brahmans were forbidden to treat the Sudra with human consideration as to his inherent rights, and in Chapters IV, VII and VIII we read: "Let him not give to a Sudra advice, nor the remnants of his meal, nor food offered to the gods, nor let him explain the sacred law to such a man, nor impose upon him a penance." "For he who explains the sacred law to a Sudra, or dictates to him a penance, will sink together with that man into the hell." "But a Sudra, whether bought or unbought, he may compel to do servile work, for he was created by the Self-Existent to be the slave of a Brahman."

"A Sudra, though emancipated by his master, is not released from servitude; since that is innate in him, who can set him free from it?" "A Brahman may confidently seize the goods of (his) Sudra (slave); for as that (slave) can have no property, his master may take his possessions." "No collection of wealth must be made by a Sudra, even though he be able (to do it), for a Sudra who has acquired wealth gives pain to Brahmans." "But let a Sudra serve Brahmans, either for the sake of heaven, or with a view to both this life and the next, for he who is called the servant of a Brahman thereby gains all his ends."

The life of the Sudra was held in low esteem and in the sacred book Bandhayaira we learn that "the penalty for killing a Sudra was the same as that for killing a flamingo, a crow, an owl, a frog or a dog." We shall search in vain among such teachings for the doctrine of the brotherhood of man that some Swamis claim for Hinduism. Even the rights and comforts of their religion were expressly denied to the Sudra, and with penalties for any violation that show the heartless and cruel treatment of the Sudra, for in the "Gautama," Chapter XII, it is stated that if a Sudra were "to listen to a recital of the Vedic texts, they were to pour molten lac or tin into his ears, and if he repeated the sacred words his tongue was to be cut out, and if he remembered them his body shall be split in twain."

For a long time no Sudra was allowed to appear in the streets of Poona before 9 A. M. and after 3 P. M., lest his lengthened shadow or doublet should fall upon the twice born Brahman, and bring ceremonial defilement to this thrice arrogant Pharisee of Hinduism. It was a practical illustration of the logical sequence of the absurdity of the law of caste, but so unreasonable and inhuman that English rule removed this old social statute from the street etiquette of Poona, and henceforth the Sudra, as well as the Brahman, enjoyed the unchallenged freedom of the city during all hours instead of being tabooed from nine to three.

We may wonder why the majority submitted to such

grievous and humiliating wrongs that entailed so much inconvenience and hardship, but we must get their view-point and remember that to them it was a matter of inheritance and there was no dissent, for it was natural, as all things continued as they had been from the generations of old, and they had no other thought but accepted the situation as a necessary and fixed institution by divine enactment, and from which there should be no departure. In fact from the earliest childhood the law of caste was fundamental in the teachings and practices that they learned from their parents and they grew up as the product of such antecedents.

In the native state of Travancore a most invidious caste distinction was imposed upon the lower castes and outcastes by the ruling classes, prohibiting the women from wearing any garment above the waist; but when some of the women became converted to Christianity they insisted upon wearing a loose jacket. Bitter persecution followed, and it was not until some thirty years later, or in 1859, that the legal right to wear this modest waist was granted them. The tyranny of caste is much greater in Southern India than in the northern portion where Mohammedan influence has operated somewhat as a social leveller, although in many places it has taken on from her Hindu neighbours some of the evils of caste, in spite of the doctrine of their religion that all are equal in God's sight. However, a Sudra ranks much higher in the South than in the North. Besides, the Sudras are so numerous, progressive and influential in public affairs, that they are practically an upper-clean caste, as well as the dominant class in Travancore.

From the "Official Census Report" we learn some remarkable facts as to the extremely sensitive adjustment of the social consciousness of the Brahmans, for they claim to suffer pollution not merely by the touch of the Mayar, but beneath him is the class of untouchables whom he must keep away at certain prescribed necessary distances according to their scale of gradation, and which has been definitely fixed in accordance with supposed ascertained facts. For example, people of the Rammalan group, including masons, blacksmiths, carpenters and workers in leather pollute at a distance of twenty-four feet, toddy-drawers at thirty-six feet, Palayan or Cheruman cultivators at forty-eight feet; while in the case of the Paraiyan (Pariahs) who eat beef, the range of pollution is stated to be not less than sixty-four feet. Some consolation may be taken here from the fact that in an earlier publication the extreme range of the social polluting X-rays of the Pariah is stated to be seventy-two feet. So there has been eight feet of progress for the Pariah.

"In some provinces teachers will object to the admission of low-caste children in their schools, or if they admit them make them sit outside in the veranda." However, even these seemingly extreme examples of long-distance susceptibility to pollution are exceeded in the case of certain haughty Brahmans who have become so thoroughly possessed with their superiority over the common herd, that they claim to be susceptible to the polluting influence of a certain class of untouchables even at the distance of three hundred feet, and hence they are obliged to take great precaution when walking in public places and on the highway; whilst in the crowded streets it is to be presumed that necessity knows no law and they close their eyes against such social distinction.

As an illustration of the actual situation a writer to the *London Times* relates the following occurrence: "In Cochin a few years ago I was crossing a bridge and just in front of me walked a respectable-looking native. He suddenly turned, running back to the end of the bridge from which he had come, and plunged out of sight into the jungle on the side of the road. He had seen a Brahman entering on the bridge from the other end, and would not incur his resentment. In the native state of Travancore it is not uncommon to see a Panchama witness in a lawsuit, standing about one hundred yards from the court so as not to defile the Brahman judge and pleaders, whilst a row of peones, or messengers, standing between him and the court, hand out its questions to him and pass back his replies. No doubt the abject ignorance and squalor, and the repulsive habits of these unfortunate castes, help to explain and to perpetuate their ostracism, but they do not exculpate a social system which prescribes or tolerates such a state of things. Naturally the Panchamas are poor, dirty, ignorant and, as a consequence of many centuries of oppression, peculiarly addicted to the more mean and servile vices."

Whilst Hinduism has never attempted to do anything for the social elevation of the depressed classes, it must seem hard at times for the Brahman, who once had the Sudra under his feet, to be compelled to appear before the judge of a much inferior caste to have his lawsuit decided by one whom he had spurned as belonging to an unclean and degenerate class of beings. When subjected to such humiliation, and seeing that the tables have been turned, he must begin to think that a Daniel has come to judgment through British rule; for the countless social groups meet on a common level of justice in the courts that are supposed to recognize no caste, though abuses still prevail.

The Pariahs was a general term that designated the lower classes of the Hindus or Sub-Hindus not embraced in the four highest clean castes, but in the official report for the sake of convenience they are made to include all the depressed classes, and called Panchamas. They number no less than fifty millions or one-fourth of the entire Hindu population. Some by the sheer power of their inherent virtues have risen from their depressed situation in which they were born and through prosperity have been advanced in the social scale, so that probably one-half of the Sudras of to-day have come from the Panchamas. Owing to their social disabilities and neglect of even the rudiments of an education, their ignorance and poverty are deplorable, with little hope for immediate elevation.

The origin of caste in India may have been the necessary result of the instinct of self-preservation among the members of the Aryan race, who foresaw that the continuance of indiscriminate intermarriage with the aboriginal inhabitants would mean the ultimate assimilation of their distinctive racial traits, and the extinction of their identity as the superior white people by being absorbed by the vast hosts whom they had subjugated. Time wrought many changes and introduced innumerable subdivisions among the once original four castes which have been split up, in many instances, into indefinable differences that only the initiate can discriminate; and this is true of the higher as well as of the lower, for there are nearly two thousand Brahman castes in India to-day, and many thousands among the lower classes.

Strange as it may seem to us, every Hindu appears to be proud of his own caste, no matter how low and despised it may be, and he clings tenaciously to the requirements of his particular caste as the Brahman does to his, and would scorn a proposal to marry below his own despised caste. No one would deny them the possible satisfaction that they may derive from such feelings of pride, for they have so little for self-congratulation. This caste spirit that permeates all the social strata provides them at least with a sense of social aristocracy by being able to despise those that are still lower down. They imitate their superiors in observing caste just as they do in the excessive use of jewelry, and whilst lacking in quality, they surpass in quantity for they wear it on the forehead, ears, nose, neck, arms, wrists, fingers and even on the toes, and we saw some wearing heavy rings of pewter, several pounds in weight, around their ankles, and only an extreme sense of vanity could have relieved them of the discomfort.

We may well ask, What do the leaders of the National Movement mean when they cry out, "India for the Indians," whilst denying the inalienable rights of common humanity to fifty millions of the people of India, and by every act violating the doctrine of the brotherhood of man by their rigid insistence upon the observance of the inexorable law of caste? When they grow eloquent in demanding that the Indians should own and rule India, they ought to define the particular class of Indians that they would include in that category; and they should also mention the fifty millions whom they would exclude, and doom to a hopelessly depressed condition through the continuance of the caste system. There is no hope in sight for the redemption and elevation of the degraded Pariah millions if British rule should be supplanted by the arrogant leaders of the upper castes. The present government has endeavoured to secure equal political rights for all, and many of the Sudras and even outcastes occupy prominent positions among the officials, and work together, side by side with the higher castes, who would have abhorred them had it not been for the enforcement of British justice.

It is estimated that there are no less than twenty thousand different castes in India, ranging from the highest of the Brahman and Rajput class to the lowest castes. Nor does this numerous group of class distinctions descend to the depths of degraded humanity, for we must go far below every social strata that has been dignified by the name of caste to that vast population of depressed beings known as the outcastes and who number as many as fifty millions of souls. This is an exceedingly interesting type of humanity, for they have been the main constituency that has furnished the Christian converts.

We must always remember that strictly speaking there is no national type in India, such as exists in the various countries of Europe, and in the strict sense these outcastes are not Hindus. We must go deep down on social stilts to descend to the lowest of the outcastes, the Pallars, Pariahs and the Palayars who are regarded in more respects than one as unclean; yet it is from this class in Southern India that Christianity has won the great majority of her converts, and transformed many of them into representative citizens. These have been the submerged class, despised and ostracized by Hinduism, and excluded from the temple as though their touch were pollution, for the sacred places would be defiled, as they have been stigmatized as the "untouchables" and contact would mean social and religious defilement. Their state has been doubly deplorable in being proscribed and placed under the ban of religion and excluded from all its possible benefits. They were often treated as inhuman beings and worse than the animals, for often the Panchamas were not allowed to take their water from the public well but were obliged to go long distances for it, unless they could prevail, as in certain cases, upon caste women to give them the necessary water, for often individuals were far more charitable than the law of caste that governed them.

It is certainly paradoxical to claim, as certain Swamis do, that the doctrine of the brotherhood of man has been embraced in the teachings and practices of Hinduism, which by formal enactments and social usages has for centuries perpetuated the caste system, and predetermined the superior condition of some favoured millions before they were born, whilst dooming to an appalling social condition the tens of millions of others by an irrevocable law, that has been based upon the artificial distinctions of a remote ancestry. Every succeeding generation is supposed to be born into distinct groups of widely differing social standings, and without any reference to their personal worth, moral character or intellectual culture. The worthless and unscrupulous Brahman beggar is held superior in the

A HINDU FESTIVAL

scale of humanity to the noblest and most influential citizen, who by a life of consecrated service and generous deeds has proved himself to be one of God's noblemen and a benefactor of mankind. All this avails as nothing in competing for the honours of social standing in the community when matched against the man who has the honoured distinction of wearing the twofold string or sacred cord of the twice born, and which was inherited, and not acquired by merit.

Hinduism denies in teaching and practice the noble sentiment expressed by Pope in his "Essay on Man":

> "Honour and shame from no condition rise;
> Act well your part, there all the honour lies;
> Fortune in men has some small difference made;
> Worth makes the man, and want of it the fellow;
> The rest is all but leather or prunello
> Stuck o'er with titles, and hung round with
>   strings;
> Go if your ancient but ignoble blood
> Has crept throught scoundrels ever since the flood.
> An honest man's the noblest work of God."

Although the Brahmans aggregate but fifteen millions of the vast Hindu population of two hundred and seventeen millions, they are thoroughly mastered by the sense of their superiority over all others and have no consideration for the low castes and outcastes, although millions of these faithful toilers may be engaged in the most important and necessary occupations, such as weavers, leather workers and scavengers, as well as the blacksmiths, carpenters and farmers.

Strictly speaking, the caste system, socially and religiously, may be regarded as a close corporation and governed by inflexible laws that hitherto bound them to the strict observance of hereditary marriage alliances, and the prescribed rules pertaining to the preparation and eating of certain food, although the latter under special circumstances is often modified through the influence of Western education and civilization. Nevertheless, "Caste like some hideous spectre haunts every grade of Indian society and awes every individual of each grade. The squalid wretch that ekes out a bare subsistence on rice and water is as much afraid of it as the wealthy Brahman. Neither intelligence nor character seems any defense."[1]

All have been enslaved by its dreaded power and fear the anathemas of this monstrous tyranny. One of the strange features connected with caste is that all classes, even of the lowest and most depressed, calmly submit to it as though they believed that they were irrevocably destined by fate for this degraded state, and hence through the centuries there has been no revolt nor strike for freedom. It shows the supreme power of an undisturbed religious belief, for the history of caste is an amazing illustration of the countless multitudes submitting to grievous wrongs imposed by the small minority for centuries.

Whilst the various castes have claimed to have a traditional occupation, and the descendants of the priests became priests, and the sons of potters became potters, and so through the entire category of pursuits, there have been some radical changes in recent years due to education and the introduction of new industrial pursuits in connection with changed conditions of modern civilization, and especially the government's refusal to recognize any distinctions of caste, but to select

[1] W. Raju Kaidu.

all officials and workmen according to their qualifications alone, and without any reference to their particular caste. Once these caste lines were so clearly defined and observed that there was even an hereditary criminal class, and which was only open to those whose ancestors had been associated with its distinguished or notorious members. But all this has been revolutionized by the tempting offers of the government for the fittest employees irrespective of their caste and hereditary functional occupation.

In certain instances in Bengal, according to a recent census, less than twenty-five per cent. followed the traditional occupation, and in some cases even much less, and scarcely one in six of the Brahmans entered the priesthood, although all the priests are Brahmans. Not only are there frequent departures from the ancestral trade but even new ones are formed, and Mr. Risley in the "Census Reports" mentions a rather unique example of this class, known as the *hail-averter*, and organized as a shrewd corporation that found profitable employment among the unsophisticated farmers whose crops had suffered from the destructive agency of the hail. Unfortunately for the unscrupulous promoters there was an unusual season, when hailstorms became an epidemic of prolonged duration, and the farmers became skeptical and withdrew their patronage; as a consequence the hail-averters became bankrupt and ceased to exist as a caste.

The lines of distinction are often so firmly drawn between the various castes that it may become very embarrassing for those who employ servants, and we had an experience the day we visited a rock hewn temple some miles beyond Mangalgheri. The night previous we drove to a bungalow, and arranged for an early start next morning. We were up before the sun and had our breakfast at the appointed hour, for we had a long day's work before us, and as the driver did not appear with the horses we grew impatient. For some reason that servant was missing and we appealed to the cook and waiter to help us in our dilemma, but these servants, though poor as beggars, absolutely refused to assist us in doing anything that did not belong to their caste, and we lost more than an hour in wrangling and waiting until another servant could be secured to care for the horses.

One of the noblest missionaries, Dr. Harpster, concluded that he had at least conquered the spirit of caste among the trusty servants in his own home, owing to his personal influence among them for so many years; but he had presumed too much, as I learned from one of his embarrassing experiences. He was at the head of the great missionary work in Guntur, and during one of the commencements of that college he had a special dinner prepared for the resident missionaries, and also for those native graduates who were about to enter the ministry. At the appointed time the feast was ready and all the invited guests were seated about the table in American fashion, though differing in dress and complexion. There had been no delay on this occasion, for the feast was inviting and there was enough and to spare.

For some of those natives it was a red letter day, and the feast of a lifetime. There was no anxiety among the host and hostess, nor among the guests. The great soul of Dr. Harpster overflowed with joy and gratitude as he beheld at last an illustration in India of the exemplification of the doctrine of the Fatherhood of God and the brotherhood of man, and he gave profound thanks, for here were representatives of various castes, not from the Brahman or highest, but from the respectable Sudra down to the lower and even outcastes, who had been elevated through Christian education to become the sons of God and brethren in Christ Jesus.

It was an auspicious event that seemed to forecast the approach of the millennium for the millions that had so long been doomed by the caste system, and Dr. Harpster was elevated with the visions of the coming kingdom. He occupied the head of the table and rejoiced in that happy family, for he had no misgivings. The dinner was to be given in courses and the waiters began to serve the soup, but not to each one of the guests, for there were among the Panchamas a few from the Pariah outcastes and some degrees in the social scale below the servants. That concession was too much even for the waiters, and they stood upon their dignity. Dr. Harpster was too optimistic on this occasion to suspect its seriousness and he beckoned to the waiters to serve the rest, thinking that they had been unintentionally overlooked. The waiters eyed one another but refused to serve the untouchables even though they had been educated in the Lutheran Guntur College and recently elevated to the Christian ministry.

Then Dr. Harpster realized the embarrassing situation and he remonstrated and appealed to what Christianity had done for them and their people, but they stood firm by their antecedents. His patience became exhausted and fired with indignation because of their disobedience and disrespect shown to his invited guests, he arose and with his Websterian attitude commanded them to go to the kitchen at once and serve all the guests henceforth without any invidious discrimination. They eyed him intently and shook their heads, for they would serve no outcaste, contrary to their religious customs, and when he threatened they eyed one another with a significant look for a moment, and then they rushed out of the house, across the lawn and disappeared for that day. Dr. Harpstér was chagrined for he had been outwitted in presuming so much upon this happy love feast with the various social groups; for the kingdom had not yet come to his servants, and the guests had to serve themselves, for even his most trusty servant of many years joined the caste strikers.

In America we rejoice in the complex and democratic character of our public assemblies and banquets, for they are most cosmopolitan, and the doctrine of the Fatherhood of God and the brotherhood of man is illustrated in a practical manner. In fact it has been realized in a preëminent degree in our country where as many as 1,100,000 emigrants from various parts of the earth have been landed upon our shores within a single year. We welcome them, associate with them, educate them, and make them worthy citizens by sharing with them the advantages of our best institutions, and as many as twenty-six distinct nations have been represented in one of our public schools in the city of New York at one time. Thus we exercise a tremendous assimilating power over them and their children, and soon they cease to be known as English, German, French, Scandinavian, Irish or Italian; for by this universal process of assimilation we transform them all into American citizens like ourselves and hence the foreign names alone survive to remind us of foreign origin and which are seen among the leading manufacturers, merchants, bankers, statesmen, educators, as well as the various professions; for all these places of usefulness and influence are open to them.

This assimilation and recognition of the brotherhood of man becomes even more thoroughly effected through intermarriage with the various Indo-European races, for we all come from a common stock of ancestors. We all are familiar with the saying, "Scratch a Russian and you will find a Tartar," but whilst that is only partially true and in a very limited sense, we may say in truth and without any qualification, "Scratch an American and you will find a European—German, Scandinavian, Englishman, etc.," and if you probe deep enough you will find our remote ancestors among the Indo-Europeans; hence we should unite in this common bond of brotherhood, and to which also the Aryan Brahmans belong as the lineal descendants of the same ancient stock, although in the absence of the historical and philological sense they have become so completely self-centred in their ethnological vision as to recognize no affinity with any other people.

Try to imagine what the condition of America would be had our ancestors tyrannized the political, educational, religious and social history of our country with the caste system. Then the names of many of our eminent Presidents would never have found a place in our American history, and there would have been no Lincoln, Grant, Garfield and McKinley. Most of the greatest statesmen, educators, inventors, reformers, public-spirited men and benefactors would have remained in obscurity and with undeveloped powers for good; for by the immutable law of caste each man would have been destined to follow the hereditary occupation, and all personal ambition, individual traits and resources would have been paralyzed and the greatest possibilities would have been prevented by not allowing them to mature.

We can only estimate the loss by recalling a few names of those who rose from obscurity to places of eminence in the world. Because some were born in the plebeian state as a shoemaker, blacksmith or labourer in the factory, that did not prevent them from rising to positions of preëminent influence and honour as the familiar names of Carey, Elihu Burritt and Livingstone demonstrate; and the names of hundreds of others in England and America might be mentioned, including Lincoln, Grant and McKinley who rose from a lowly birth to positions of the highest eminence, and received from their nation undying fame and a proud immortality. The magnificent monuments erected by a grateful people testify not only to the esteem in which they were held, but show the possibilities of young men, when born free and untrammelled by the fetters of caste. Little did Livingstone think the day he strolled into Westminster Abbey as a missionary, and looked upon the monuments of the mighty, that the day would come when, after a life of self-sacrifice in battling against the terrible evils of the slave trade in Africa, England would bestow upon him the distinguished honour of laying his mortal remains at rest among the kings, statesmen and great heroes of her country in that famous Abbey.

We know what disastrous bankruptcy of human

achievement would have befallen our own country had its founders brought the inexorable law of caste, with its unmitigated evils, with them as it prevails in Hinduism throughout India. Then there would have been stagnation, for all progress and brotherhood would have been throttled by the relentless grasp of that inhuman evil that for so many years has been the curse of mankind in India. Then Edison, the modern wizard of the most beneficent discoveries, would have been confined to his inherited occupation, and doomed to a life of ignorance and poverty, with undeveloped inherent powers, and all the world would have been much poorer.

It is difficult for us to realize the situation of the caste system in India, for accustomed to our Western ideas and democratic fellowship with society that is composed of a variety of members, we are not shocked when a young man from lowly and obscure parentage rises by his inherent worth and marries in a family of prominent social standings, and there is no feeling of disgrace and no public ostracism. Often there are great differences in nationality and social antecedents, but other compensations of character, culture and standing are recognized, and congratulations are freely bestowed. There is no upheaval of society, no persecution, but a happy home has been formed and in which all rejoice.

In Hinduism such a state of union is forbidden. The parents make the marriages, and strictly within their own caste, for any transgression of that law would mean bitter persecution, and the entire family would be involved in the disgrace. The matter is all the more serious in Hinduism where every woman is supposed to be married at an early age, and where it is regarded as a disgrace not to be married.

An incident from the well-known Woman's Hospital at Guntur will illustrate the situation. It was at a religious service held in the court of the hospital on a Sunday morning that I met an interesting member of a higher caste, whose wife had just recovered from what his friends and native doctors in his village had regarded as an incurable disease, and on the following day would return home. The husband was a man of culture, and as he loved his wife, his heart was filled with gratitude towards the medical missionaries, and he freely expressed himself. He also declared that he believed in Christ and the Gospel and that he no longer believed in Hinduism, and that he would be baptized but dared not, for that meant to break caste.

He and his wife would be willing to make the sacrifice and suffer all that it involved, but he said: "What would become of my daughters? Whom will they marry?" That was a very serious question in that country where it was considered as a disgrace for a woman not to be married. But where he lived there were no Christians of his caste, but only of the outcastes, and he could not marry his daughters to that ignorant, poor and degraded class, and neither would we favour such a shocking alliance, for after baptism the father and mother with their children would be treated as outcastes, they would be ostracized by their own caste, and none of the sons of their caste would marry the daughters, and amid such persecutions their condition and outlook for the future would be too deplorable for the father openly to follow his religious convictions. Those who condemn him may ask themselves whether they would be willing to make such a personal sacrifice by marrying their daughters to an actually degraded people.

Stanley Rice, who for nineteen years was a member of the Civil Service in India, and who had ample opportunity for observation, writing of the respectable character of the Sudras of Northern India, who are as much superior to the Panchamas as the Brahmans are to them, reminds us that it is difficult for us to appreciate the disabilities under which the Sudra is placed who contemplates the acceptance of Christianity; for in the vast majority of cases it means to identify him with the lowest or Pariah class, and that social stigma and ostracism is too great a sacrifice for many caste men to make. He states that "caste is essentially a social distinction with a religious sanction." To lose caste subjects him to persecution, and the denial of religious rights, and also ordinary comforts, for "the barber will decline to shave him, the washerman will not wash his clothes, his quondam friends will refuse him fire and water, and he may be in straits to get food itself." "The Pariah lives in almost inconceivable squalor, in the most superstitious ignorance, and in a condition of morality that hardly bears investigation. There is a marked difference between the mode of life of a Christian and a Hindu Pariah. Habits of clean-livers, of truth, of thrift are engendered, and missionary effort in this respect is certainly justified of her children." "Caste is dearer than ethics, than wealth, than anything short of life."

J. A. Sharrock, a missionary for twenty-seven years in Southern India, declares that whilst the Church condemns the spirit of caste and preaches against it, they tolerate it, and the converts practice it. He refers to a certain occasion when he allowed a Pariah man and his family, whom he had baptized, to sit with the others in the church, but the native Christians remonstrated with great demonstration and threatened to leave the building. Then he went to the door and bolted it to prevent their escape from the church, but the incensed members overpowered him, and the three hundred forced their way out, for their conversion to Christianity did not change their convictions as to caste nor remove their prejudices against associating even in the church with the Pariah outcaste. The curse of caste has been the greatest foe and barrier against the progress of Christianity, and yet it has triumphed, and I am persuaded that there are thousands of silent Christian believers among the better class of Hindus, but who feel that they cannot afford to make the necessary sacrifice of social ostracism and persecution.

In the Guntur Mission I spoke with a Brahman whose wife and children abandoned him when he became a convert; it was some years before a reconciliation was effected through their own conversion. Few men are ready to make such sacrifices, and should they be encouraged? It is easy to say that the Hindu should, but would you do it? This is one of the serious domestic problems that the missionaries encounter, and it is the greatest barrier to their work. The man ostracized by his caste is in a deplorable and almost helpless condition, for socially he becomes a nondescript, and where shall he find his social level? Strange as it may seem there is a terrible truth in the saying that in the Hindu system of caste it is as "impossible to fall downwards as it is to fall upwards," and no wonder that men hesitate and count the cost before breaking with their own caste.

As an illustration of the persistency of caste in a country where it is dearer than "ethics, wealth" or any human possession, and where the difference between theory and practice, even among Christians, is clearly in evidence, I submit the following protest that appeared in a recent issue of the *Christian Patriot*, published in Madras, and without any dissent or comment from the editor.

"*The Middle Wall of Partition.*

"SIR:

"I regret to inform you that at a recent mission prize giving a rather painful distinction was observed between the Indian and the foreign guests who had been invited. On arrival all were received at the same entrance and led through the same passage and then suddenly turned into distinct places set apart for white and black (the sheep and goats).

"I thought that in Christian circles, at least, race distinction among specially invited guests would not be so rigidly observed.

"I trust that the better spirited Christians in the West will take pains to notice not so much what their agents out here print and publish but rather what they practice in actual life, as regards those whom they speak of as their Indian 'brothers and sisters.'

"A BLACK GUEST."

That is the practical situation, which is likely to continue for many years to come. We can hardly condemn it, and disallow the proud Aryan in India the exercise of the same inherent convictions that we hold to be our right in discriminating between the rank of people with whom we associate. We claim this liberty, and we not only have drawn a colour line, but even instituted the "Jim Crow" cars in some states, so that the whites may not suffer the blacks to ride in the same coach. Whilst we have removed many disabilities from the coloured race and given them protection, teachers and education so that they have been elevated and fitted for honoured places of usefulness, nevertheless that colour line is instinctive in the minds of all, and any suggestion of a possible union of the races by an amalgamation through miscegenation would be met with universal abhorrence, not only by the American people but by all the white races. We want to co-operate with them in every possible manner by which their highest welfare may be attained, but we have an innate and inexorable conviction against intermarriage, and any violation of this innate and inflexible law through the forbidden marriage of those who should not be joined together meets with universal condemnation and disgust. The degenerate violators commit a crime against society as well as against their own pitiable offspring.

I am convinced that too much emphasis has at times been placed upon the duty of intermarriage between the high and low castes in India, as though such humiliation, and in some cases degradation, were regarded as a cardinal virtue and duty of Christianity. In many instances there is a vast difference that is not artificial but most real between high castes and outcastes, and who would have his own daughter make the descent? The descendants of future generations will rise under Christian influences and the great social chasm will become closed in time, and then the situation will be changed, but the Panchamas must first become the equals of the higher castes in respectable habits, moral character and culture, and I am speaking of present conditions as they are, and not as we may idealize or wish they were. I could appreciate the justifiable feelings of the father I met at the Woman's Hospital in Guntur as he expressed the grave difficulties in his way to make a public acceptance of Christianity by being baptized, for that would have doomed his daughters to marriage with a despised and low people in his village, if they married at all; and a woman of refinement would rather a thousand times live and die an old maid than to descend to such social depths as exist among millions of the lowest of the Panchamas. Of course I do not include in this unsavoury category the many millions of that elevated and highly respectable class of Sudras, who were originally under the ban of the Brahmans, but who are now often competing successfully for the highest positions of culture, wealth, influence and honour among the leaders and best men of India.

Our social ideas with reference to the survival of the fittest, and that God is no respecter of persons, would strike the Brahman class as a preposterous heresy. Were he to study the political history of our country he would be astounded to learn that a boy without any distinguished ancestors, and born of very poor, obscure and unlettered parents, amid the most adverse circumstances, in a very humble cottage in the wild wilderness, remote from all refining, elevating, social and educational advantages, was able by his own moral force and virtue, in spite of all the unfavourable antecedents and environment, to rise to the very pinnacle of national fame and lasting honour.

The Brahman would be amazed at such a story and

would be unable to comprehend the possibility of such a rise from social obscurity to the highest position of responsibility and honour in the gift of the American people, and wholly because of his moral worth and the development and exercise of his personal powers. And yet the poor boy became the noble Abraham Lincoln, known and honoured throughout the world as one of God's chief noblemen. There is much truth in the lines of J. A. Edgerton:

> "When Lincoln died, a type was lost to men.
> The earth has had her conquerors and kings,
> And many of the common great, through all;
> She only had one Lincoln. There are none
> Like him in all the annals of the past.
> He was the growth of our new soil; the child
> Of our new time; he was American;
> Was of the people, from the lowest rank;
> And yet he scaled with ease the highest height.
> Mankind one of its few immortals lost
> When Lincoln died.
> He led a splendid fight for liberty,
> And when the shackles fell, the land was saved,
> He laid his armour by and sought his rest."

There is unreasonableness as well as injustice in the system of caste. Whilst we are not indifferent as to remote antecedents, we are not so seriously concerned to know who a man's great-grandfather was as to know who the man himself may be, and by his personal character and fitness judge and accept him. If he is lacking in culture and moral character, the virtues of distinguished ancestors cannot atone for his personal delinquencies, for it is not birth that gives man his station, but the development of personal virtues. But with the Hindu all this is reversed. No matter who the man may be, how cultured and noble his character, what virtues or vices he may possess, how capable or how stupid he may be—these do not necessarily determine his station of honour or dishonour in society but who were his ancestors, and not merely the immediate, but even the remote ones. A man is seriously handicapped by the fatalism of such an unjust law in making him responsible for all his ancestors, whatever crimes they may have committed, and by whom it was determined that the man should be born in a certain social group of low castes or possible outcastes.

No wonder that for centuries stagnation characterized the social and industrial condition of India, for there was no stimulus for development, no incentive for the young men with minds to become hopeful and ambitious for advancement and success in society and the state. No new avenues were opened to them but all closed by caste, and their future destiny was confined to the treadmill routine of the hereditary occupation and which was fixed at birth by their father's station. There was no freedom of choice in the struggle of life, no opportunity for developing the mind and personal gifts by the exercise of will power in devising improved conditions; for fate had mapped out their earthly career the day they were born, and they dared not deviate from the record.

An observing traveller in India will often be impressed with the deplorable condition of the depressed classes and the wide breach that separates them from the Brahman aristocracy. This was forcibly brought to mind the day that a college professor in Conjeverim accompanied me to one of the celebrated temples, for whilst he was an intellectual and influential man in that city, he was not permitted to cross the threshold of the temple because he was a Tamil, and not having been born of a higher caste; and while he was in no way responsible, but made the most of his life, he was excluded, although the lowest Brahman beggars, monkeys, goats, cows and bulls were freely admitted.

I reasoned with the priest and remonstrated against their irrational conduct in making such an invidious and inhuman distinction that I supposed the local professor felt most keenly. They had no reason to offer in defense, but excused their action by referring it to the god of custom, and which is the highest court of appeal in Hinduism and recognizes no modern reasoning. However, the humble professor was not so sensitive as I imagined, for he had been reared under the caste system, and had inherited the spirit of submission to the upper classes, and never counted the cost but yielded as a matter of course.

We had an interesting illustration of the power that caste exercises over the mind and conduct of the individual the day that we drove from Delhi to Ktub Minar to see the famous column and ruins of that ancient site. Our driver was poor as the men who follow his lowly occupation, and he was not well fed nor well groomed. His meagre income did not permit him to enjoy anything beyond the bare necessities of life, the plainest food and clothing, and his limited resources were apparent in the quality and extent of his simple wardrobe, for it was lacking at both ends and mostly confined to his loins. He had a sad and hungry look that excited my sympathy, and I resolved to make it an unusually happy day for him, and that once at least he should have enough to eat, and if possible the best and most bountiful meal of his life.

As the drive was a long one the hotel provided our luncheon and I arranged with the head waiter to put in a liberal supply, for I wanted the driver to have a feast that day, and such as would gladden his heart as well as satisfy his hunger. The drive was one of unusual interest and we visited several historic places on the way. After the noon hour, we selected a place in the shade of the ruins and sat down for our tiffin, but having a thought for the inbred religious scruples of the Hindus, and which especially dominate their table etiquette, I avoided all possible offense by handing to him the major portion of that choice luncheon before we tasted a morsel.

I expected to see a wonderful transformation in the expression of that sad face, and I thought that for the time being he would be one of the happiest men in India, for I had no thought of the demon of caste so controlling this humble and hungry mortal that he would not be able to enjoy the feast prepared, and which we relished. I am confident that he had never enjoyed such an excellent meal and I was prepared for a happy smile of gratitude, with much bowing, but imagine my disappointment at his stolid indifference, for instead of joyfully accepting that feast with thanksgiving, he would not so much as touch the tabooed things, but with a possibly still sadder look, bordering on despair, he shrugged his shoulders significantly and said: "I am very sorry, sir, but my caste will not allow me to eat it." He did not intend his remark as any reflection upon us, and he added: "But I am hungry and I will thank you for some money that I may buy some bread to eat."

I gave him the money, for I understood his bondage and how the tyranny of custom had fettered him, both mind and body, so that he could not do otherwise, and did not seem morally responsible for his absurd refusal of the food that I offered him. It was a feast compared with what he bought to satisfy his hunger, and I pitied him as I saw him eating that frugal meal, without any variety, but only composed of the plain black and dry bread. He followed his religious caste convictions, although at the sacrifice of gastronomical satiety.

As I scanned him the contrast was suggestive, and I thought that the dominant principle for one's religion should exist somewhere in the mind and heart, and not down in the region of the stomach. His ethical code became faulty in practice, for he insisted that I should give him an extra amount of money to secure provision to feed the horses and that the sum which he stated was absolutely necessary, for he had brought no money with him. I gave him the required rupees as requested, and learned later that he had deceived me and withheld from the horses the full quantity to satisfy their hunger by retaining one-half the money given him, but his religious scruples were not so inflexible with reference to the practice of this moral code.

Such artificial discriminations that the caste system enjoins appeared irrational to us, and productive of much evil, for they are based upon the mere accidents of birth and not personal merit and the character and worth of the individual. The student of Hinduism is impressed with its phenomenal coherence, solidarity and dominant power for so many centuries, and in controlling the minds and lives of two hundred millions of followers at the present time. The amazing feature of this fact is, that whilst it is so strongly intrenched in the hearts of the people and has shaped their destiny, all this has been effected without any ecclesiastical head corresponding with that of the pope, patriarch, or ecumenical council or synod. This is without a parallel and challenges an explanation.

We can only account for this fact by referring to the unique and invincible system of caste that controls the many divisions of the separate social groups into which Hinduism has divided itself, for the various members of the lowest as well as the highest groups recognize their identity as a part of the complicated system, and submit as if controlled by an innate law of conscience that insists upon the observance of caste, no matter what the cost may be. No doubt Hinduism owes much of its tremendous power to the vitality and supremacy of caste. We may regard its sway as an unmitigated evil, especially for the depressed classes, and yet they themselves insist upon caste observance.

All this has only been possible in virtue of the peculiar character of the family system in Hinduism, and which grows somewhat like the former Oneida Community; for when the sons marry, instead of going forth with the bride to form a new home for themselves, they bring her to the ancestral home where the children, parents, grandparents and great-grandparents all live together and the old man holds the purse and gives the orders, and receives obedience from this ever enlarging social and domestic corporation. In the strictest sense they are the product of their antecedents and from their inherited ideas and customs there is no departure, for they recognize no law of progress, but all bow to the standards that have been fixed by the inexorable law of the past.

Within that close corporation no foreign ideas nor customs intrude, but all things continue from generation to generation as transmitted by their forefathers, and no one conceives of doing otherwise, for the orthodox Hindu mind is not supposed to exercise itself with such liberties. Hence the children become imbued with the spirit of caste by precept and by example so that it becomes an inherent asset of their being, for there was little change or development in the monotonous routine in the life of the ordinary Hindu for many centuries, beyond the growth in years, inasmuch as their ideals were in the past, and custom was finality for their individual conduct. They preserved the purity or impurity of their particular caste by confining their intermarriages to restricted degrees of relationship, and which has been attended by many evils.

English rule and education in India have become powerful solvents of some of the worst features of caste, for the government decreed in 1831 that "no native be debarred from office on account of caste, creed or race, and that a son who had left his father's religion did not thereby forfeit his inheritance." Even some of the higher Hindus have gone into the most tabooed leather business because they saw it to be remunerative, although still under the ban of caste, and the beggar Brahman would not take food from them, for that would be pollution, although he would not be polluted by the touch of a cat or even a dog, and such discriminations seem irrational.

FESTIVAL PROCESSION AT MADURA

TEMPLE DANCING GIRLS

The opening of the railroad became an effectual entering wedge into this hitherto inexorable system that had separated all classes, for the common seat in the coach became eventually the meeting place of all conditions of men who could pay the fare, for that ticket entitled one of the hitherto untouchables to the seat beside the haughty Brahman. No provision was made on this fast line of universal progress for that hoary system of caste that for so many years had made all progress impossible. This startling innovation came from the West, and all readily recognized its superior advantages as a means of transportation in that hot country of long distances, and with which the uncomfortable springless bullock cart could not be compared. But it was run on an altogether too democratic basis, and the Brahmans demurred and entered vigorous protests to secure immunity for themselves which would not subject them to the grievous outrage of putting one of the depressed classes in the same compartment with them. However, the railroads were not built by the caste system, and the trains were not scheduled to run for the exclusive convenience of the Brahman aristocracy; so they had no alternative except to walk or ride in the slow and uncomfortable bandy cart, and hence they ungracefully submitted by gathering themselves as closely together as possible, and trying to keep the untouchables at elbow distance, lest the actual touch should cause pollution.

The public educational system is a great leveller of caste, for the upper castes, in order to keep pace with the lower ones in competing for honours and government positions and stations of influence, must have their children educated. But all caste distinction is ignored in the public schoolhouse, for the high and low, Brahman and Panchama, meet and sit together, although some exceptions have been made where the Pariahs sit outside in the veranda. They not only compete for rank in the class room, but the latter have even carried off the coveted university honours.

In many respects the Brahmans are the favoured class and not so restricted as to the character of their particular employment; for whilst they furnish all the priests they also find occupation as soldiers, farmers and servants, and it seems rather incongruous to find the high caste Brahman doing service for a low caste employer, whose bread he would not receive and at whose table he would not eat. Such self-conscious superiority often hangs upon a very slender thread not visible to the eyes of mortals, for even that sacred or twice born cord which the Brahman wears is too plain and limited to conceal his menial service. The young men who have been members of the Panchama class, but who have received their education in the Christian missions, and developed so as to outrank the leading Brahmans in the place, so far as intellectual influence and service for the social betterment of humanity are concerned, become convinced that the caste system is as artificial as it is unjust, and their influence is directed against it.

The Gaekwar of Baroda, who has taken an active part in a wide-spread movement to secure the amelioration of the degraded state of the untouchables who make up one-fifth of the Hindu population, declares that "want of education is practically universal among them, for they are unable to attend the ordinary schools owing to the idea that it is pollution to touch them. To do so is to commit a sin offensive alike to religion and to conventional morality. Of professions as a means of livelihood those depressed classes have a very small choice. Here too the supposed pollution of their touch comes in their way. The common man, who never bothers to search for the reason of a practice that is sanctioned by custom or what he calls religion, believes it sin to touch one of the depressed classes, the expiation of which is a bath, the shaving of the face, the handing over of a substantial fine to the Brahmans. That his fathers did it before him, and that the nebulous collection of custom and superstition which does duty for religion with him prescribes it, satisfies his reason. You cannot argue with him for his religion is beyond argument, being based on facts which if written are more or less inaccessible, and not open to logical attack. The more educated put forth a complicated occult theory in justification of this practice.

"To touch a dead animal or leather destroys sanctity; so does the touch from some of the animals—and so on until it culminates among some Vaishnavas who cannot eat food cooked by their own wives. It is pollution, it is loss of sanctity to do so. What can be more absurd? The polluting power of a cat is very small, of a dog it is greater, but nothing equals the pollution of a Pariah. The degrading of a man below beasts is the culminating point of this fabric of sanctity.

"The religion which commands the trampling down of millions of our fellows into perpetual ignorance, and consequent vice, disease and misery, is a false one. If the Indian people wish to progress and to make the most of their national influence they must give up these old false ideals, and limit the tyrannical and despotic sway of religion, which is crushing out the life of our people by driving out of them all sense of personal pride, individuality and ambition. The absurdity and injustice of the theory divide men into divisions based not on personal merit but on mere accident of birth."[1]

The Brahman who has so long been accustomed to lord it over the low castes does not even bow his head when addressing them, and the self-centred priests do not even deign to bow before the images of the gods of the Sudra and lower castes when officiating at the simple altar in the homes of these people. No wonder that the distinguished native jurist, Jagendra Nath Battacharya, arraigns the practice of caste in the severest terms when he declared that "nothing can be more sinful than to speak respectfully of persons who are enemies of mankind, and to whitewash rotten institutions by esoteric explanations and fine phrases. For purposes of marriage and interchanged hospitality each caste is an independent and exclusive body."

"The Vedic rites and prayers which the three higher castes are required to perform are all prohibited to the Sudra. The latter can be taught to repeat only those prayers which are prescribed. But the Brahman who enlists even a good Sudra among his disciples is lowered forever in the estimation of the people; while ministering to a Sudra of a low class, he is degraded altogether." "Under no circumstances is he to eat any food cooked with water and salt by a Sudra, or touched by a Sudra after being so cooked."

[1] *Indian Review*, December, 1909.

VIII

HINDU TEMPLES

THESE are found in all the cities, towns and villages of the empire, from Cape Comorin on the south to the Himalayas on the north. And whilst there are some large and magnificent ones in Bengal and the Madras Presidency, every village has its temple and shrine, however small and insignificant they may be, for the people are passionately religious and devoted to their gods. Among the thirty or forty Dravidian temples in the South, there are few that antedate the fifteenth and sixteenth centuries, and some belong to an even later period. By far the most magnificent of these temples are located in Southern India and are easily reached by rail. The towering pyramidal gopura is the most distinctive feature, and this is the first object seen among the buildings, for it is the most conspicuous as well as picturesque object in the landscape.

On our way north from Tuticorin, we received our first impression of the Dravidian temples at Madura. These are the religious centres of every community, and the chief attraction for the traveller who is interested in the study of humanity, for here we find a wonderful panorama of human interests spread out before us and ever changing with a sort of kaleidoscopic effect that prevents all monotony. It was a strange and different world in which we found ourselves, for the transformation from the West to the East is so great that an eye-witness alone can appreciate it. You cannot express certain qualities and feelings in cold type upon the page, no more than you can define a mother's sorrow by a chemical analysis of her tears. To know the exact flavour of a luscious peach you must eat it yourself, and to know and feel certain conditions in India, you must see them, for they are so utterly foreign and strange to us.

After all, nothing is so interesting as the human element, and hence I have given it a prominent place in this work. It is never absent in India, with its teeming millions, and the thousands that crowd about the temples on every festival occasion; and I shall endeavour to describe some of the scenes witnessed, trusting that by the aid of the imagination the reader may also be enabled to see them.

Imagine a quadrangle 847×729 feet, enclosing the great temple and group of related buildings,—having four large gopuras and five small ones, the largest reaching to a height of about one hundred and fifty feet. The gopura is an imposing structure, and serves as the gateway to the temple, and somewhat resembles the pylon of the ancient Egyptian temple. These lofty and picturesque towers add greatly to the grandeur of the architectural effect, as well as to the solemnity of the sacred buildings. The great temple is not the only attractive feature in the enclosure, for there is the so-called hall of one thousand pillars, with some remarkable carvings. The monumental gateway is covered on all sides with raised figures and designs of great variety in stucco. The original purpose may have been purely decorative, and in addition to the many geometrical designs, there are figures of animals, gods and goddesses, and some of them have brilliant colours.

The decoration is cheap and easily criticized from the standpoint of art, for there is much that is grotesque and inartistic, and distance lends enchantment; but the general effect is picturesque and most imposing to the swarms of illiterate pilgrims. The lavish prodigality of decoration, and the prevailing bright colours of red, green and blue must impress the minds of most of the Hindus as something bordering on the marvellous.

About the gateway many beggars were congregated to solicit alms from the multitudes as they entered and withdrew. One of them was of special interest, and made a profound impression upon me, for he was the first devotee of the bovine cult that I had witnessed, although the spectacle became one of the familiar objects seen about the great temples. I have introduced him to the reader through a photograph that I took of him, for he appeared much pleased to have his picture taken, and he posed for the occasion by assuming his devout attitude, that showed his attachment and faith in the sacred animal by alternately rubbing his hand over its back and then taking hold of the tail and pressing it to his lips with intense fervour. The people crowded about us and looked on with evident curiosity, and shut out of view the ascetic, who, not to be frustrated, changed his position and sat directly in front of the animal with his head resting against its jaw. He had an abundant growth of black hair that fell over his shoulders, and his long whiskers were in striking contrast with his pale ashen face. He was by no means indifferent to his appearance for he brushed aside the hair that had almost concealed his face, and several times he stroked his long flowing beard; but he showed no concern as to the effect of his scanty wardrobe, for his sanctity was supposed to be a sufficient covering, and which was abundantly supplemented by his long and heavy growth of hair and whiskers. He was an interesting representative of that ubiquitous type of ascetics that attract the special attention of travellers, and we never lost our interest in them, for they were a marked example of some of the strange and irreconcilable freaks of that complex system of Hinduism.

Passing through the gateway we entered a large area that was converted into a bazaar, where many articles were offered for sale, especially cheap jewelry, made of brass and coloured bits of glass instead of precious stones, for the poor of India have a passion for display in jewelry as seen in their peculiar and profuse ornamentations. There was a din of noise, and the atmosphere was musty and laden with pungent odours of undefinable ingredients, for the animals that freely roamed about had converted it into an unclean and malodorous place. The sunshine was excluded, and the fictitious sanctity from the cow could not neutralize the stale and offensive elements that entered into that atmosphere, and make it agreeable to the olfactory nerves of any one except the devout Hindu.

Crowds swarmed through the temple apparently drawn thither, like ourselves, out of curiosity and to see the objects of interest and study the faces of strange looking men and women, for there was no particular place set apart for worship, and where the people engaged in special religious devotions during certain hours of the day, the throng moved aimlessly about, but with what thoughts and silent prayers we know not. There was no special demonstration or outward devotions that would correspond with our idea of congregational or private worship, although certain individuals stopped for a moment in meditation before some shrine and then hurried on, but without any apparent concern for any one else. The sacred image of the god Siva, confined within its holy shrine, was the centre of religious attraction for the Hindus, and in order to deepen the mystery of the divinity, its sanctuary is but faintly lighted by the small taper of the primitive lamp; yet this dim religious light was no less obscure than the purpose that seemed to have brought the people there, for many gazed upon us with as great curiosity as they did upon that image, and much longer. There were numerous priests in attendance to direct the visitors to see the sights, and to collect from them as much as possible for the support of the temple.

It was a relief to escape from the crowded building to an outer court where there was a beautiful arcade about a large tank of water, a necessary equipment in connection with the daily religious ablutions, for the sacred bulls, though impelled by a different instinct, followed the example of the Hindus, and even exceeded them in the number of times that they bathed. No doubt the excessive heat led them so frequently into that tank, although the water was quite warm, and of course no one disturbed them, although there were some very offensive features connected with their gross violation of our Western standards of common propriety that shocked us, but it did not offend the sense of the strict religious etiquette of Hinduism; inasmuch as those animals are so sacred, and everything that proceeds from them is so potent in securing salvation for the Hindu that special rights are accorded to the bulls and cows and which would be denied to man. The most and perhaps famous of these places is the Mahamokam tank at Kumbhakonam.

In a sheltered corner stood several large elephants that were employed in special services about the temple, and to give impressiveness to the religious ceremonies connected with the spectacular festival processions that we witnessed on the following day. The Juggernaut car processions are not confined to the temple at Puri, that contains his original and sacred image, but as he is one of the manifestations of Vishnu, therefore his temples are in every large town, and even some smaller ones have their Juggernaut image, and their annual car procession, on the great festival day, while the ceremonies attending them are similar to those seen at the central seat at Puri, although on a less elaborate scale.

In various cities in Southern India we saw the colossal Juggernaut cars, sometimes enclosed in a shed or with a covering above it, and kept near the temple in readiness for the next festival. Some were of enormous size, and nearly fifty feet in height, with ponderous wheels and massive beams for axles; the wheels were without the modern hub, spokes and felloes, and made of very heavy planks, so that we can easily understand how several hundred men at least, tugging at long ropes, would be required to draw the car through the rough streets.

The body of the car is made of lighter material and built in a somewhat pyramidal form, although it is square and wide at the base, resembling a small cottage. We saw a much smaller one drawn by one hundred or more men and women through the main street in Guntur. The idol was seated on the car beneath a canopy, and was gaudily dressed in bright colours with a profusion of jewelry and looking like some oriental doll. On either side of the image stood a boy who was fanning it, not to keep the god cool nor to keep the flies from its face, but, in accordance with Eastern custom, in showing marked respect and reverence for a superior personage, for that was a representative of Juggernaut, the lord of the world in the eyes of the Hindu worshipper of Vishnu.

It was a hard pull to draw that car up a slight incline and the men and women pulled most strenuously, but rested at short intervals. They perspired freely and some leaned against the buildings for a rest until ordered to move again. They did not appear to be in a very serious mood, especially the young man whom I addressed, for in reply to my question as to why they were drawing the car with the image through the streets, he said that the god had been in the temple for six months and was sick, and they were taking him out for an airing.

The car procession that we witnessed at Madura was an unusually attractive one for it was the annual celebration of their great religious festival, and thousands of people, men and women, crowded the main thoroughfare, and only the centre was cleared for the procession. The street was unusually wide and adapted to such spectacular display. The women mingled freely in the crowd and many were dressed in costumes and adorned with rich jewelry that indicated their financial rank at least, and their general appearance and excellent behaviour were evidence that they belonged to the better class. Their bright and happy faces showed that they enjoyed the freedom of that day, and that they did not belong to that unfortunate class of women, found in some quarters of India, who voluntarily enslave themselves by keeping indoors and in their secluded apartments behind the pardah. Large groups allowed themselves to be photographed, and it seemed to afford them much amusement.

It was an unusual opportunity to behold all classes, the rich and the poor, the high and the low, the prince and the pauper, for the people of Madura were on the street and all enjoyed that gala day with its brilliant street attractions. Of course, with the rich display of wealth and the cheerful countenances there was abject poverty, and many faces scarred with the sad marks that showed the terrible struggle for existence through which they had passed. The regular contingent of that worse than useless population, the ascetics and mendicants, mingled with the crowd, and the wild look of some of these religious fanatics clearly indicated that they should be treated in some asylum. It was an interesting study of the extremes of humanity, for the utmost freedom and good-will prevailed, and all were patient and courteous. There was no intoxication, and I saw none of that disgusting class of half-drunken fools who often become a terror and a disgrace on a public holiday in our country.

There was great excitement as the procession approached, and from our commanding position we saw all that transpired. Never before had we seen such oriental splendour and barbaric display; and ancient history seemed to be reproduced before our eyes, and in imagination I witnessed the gorgeous parades of the days of the powerful native Moguls and emperors of India in centuries gone by. Those once mighty rulers seemed to live again, and the scenes of their times became visualized and vitalized by this living panorama. There was no other pageant in modern times in Madura to be compared with this annual festival, and thousands came from the villages about. A large number of elephants, richly caparisoned, added greatly to the imposing character of that procession. The proud mahout who sat on the shoulders, astride the neck, was thrilled with a sense of pride because of his conspicuous position, and he prodded the monster animal with his iron goad, even more than was necessary, to show his importance.

Everything was on an elaborate scale, and there was a great exhibition of the images of their chief divinities. These were of silver, of large size, and representing a variety of animals and fouls, borne on the shoulders of four men and beneath a gorgeous canopy; although the largest ones were mounted on wagons, some of which were drawn by elephants with their gaudy trappings. There were some richly decorated cars, built for that special purpose, and on which were seated some of the leading dignitaries of the city. There was great variety, and many startling surprises among the objects and decorations of that parade, but the one of chief interest to us was the elaborate car Juggernaut and which contained the image of their chief divinity. Unbounded enthusiasm was manifested as it approached and the religious feeling of the people was evident.

When the grand marshal of the day saw my interest he stopped the procession until I took a number of photographs, and for all this unexpected courtesy he only asked me to send him some of the pictures, and which I did with due acknowledgment. Imagine that marshal, unsolicited and unexpected, showing such remarkable consideration as to stop that vast religious procession of Hindus in order that an American might have a favourable opportunity to gratify his desire in getting some interesting pictures. Of all the people of the world, none are so universally and intensely patient and courteous as the Hindus, and hence my deep interest in them, for they are deserving of a far better fate than that which they have inherited from Hinduism.

One of the most magnificent gopuras is seen at Tanjore in front of one of the greatest of all the Dravidian temples, and one of the oldest, for it was built in the fourteenth century. It is unique in that whilst it was dedicated to Siva and his worship, the figures on the gopuras belong to the religion of the god Vishnu, and this apparent compromise seems to indicate the amicable relations that existed at the time this temple was constructed, and that the lines of distinction were not clearly defined. The chief gopura rises to a height of two hundred feet, and as we pass through this gateway, we see in the foreground of the enclosure the colossal sculptured stone image of Siva's bull (nandi) in a recumbent position. The material is granite, but it has grown black with age, and especially from the quantity of oil poured over it. Its chief attraction is due to vast proportions and symbolic character, rather than to any superior artistic merit, for the carving shows a decline in art, and it belongs to a later period than the temple.

Trichinopoly is almost a synonym for the rocky mount that rises abruptly from the plain, and which we ascend by about three hundred stone steps cut out of the native rock. From the summit there is a commanding view of the level country on all sides. There was an insignificant temple of Ganesa that crowned this elevation, and several shrines in caverns on the sides, but of no special interest, although the attendant priests pled for our attention and rupees in behalf of their childlike ceremonies and decorations.

It is a drive of several miles to Seringham, where there is one of the largest and most interesting groups of temples in all India. They are more modern than those at Tanjore, but the picturesque effect of so many temples grouped together within a limited area is unrivalled, and one of them is the largest, and unsurpassed in beauty by any other temple of Hinduism. As many as fifteen gopuras add to the picturesque picture that attracts every traveller.

Monier Williams declares that " No sight is to be seen in any part of India that can at all compare with the unique effect produced by its series of seven quadrangular enclosures formed by seven squares of massive walls, one within the other, every square pierced by four lofty gateways, and each gateway surmounted by pyramidal towers rivalling in altitude the adjacent rock of Trichinopoly. The construction of this marvellous congeries of sacred buildings must have cost millions of rupees, and since its first construction fabulous sums have been spent on its maintenance and enlargement. It is said that kings and princes have emptied their coffers and given up their revenues for the completion and extension of its many storied towers ; rich men of every rank have parted with their treasures for the adding of column after column to its thousand pillared courts; misers have yielded up their hoards for the decoration of its jewelled images; capitalists have bequeathed vast benefactions for the support of its priests; architects and artists have exhausted all their resources for the production of a perfect shrine, the worthy receptacle of an idol of transcendent glory."[1]

The immediate approach to this maze of temples is through a great outer court, lined with bazaars, and hawkers went through the crowds of thousands of people, offering their wares for sale, for though it was a sacred city, the commercial feature was necessary for meeting the enormous current expenses involved in the maintenance of these temples. In the centre of this foreground was a monster elephant, that under the direction of his keeper performed some clever tricks for the entertainment of the pilgrims, and as a means of revenue. Inasmuch as the temple had been dedicated to Vishnu, the elephant belonged to the same deity, and on his forehead, painted in broad bands of white and vermilion, he bore a large figure of the trident, the distinctive symbol of the god Vishnu. Often this symbol is represented merely by three vertical lines, as these are more easily made than the trident. One of the most interesting buildings in the group was the great hall of one thousand columns, each elaborately carved from a block of granite, but the general effect was sadly marred by evident neglect.

We saw several of the large Juggernaut cars that are drawn through the streets by thousands of pilgrims on

[1] "Brahmanism and Hinduism."

the occasion of the great religious festival. Chidambram should be included in the places seen as we journey north, for the temples are of unusual interest, and the place is holy, and these are sufficient reasons to attract the traveller in search of knowledge. Unfortunately the railroad was located too far away from the city, and the carts are the most forbidding that I saw in India, and are likely to continue until there is a demand for something better through the increased number of foreigners visiting this place. There was also difficulty in getting anything that a foreigner could eat, beyond fruit, except at the home of a missionary.

During years of travel we had suffered much from wretched vehicles driven over cobblestone streets, but never did we get such a punishment as that which was inflicted upon us the day we drove from the station to Chidambram, for even the streets of Cordova are better. The covered cart was so low that we could not sit upright but were obliged to recline on our elbows or else lie flat, and the jolting was too severe for either position, for the man drove as furiously as Jehu.

However, we have not regretted having passed through that ordeal, for the famous old temple of Siva, and the unusually lofty gopuras, richly repaid us for the temporary agony endured in that low and springless bullock cart. The temple was provided with a band of musicians and they played their strenuous instruments incessantly and during all the hours that we spent about the sacred precincts. There was a great variety of instruments, all unfamiliar with the exception of the tom-toms, but no matter by what name you might call them, the quality of the music would not be improved. In fact it seemed like a contradiction of terms to call it music, for there was only a deafening din of discordant sounds that became excruciating to sensitive nerves; and each one seemed to be bent upon making all the noise he could and without any reference to the other musicians. Again and again we pled with them to stop but this only stimulated their enthusiasm and they blew their horns louder than ever and beat the tom-toms as if testing their strength; for they could not understand our language of disapproval and evidently interpreted our signs and violent gesticulations to cease as expressing our applause and grateful enthusiasm. In fact the treasurer of the temple emphasized the fact of our being so highly entertained by the band of musicians when attempting to extort an unusual gratuity as we were about to leave the temple. Their music had no charms for us, and what strange conceptions of divinities they must have in supposing that such rasping sounds are pleasing to them.

But in spite of this band of intolerable musicians that followed us there were some rich compensations that we enjoyed, for it was in the great temple that we got our best and clearest view of the sacred inner sanctuary and which contained the image of their deity. The golden interior was well lighted, and it sparkled with the many jewels and ornaments in gold. The small stairway leading into the shrine was made of silver with many ornaments about it in gold, and we spent some time in studying this famous shrine, for the priests were courteous and patient and gave us all the time we desired. In one of the large rooms connected with the temple we were permitted to get a close view of the many curious representations of some strange animal divinities.

These sacred objects were treasured in this place until the annual parade, when they were carried in the processions. They were of large size and in appearance similar to those seen at Madura, and I suspect they are merely silver plated, but their effect upon the illiterate people is the same. The attendant priests endeavoured to awaken our enthusiasm in these sacred symbols by telling us of their marvellous potency among the people in former years, but all the stories were too incredible to even interest us.

It was different with the natives, for Hinduism had not died out in that city, and we were surprised to see the construction of a new temple, and on a magnificent scale and at enormous expense by a wealthy citizen of Burma, but who was formerly a native of Chidambram. He had grown to be immensely rich and had returned to erect this costly edifice out of gratitude to the divinity that had so greatly prospered him. Some of the square pillars with sculptured capitals cost as much as eight thousand rupees each and there were many of them, and from the expense of these we could estimate the immense cost of that temple. Whilst it was a generous act it was not wholly unselfish, for it was a meritorious act, and great blessings were in store for him in the next life. My only regret was that he had not given the money to feed and educate the depressed classes, for there was no need whatever for this additional temple in that city, and from which these unfortunate mortals may be excluded, just as we were not allowed to cross the threshold of the chief temple of this quadrangular group, although we were freely admitted to all the others; but whether the new one will be reserved for the exclusive twice born I know not.

Conjeverim is one of the seven holy cities of India, and in point of sanctity is the Benares of the South. There are two towns, not far apart, and known respectively as Great Conjeverim, and Little Conjeverim, the former containing an enormous temple, with one of the most attractive gopuras with ten stories, towering to the height of nearly two hundred feet. The group of temples in extent and picturesque beauty is scarcely excelled elsewhere and I found much of interest in the interior, although I was often unable to understand the priest who had refused the professor from the Christian college to accompany me within the sacred precincts.

I visited the large Brahman school and became greatly interested in the teachers who spoke English fluently, and they cheerfully answered my questions respecting the temples, schools, city and people, and even some of the students volunteered their information. But I found them utterly unyielding when I protested against the injustice of excluding an intelligent and respectable college professor from the temple merely because his remote ancestors belonged to the Tamil race and were tabooed as a low caste. I tried to reason with them but in vain, for the only reason that they presented and which controlled them was custom, and that was an inheritance that was inviolable. This exclusive act did not appear so unjust and invidious as it did later in the day, when I myself was refused admittance into a new temple. This had become a very personal matter, and the black Tamil professor seemed embarrassed at my situation, for he did not anticipate it, but he had no influence whatever with the Brahmans who despised his low caste.

I maintained my good humour and tried to reason again with the unreasonable priest. He allowed all the bulls and cows and goats and ignorant rabble, regardless of character, to enter and roam about at their inclination, but I was not allowed to cross the threshold. I could see no rational ground for such discrimination against an American in favour of Hindu beasts and a promiscuous crowd of natives, and I told them so, but we had a different point of view and they did not seem to realize the absurdity of the situation as I did, for the law of caste and custom controlled their mind, and they could not think differently. Adjoining the great temple was one of the largest and most attractive of all the cars that I had seen, with magnificent carvings, and which was drawn through the city during the great religious festival.

At Little Conjeverim I found another temple that was so exclusive and holy that the presence of any foreigner would have meant pollution, although the animals and naughty-nautch girls were not excluded, but the latter were considered as a necessary evil for the temple requirements. Their faces were against them, and a shameful reflection upon a religious institution, and so were some of the religious carvings, and which would not be tolerated in any of the frequented cities on the main line of travel; for Conjeverim is on a branch road between Chingleput and Arkonam. We may easily infer the character of the figures on the interior of that temple and enclosure from the shocking immoral specimens that are exposed to the public gaze some rods away. These are carved upon the pillars of a portico of recent construction and which serves as an ante-approach to the temple, a sort of public announcement or exhibition of the performances that take place within the temple itself. The exposure for sale in any public place of a photograph of these grossly indecent figures would mean punishment in the state prison, in accordance with the law, but they are allowed to the Hindus for religious uses at their temples.

No worse indictment could be brought against Hinduism and which is so exacting respecting caste, but lacks moral discrimination in the selection of symbols for their temple decorations, for many are grossly immoral and disgusting. The debasing moral effect of these salacious figures upon the minds of the young who stood about was apparent, for they could only engender lascivious thoughts, and it passes our comprehension to understand the motive of the leaders in sculpturing such lewd representations. To say that they are images of their deities, and only symbolize the laws of procreation only makes bad worse, for it is unspeakably vile to make these public exposures of such figures. It was a great relief to turn to that most attractive structure in the city, the hall of pillars, with their remarkable sculptured figures of mounted horses and hippogriffs, for the carvings show the skilled workmen. Fortunately they are well lighted, for the sides of the building are open, and excellent photographs can be taken.

Whilst there are many large and magnificent temples among the Hindus, the great majority of the buildings are small, but they answer the purposes of Hinduism for there is no congregational or associated worship

TEMPLE ELEPHANTS AT SERINGHAM

A RIDE FROM JENPORE TO ANBER

but the chief object of interest in the temple to the Hindu is the shrine that encloses the image of the god and where the priest officiates for the people who come and go, spending but a few moments before the idol as they bow and perhaps utter a prayer and then hand an offering to the priest.

The priest, who must be a Brahman, is practically the worshipper for the people and serves them as a proxy, and so thorough a substitute does he become that the interested persons need not necessarily remain to witness the ceremony. The priest rings the bell before the image to announce his presence, utters some mantras, makes an offering of flowers and water to the deity, though they treat these idols as though they were living beings, for they bathe that image, clothe it, and serve it with a meal in the morning, at noon and in the evening, and it is put to bed. It is also entertained with music and dancing. The name of the deity is frequently repeated by the use of the rosary which is common among the Hindus, for they believe there is special merit in the frequent repetition of the names of the most potential gods in their pantheon.

IX

THE VILLAGES

THE innumerable villages are the swarming hives of humanity in India, for ninety-five per cent. of the entire population of the country live in villages and towns that are scattered throughout the vast empire, and only five per cent. of the people are found in the cities. Hence, the smaller towns are of special interest, for they have been least affected by modern civilization, and in many of them we see the Hindus as Hinduism has made them from generation to generation, and what they would continue to be without the social and educational influence of Christian civilization. Ignorance and poverty abound in these places that have not been specially touched by Western ideas, and the primitive character is seen in their simple dwellings and mode of life.

The poorest occupy shanties that can scarcely be designated as houses, for at times there is but one room, enclosed by straw mats, suspended from slender poles, and some mud hovels are built of bamboo covered with mud, and this is often spotted with the disks of cow-dung drying for fuel, and which is an important item in the culinary department of these very poor people. The roof is thatched and the majority of the houses are provided with several rooms and the necessary courtyard, while the better and well-to-do or rich class have large and comfortable houses. It is only distance that lends enchantment to these villages, for the picturesque effect produced by a distant point of view vanishes as we approach them. There is a sameness, and little of special interest in the architecture and life of the people in the different ones to relieve the monotony, for the conservatism of centuries characterizes the Hindu who looks to the past for his ideals and ideas for the future.

As the majority of the houses are occupied by the poor, there are no luxuries, nor even comforts beyond the immediate necessities, and furniture is most conspicuous for its absence. There are the few cheap rugs and low stools, and string bed, and the indispensable clay vessels for water and cooking utensils, with a possible brass bowl, and with these the inventory of the household furnishings of millions of the poor is complete. But the interests of the wife and mother are centred in that humble dwelling place as the sphere of the world in which she lives, for her horizon of interests is limited. Hence she makes the most of her situation, prizing what she has, and she keeps her kitchen scrupulously clean, and practices the strictest economy. Outside these limited apartments may be found the necessary accompaniments of the old churn and the primitive stone pestle and mortar for crushing or "grinding" the grain.

This is a plain picture of the manner in which millions of the poor people live or exist from year to year; and there is an awful gulf between the social fruits of Hinduism and Christian civilization. Of course they can indulge in no luxuries and have neither inclination nor opportunity for the culture that comes from education; for the common labourer receives but about five cents per day, and the majority of the poor cannot afford rice but eat the common millet. Fortunately the food is much cheaper than in our country, and hence with an increased purchasing power of the rupee for cheap grain, and the scanty piece of clothing that he needs, his pay per day serves him with the equivalent of a half dollar for our working men. Besides his humble dwelling place is given him free of rent. Since he is a vegetarian he is not affected by the high price of meat, and he does not support the saloon nor smoke five cent cigars.

In many respects India is an exceedingly cheap country in which to live, for the warm and even hot climate saves them all the increased expense of Northern climates in providing the necessary furs and heavy clothing. So far as the men are concerned a narrow strip of white cotton cloth twisted around their loin satisfies all the climatic as well as social requirements for the greater part of the year, and hence their expense of clothing is reduced to a minimum; about three-fourths of the people wear no shoes and even the rich go without the aristocratic stockings except in cases where they have adopted European customs.

The majority of the inhabitants of Southern India, the Deccan and Bengal, including even the poor Brahmans, go without a head covering. They pay no tailor prices to make their clothes, according to the strict regulation fall or spring style, and cast away those that are out of the latest fashion, but they buy several yards or more of cheap white cotton cloth, and without needle, thread or button, each ties it about his loin, just as his ancestors did many generations ago, and he wears it with daily washings until it is worn out. Even the women are saved much expense and embarrassment because of their disregard to the style of the new spring or fall hat, for they never wear one, and so far as the tailor-made suit is concerned they never conceive of it.

Their dress is never out of style, for there is no such thing as a new style, except in the new and cheaper material that has been furnished by modern manufacture. Hence they suffer little exhaustion from being fitted by the dressmaker and they suffer no disappointment and loss of patience from misfits. With the exception of the simple bodice about the waist, every woman clothes herself and wholly independent of any dressmaker, for the long Sari remains uncut as when she bought it, for she ordered the necessary number of yards that were cut from the original piece, and this she arranges gracefully about her person, in the same manner and style as her great-grandmother wore it, and which is most admirably adapted to all the requirements of their climate and life.

However, with strictest economy so poor are the millions with their scanty income that they eke out a miserable existence, barely sufficient at times to keep body and soul together. Sir William Hunter, after many years of observation among them, declares that "Forty millions of the people never at any time had enough food to eat—and that seventy millions of Indian peasants are in a condition of hopeless poverty." No doubt the fearful mortality is largely due to their extreme poverty, for being underfed, the system, being weakened from lack of sufficient nourishment, becomes more susceptible to disease, and an easy prey when pestilence comes, for being below the normal strength they are unable to resist and yield the more readily to disease as well as that scourge of the bubonic plague.

Their poverty is due to various causes and for some of which they themselves are directly responsible. Were they to employ the more modern and scientific methods of our Western farmers there would be a large increase in the food supply. The arable land with proper cultivation would yield far richer returns, and gradually they are introducing in places improved methods and implements for farming, and with encouraging results, although the process of such innovations are slow. The fertile plains readily yield two crops annually and there is an abundant variety of cereals, vegetables and fruits. The farmers suffer greatly from famines owing to severe droughts from lack of rain, and which are likely to continue because of the peculiar climatic conditions of the country, although increased irrigation has done much to meet the difficulty.

In accordance with ancient custom they continue the wasteful expenditure for marriages and funerals, never reasoning whether they can afford it, but blindly yielding to hereditary custom, though it often involves them in bankruptcy and great suffering for many months and even years to come. The poor and ignorant peasants pride themselves in the observance of the law of custom, though they become hopelessly impoverished by such an unreasonable act, and their only compensation is the strange satisfaction of having assumed the semblance at least of aristocracy.

The native passion for jewelry leads to excessive extravagance even among the poor, for whilst much of the jewelry is of the baser sort, still it is an expenditure that amounts to considerable in the aggregate which should be spent for bread and the necessities of life and especially with a preference for a little education as an adornment of the mind. Never have I seen such an extravagant and barbaric display of jewelry as that which is worn by the Hindu women of Southern India, for they wear it from the crown of their head to the end of their fingers and toes.

On that remarkable festival day in Madura they wore a number of pieces on their head, including the crown, frontlet, another piece at the back of the head and two more on either side, two for each ear, one for the lobe and another set under the rim of the upper part, another on each side of the nose, and the third suspended from the septum of the nose, which must be very annoying and much in the way when they suffer from a severe attack of influenza. Then there were the conspicuous necklace, the armlets and bracelets and many rings on their fingers, the girdle about the waist and the immense rings about the ankles, some of them weighing a pound each, and most uncomfortable were it not for the overmastering vanity of the wearers and which seemed to make them oblivious to the discomfort. A number of them even wore very elaborate rings on their toes, but no amount of jewelry could make such feet attractive, and the rings only tended to make the monstrosities the more conspicuous.

I could allow them to indulge their excessive fondness for jewelry even to the adornment of the pedal extremities, for there is no accounting for taste, but I had a feeling of revulsion when I witnessed for the first time that most barbarous and repulsive fashion of slitting the lobe of the woman's ear, and then forcing a cylindrical ornament or block, resembling a spool, through the opening and which becomes lengthened to the extent of several inches in extreme cases. I have seen the pendant of gold, silver or some baser metal suspended from this greatly distended lobe that was supported by two mere shreds of flesh, a most revolting practice; yet these natives said it was beautiful, but that is proof sufficient that they lack refinement and culture, and that they have no eye for the beautiful. The degradation of woman, at least among the lower class, was evident in this barbarous custom. The beautiful and expressive lobe of the ear is an important feature of the graceful setting for the face, but the Hindus had horribly disfigured it into a most repulsive object that excited my commiseration for these unfortunate women who had been made hideous in their old age.

Among the various industries of the towns and villages none interested me more than that of the potter, for often he displayed exquisite skill with his primitive potter's wheel, that was as plain as those used in ancient Egypt, and yet he easily converted the shapeless but pliable lump of clay into useful and graceful vessels. The village potter is an absolute necessity in the East where his wares have been indispensable from time immemorial, and one of the common and universal mounds of remains about the sites of ancient cities in oriental countries is that of broken pottery, the vast heaps of ruins composed of the fragments of these frail vessels of clay; and could they speak, how much they would tell of the gossip of the domestic life of the people. In fact many fragments do speak, for often men in need of better material used these pieces instead of parchment or papyrus, and many important inscriptions have been copied from the ostraca of ancient Egypt. I looked in vain among the potters of India to see them making vessels with the hands alone, and without the use of the wheel as I saw among the Samoans, although such examples may exist. Thus the ancient Egyptians and Etruscans made their earliest pottery as the abundant examples in their countries and museums show.

The barber is one of the ubiquitous and easily recognized functionaries in India, although his place of business is not stationary and designated by the conspicuous bright coloured barber's pole. The poor village barber is very poor, and he has no tonsorial parlour and easy-cushioned chair for his customers, but he is generally of a peripatetic character, as well as indispensable to every man, for no one shaves himself, and the men know nothing of the luxury and time-saving element that we find in using the safety razor at home, and at our personal convenience, and where we are never obliged to wait for the "next one" ahead of us. The Hindus enjoy no such liberties nor conveniences, for that would be most heterodox and a gross violation of custom, the thought of which would not be tolerated, and hence the progressive Hindu, whilst remaining orthodox, cannot introduce such a boon into his home. Hence he goes out-of-doors to meet the barber as he walks through the streets for his regular customers and sits in the open upon a plain low stool without a back, and with his face towards the barber, who shaves his head as well as his face, cuts his nails and cracks his joints. The reason for doing this work in a place opening on the street or under a shed or tree is to avoid the pollution that would come to the home should any of the hairs or pieces of nails fall upon the floor. The barbers receive but a pittance, less than ours receive in tips, but the power of custom keeps them from strikes.

The shoemaker is a cobbler and when I saw the rude and clumsy shoes that he made I did not wonder that so many preferred to go barefooted, for whether from necessity or from choice, there was little comfort in wearing such hard shoes. However we cannot expect the cobbler to do skilled work with the rude tools at his disposal. He seems to follow his trade without taste or ambition to improve upon the past, and he has none of the interest and ideals expressed in the doggerel:

> "If I were a cobbler, it would be my pride,
> The best of all cobblers to be."

The same might be said of the blacksmith and carpenter, and for similar reasons. Because of the universal passion for jewelry and the excessive demand by the rich also, it is not strange that the jeweller has often excelled in his special art, and yet let no one for the mere sake of sentiment boast unduly of his work, for it is primitive looking, and was greatly surpassed by the ancient Greeks and Etruscans, with whom the best Hindu jewelry cannot be compared.

The weaver's loom is seen about the villages, but it is generally of the most primitive character imaginable. All was in the open for inspection, in some lane or retired place, and if possible where the simple frame could be suspended between two trees. The warp was prepared by "setting up rows of sticks for supports and winding thread between them." The cloth was very narrow and the process was a very slow one, and must have been made at starvation wages to sell it at such low figures. The dyers used bright colours and much went to waste upon the ground. There are nearly six millions of weavers using the hand looms, although the large mill looms have been introduced in the cities.

We had often heard that the sun was the white man's enemy in India, and so painfully did we realize it that often we wished that there had been no sunshine during the period of our travels. I have a vivid recollection of an excessively warm experience that I never wish to repeat. It was on a Monday and I had spoken several times in Guntur on the preceding day, and then travelled part of the night so as to have an early drive to an interesting old rock hewn temple.

Any archæologist would have been interested in that remarkable temple which will endure with the everlasting hills, and after spending some profitable hours of careful scrutiny, we left it with regret to return to Mangalgeri. It was after the noon hour, and the Indian sun was reaching its strength. Our antiquated carriage had no cover to protect us, and the slow ponies had no ambition, and the ignorant driver no capacity for thinking, and he carelessly ran against a huge ant hill, and the frail harness broke. There we sat in the sizzling burning sun whilst he made the repairs after the most primitive fashion, and then with much good advice he started the ramshackle vehicle once more. But he had not gone a great distance when that stupid fellow struck another obstruction with more disastrous results, for that rotten harness was beyond repair.

Imagine the despair of our situation when, against all the prescribed safeguards for foreigners, we found that we were obliged to walk, through the hottest portion of the day, back to the bungalow, a distance of nearly two hours. The scorching sun was overhead and the thermometer registered more than 100° in the shade on that day, but unfortunately we were not in the shade, and none was in sight; so we were compelled to walk across the hot desert waste without a single attraction in the landscape, and with not a single tree nor rock to cast a cool shadow. There was no breeze, but only the heat that seemed to have come from a furnace, and never was I in so great need of an automobile, and longed so greatly for one.

We tried to think pleasant thoughts so as not to increase our temperature by worry, and we trudged slowly along, though at a serious risk, but we had no alternative. It was a great relief when we reached the bungalow, and after a brief rest found that we did not suffer from the much dreaded effects of that unfortunate exposure. I pity every missionary who has had similar experiences.

X

THE SACRED BOOKS OF THE HINDUS

INASMUCH as the religious teachings of the Hindus have determined their thought and life through the many centuries of their history, we must naturally have an interest in their Sacred Books from which they have derived their beliefs and practices, for nothing is so potent as our thoughts; in them we live and move and have our being, and the character of them shapes our daily life and destiny, for as a man thinks within himself so he is and does and lives. The thoughts become the dominant cause, whilst the outward life and deeds are the fruits; for thinking precedes the doing, and the deeds correspond with the character of the thoughts.

That which interested me most in India was not the primitive character of their dress and culinary department, for these are adapted to their needs and the peculiar conditions of their climate and civilization. To appreciate the distinctive feature and power of Hinduism over the lives of the many millions for centuries, we must go deeper and farther back to the religious sources that have made the Hindus the unique people of the world, and the most excessively religious of any nation. In their Sacred Books you will find many rules for sleeping in accordance with strict religious requirements. They have inflexible rules for eating, and they are justifiable in their insistence upon always eating with the fingers of the right hand because freer from defilement. They have their table manners religiously enjoined, and from which there must be no departure, although we would not approve of some of the etiquette, for they exclude the wife and mother from the social fellowship of the table when eating their meals. The "Laws of Manu" are very explicit on this important exclusive relation, for in Chapter IV we read the commandment for men: "Let him not eat in the company of his wife, nor look at her while she eats, sneezes, yawns, etc."

There is an evident lack of domestic sociability among the strictly orthodox Hindu who observes the "Laws of Manu" on this point. Another imperative injunction for man from this Blue Book of Hinduism is: "Let him not step over a rope to which a calf is tied, let him not run when it rains, and let him not look at his own image in the water."

"Let him keep his right arm uncovered in a place where a sacred fire is kept, in a cow-pen, in the presence of Brahmanas, during the private recitation of the Veda, and at meals."

"Let him not interrupt a cow who is suckling her calf, nor tell anybody of it. A wise man, if he sees a rainbow in the sky, must not point it out to anybody." Reasons not given.

"Let him not give to a Sudra advice, nor the remnants of his meals, nor food offered to the gods; nor let him explain the sacred law to such a man, nor impose upon him a penance."

"For he who explains the sacred law to a Sudra, or dictates to him a penance, will sink together with that man into the hell called Asamvrita." (A most horrible and loathsome hell it is.)

We often hear unqualified and extravagant statements made in reference to the lofty spiritual and ethical teachings of the Sacred Books as though they even surpassed our own Sacred Scriptures, and hence I have made certain selections from the volumes of translations made under the supervision of Max Muller. In his preface to the "Sacred Books of the East" (in his volume on the Upanishads), he gives what he regarded as a necessary caution and from which I quote the following:

"Readers who have been led to believe that the 'Vedas' of the Ancient Brahmans, the 'Avesta' of the Zoroastrians, the 'Tripitaka' of the Buddhists, the 'Kings' of Confucius, or the 'Koran' of Mohammed are books full of primeval wisdom and religious enthusiasm, or at least of sound and simple moral teaching, will be disappointed on consulting these volumes. Looking at many of the books that have lately been published on the religions of the ancient world, I do not wonder that such a belief should have been raised; but I have long felt that it was high time to dispel such illusions."

Some scholars "are more inclined, after they have disinterred from a heap of rubbish some solitary fragments of pure gold, to exhibit these treasures only than to display all the refuse from which they had to extract them. . . . True love does not ignore all faults and failings. . . . To watch in the Sacred Books of the East the dawn of the religious consciousness of man must always remain one of the most inspiring and hallowing sights in the whole history of the world. . . . What we want here, as everywhere else, is the truth, and if the whole truth must be told, it is that, however radiant the dawn of religious thought, it is not without its dark clouds, its chilling colds, its noxious vapours."

"We must have thoroughly faithful translations of their Sacred Books. Extracts will no longer suffice." We cannot know India from the "Taj Mahl," nor Hinduism from the anthologies made by partisans.

We find in the Sacred Books of the East "by the side of so much that is fresh, natural, simple, beautiful and true, so much that is not only unmeaning, artificial and silly, but even hideous and repellent."

"It cannot be too strongly stated that the chief, and in many cases the only interest of the Sacred Books of the East is historical; that much in them is extremely childish, tedious, if not repulsive; and that no one but the historian will be able to understand the important lessons which they teach."

In his "Gifford Lectures" he refers to Christianity which "if only properly understood, it is infinitely superior to all other religions." Lanman, the Sanscrit scholar of Harvard, after quoting Emerson's paraphrase of the Katha Upanishads, adds in closing: "What a prospect, dark and void, this supreme spirit before whom all human endeavour, all noble ambition, all hope, all love, is blighted! What a contrast, a relief, when we turn from this to the teachings of the gentle Nazarene!"

The "Rig Veda" is the oldest and of great interest as it preserves the religious creed of an ancient people as well as the varying types of the oldest civilization of the Aryans that entered India at least several thousand years ago. The "Rig Veda" contains one thousand hymns or poems that express the thought and religious belief of a primitive people who were conscious of their own limitations, and their dependence upon superhuman aid. These hymns and prayers are addressed to their various gods, arranged in ten books, and are about equal in matter to the Iliad and Odyssey of Homer. This work occupies the first place in age and importance among all the Vedas, although Sanscrit scholars are not agreed as to their age, but the oldest have generally been assigned to a period of 2000 or 1500 B. C., and others belong to a much more recent date, although Kaegi holds that the collection was closed as early as 1500 B. C.

According to Bloomfield, "the hymns of the Veda are to a considerable degree cloudy, turgid and mystic; taken by themselves they will never yield to a clear picture of human life that fits any time or place." They give us an insight into the Vedic Pantheon of that age when it was composed of the personified powers of nature, and when the priests and people were worshippers of the phenomena of nature. Those mysterious forces that came from the sun, wind and rain had not disclosed their secret energy to that primitive people, who recognized the presence of divinity in every unusual object. There is much of the *quid pro quo* spirit that characterizes the mutual relation between the worshippers and their gods. The former bring their oblations of butter, with cakes and rice, and the latter accept them in consideration of certain returns, for they were given with the expectation of receiving children, health, food, cattle and rain.

Whilst many of them express the simplicity of the outpouring of the soul in times of its deepest consciousness of the need of supreme powers, they are characterized on the whole, as Kaegi states, by "monotony and endless repetition, since almost all the hymns are variations of the same theme"; but they are full of absorbing interest to every one who is concerned in tracing back the stream of humanity to the origin of religious thought and literature. The following are from Kaegi's translations: "If I asked again and again, the ever victorious Indra fulfilled my prayers." Here is an extravagant prayer addressed to Indra:

> "Grant me, O God, the highest best of treasures,
> A judging mind, prosperity abiding,
> Riches abundant, lasting health of body,
> The grace of eloquence, and days propitious."

A querulous one dares utter the following: "If you were a mortal and I immortal, I would not abandon you to misfortune nor poverty; my singers would not be needy nor in evil case, not lacking his deserts."

Indra was "the most celebrated god of the Vedic period,—the real national god of the Indians," the all conquering victor in battle, and invincible in power.

> "Through fear of thee upon the earth is shaken
> E'en the immovable, the ether,—all things,
> The earth, the heavens, mountains, forests tremble;
> The firm foundation trembles at thy going."

To that people Indra was a great god, even the Creator and upholder of things in heaven and on earth, although not always free from contradictions and confusion of ideas.

In answer to the lack of faith in Indra among men as expressed in one of the prayers, the god himself deigns to reply to the doubting worshipper:

"I am, O Singer, look on me, here am I,
And I am greater than all living creatures.
The service of the sacred rite delights me,
Destroying, I creation hurl to ruin."

Another hymn begins:

"Praise the great praiseworthy Indra,
Ruler of the world, with singing,
Him the richest man, the victor.
All the mortals, all the peoples,
Ever in their hymns praise Indra,
Him in songs and him in measures."

Kaegi adds that "the relatively few hymns to Varuna belong to the most exalted portions of the Veda. They recall especially the tone of the Psalms and the language of the Bible in general. They picture the god as the all-wise creator, preserver and regent of the worlds, the omniscient protector of the good and avenger of the evil."

"His works bear witness to his might and wisdom,
Who fashioned firm supports for earth and heaven,
Who set on high the firmament uplifted,
And fixed the stars and spread out earth's expanses.

"He mingles with the clouds his cooling breezes,
He gave the cow her milk, the horse his spirit,
Put wisdom in the heart, in clouds the lightning,
The Sun in heaven, on the rock the Soma.

"The Sun's sure courses Varuna appointed,
He sent the streaming waters flowing onward,
The mighty path of days he first created
And rules them as the riders guide their horses."

In the following stanzas from a hymn from the "Atharva-Veda," translated by Professor Jackson of

Columbia, we have a remarkable example of their belief in the divine omniscience and omnipresence :

> " This earth is all King Varuna's possession,
> And yonder lofty sky with boundaries distant.
> The ocean's twain are but the loins of Varun ;
> Yet in the tiniest drop he lieth hidden.
>
> " What though one flee beyond the farthest heaven
> One could not even there escape King Varun,
> His spies come hither forth from out of heaven,
> With all their thousand eyes the earth surveying.
>
> " King Varuna discerns all this that lieth
> Between the firmaments and that beyond them.
> The very winklings of men's eyes are numbered ;
> He reckons all, as doth the dice a player."

There is also a humorous vein in some portions of the "Rig Veda" as the following shows.

> " Poet am I ; Papa's a quack ;
> Mama the upper millstone turns ;
> Whate'er our aims—like chasing cows—
> We all are hunting after wealth."

The monotheistic conception is most prominent perhaps in the well-known Creation hymn, although there is much uncertainty and want of information in the mind of its author as the following stanzas show :

> " Then there was neither being nor not-being,
> The atmosphere was not, nor sky above it.
> What covered all ? and where ? by what protected ?
> Was there the fathomless abyss of waters ?

"Then neither death nor deathlessness existed;
Of day and night there was yet no distinction,
Alone that One breathed calmly, self-supporting,
Other than It was none, nor aught above It.

"Then for the first time there arose desire,
Which was the primal germ of mind, within it,
And sages, searching in their heart, discovered
In Nothing the connecting bond of Being.

"Who is it knows? Who here can tell us surely
From what and how this universe has risen?
And whether not till after it the gods lived?
Who then can know from what it has arisen?

"The source from which this universe has risen
And whether it was made, or uncreated,
He only knows, who from the highest heaven
Rules, the all-seeing Lord,—or does not He know?"

There is no such tone of uncertainty in the creation account given in the Book of Genesis.

The following are quotations from the hymns of the Maruts, the Mars of the Romans, for the etymology shows that originally they were identical:

"They make the rocks tremble, they tear asunder the kings of the forest. Come on, Maruts, like madmen, ye gods, with your whole tribe."

"Come hither, Maruts, on your chariots charged with lightning, resounding with beautiful songs, stored with spears and winged with horses! Fly to us like birds, and your best food. You mighty one."

Whilst they pray much for great wealth, cattle and offspring, they were conscious of sin and prayed for forgiveness as the following prayer to Agni shows:

"Whatever sin, O youngest god, we have committed

against thee in thoughtlessness, men as we are, make thou us sinless before Aditi. Release us from every guilt on all sides, O Agni! Even from great guilt, O Agni, from the prison of gods and of mortals—let us, thy friends, never be harmed; grant luck and wealth to kith and kin."

There is no assurance from the god that the prayer will be answered. The prayer is for forgiveness and temporal blessings, but not for personal righteousness, for moral and spiritual development. There is continual repetition not only of ideas but often of the very language, and the desire for temporal riches is uppermost: "Desirous of riches, we devise to-day an effective song of praise, of Agni, the heaven-touching god. The priests make thee grow, O Agni. Bestow thou on us abundance of heroes."

The following hymn to the unknown God has sublime conceptions of deity and shows the earnest longings of the soul after God.

"*To the Unknown God—Hymn 121*

"*In the beginning* there arose the Golden Child; as soon as born, he alone was the lord of all that is. He stablished the earth and this heaven:—Who is the God to whom we shall offer sacrifice?

"*He who gives breath*, he who gives strength, whose command all the bright gods revere, whose shadow is immortality, whose shadow is death:—Who is the God to whom we shall offer sacrifice?

"*He who through his might became the sole king of the breathing* and twinkling world, who governs all this, man and beast:—Who is the God to whom we shall offer sacrifice?

BATHING IN TANK AT KUMBHAKONAM

"*He through whose might* these snowy mountains are, and the sea, they say, with the distant river, he of whom these regions are indeed the two arms :—Who is the God to whom we shall offer sacrifice?

"*He through whom the awful heaven* and the earth were made fast, he through whom the ether was stablished, and the firmament; he who measured the air in the sky :—Who is the God to whom we shall offer sacrifice?

"*He to whom heaven and earth, standing* firm by his will, look up, trembling in their mind; he over whom the risen sun shines forth :—Who is the God to whom we shall offer sacrifice?

"*When the great waters went everywhere,* holding the germ and generating light, then there arose from them the (sole) breath of the gods :—Who is the God to whom we shall offer sacrifice?

"*He who by his might looked even over* the waters which held power (the germ) and generated the sacrifice (light), he who alone is God above all gods :—Who is the God to whom we shall offer sacrifice?

"*May he not hurt us,* he who is the begetter of the earth, or he, the righteous, who begot the heaven; he who also begot the bright and mighty waters :—Who is the God to whom we shall offer sacrifice?

"(*Pragopati, no other than thou* embracest all these created things. May that be ours which we desire when sacrificing to thee. May we be lords of wealth!)"

Max Müller in his lectures on the "Vedanta Philosophy," referring to the ancient Vedic hymns, speaks of the incipient traces of this yearning after one God. "Each God is for the time implored as Supreme. . . . These were indeed giant strides and we can watch them clearly in different parts of the Veda from the simplest invocations of the unknown agents behind sun and moon, heaven and earth, to the discovery of the One God, the maker of heaven and earth, the Lord and Father, and lastly to faith in one Divine Essence Brahma."

Unfortunately there was a deterioration in their sublime and at times monotheistic conceptions of deity, and which Professor Hopkins has well expressed in this brief form: "In the Vedic hymns man fears the gods and imagines God. In the Brahmanas man subdues the gods and fears God. In the Upanishads man ignores gods and becomes God. Such is the theosophic relations between the three periods represented by the first Vedic collection, the ritualistic Brahmanas, and the philosophical treatises called the Upanishads." This is a striking summing up, and in the most concrete form, of the marked characteristic teachings of each of the famous Vedas, and great was the descent in the place assigned to deity.

From the "Apastamba,—Aphorisms on the Sacred Law of Aryan Hindus," translated by Buhler, we cite the following:

"As it is sinful to touch a Kandala, so it is also sinful to speak to him or to look at him. If a Sudra listens intentionally to a recitation of the Veda, his ears shall be filled with molten tin or lac. If he recites Vedic texts, his tongue shall be cut out. If he remembers them, his body shall be split in twain. If he assumes a position equal to that of the twice born men, in sitting, in lying down, in conversation on the road, he shall undergo corporal punishment."

So sensitive is the ceremonial purity of the twice born to the polluting presence of the Sudra that he was even forbidden to read the Veda "in the neighbourhood of a Sudra." "He who in anger raises his hand or a weapon against a Brahman will be banished from heaven for one hundred years. If he strikes, he will lose heaven for one thousand years."

It is not a sin to kill in battle except "those who declare themselves to be cows or Brahmans. Persons who declare themselves to be cows or Brahmans become inviolate on account of the sacred character of the beings they impersonate." "Historical instances are narrated where conquered kings were forced to appear before their victors holding grass in their mouths or dancing like peacocks in order to save their lives." "For killing a flamingo, a peacock, a crow, an owl, a frog, a muskrat, a dog, etc., the offender shall pay the same fine as for the murder of a Sudra;" that is, he shall give ten cows. "If a Brahman dies with the food of a Sudra in his stomach he will become a village pig in his next life or be born in the family of a Sudra." Various rites are prescribed by which a man quickly attains the wishes of his heart. Some of them are too loathsome for these pages, but one of the clean ones is this: "Avoiding to sleep in the daytime, let him worship cows, Brahmans, manes and gods."

"Now a Brahman may take four wives; a Sudra one. No one should marry a woman whose hair is decidedly red."

The duties of a woman are given as seventeen in number, and "after the death of her husband, to preserve her chastity, or to ascend the (funeral) pile, after him," for "the self-immolation of widows (suttee) is a specially meritorious act, and not obligatory." Among the many crimes mentioned, and some of them are most abominable, we find the minor ones mentioned also, even that of "killing worms or insects." Of course they never enjoyed fishing, but how strange that men should become such fanatics as to prohibit killing of worms and insects, but should at the same time encourage the burning to death of widows. Such Sacred Books cannot claim a divine inspiration, for such inhuman discriminations are not divine.

They have a number of horrible hells and in the grossness of revolting descriptions they far surpass those that are depicted upon the temples or town-halls of China, and certain cathedrals of Southern Europe. There are explicit specifications for the various penalties that are inflicted for certain offenses: "For those who have committed a crime effecting loss of caste, the penalty is one thousand years in hell. For six specified crimes they must "suffer terrible pangs" after life and in hell "they are devoured by dogs and jackals, by hawks, crows, herons, cranes and other animals—serpents, and scorpions."

Here follow the unmentionables in English that they are compelled to eat. "Here enveloped in terrible darkness, they are devoured by worms and jackals and other horrible animals having flames in their mouth. They are tormented by frosts, walking in" unspeakable horrors; "departed spirits eat one another, driven to distraction by hunger, beaten, suspended by ropes, shot with arrows or cut in pieces, walking upon thorns, bodies encircled with snakes, tormented with grinding machines." "Now after having suffered the torments inflicted in the hells, the evil doers pass into animal bodies. Mortal sinners enter the bodies of worms or insects. Minor offenders enter the bodies of the birds. Those who have committed a crime causing defilement (*i. e.*, ceremonial) enter the bodies of low caste men, such as Kandalas, who may not be touched.

"One who has stolen grain becomes a rat. One who has stolen perfumes becomes a musk-rat. One who has stolen a woman becomes a bear. Women who have committed similar thefts receive the same ignominious punishment; they become females to those male animals. A criminal in the highest degree shall have leprosy —one who is a Brahman, pulmonary consumption. A killer of a cow, blindness. A usurer becomes epileptic. Thus, according to their particular acts are men born, marked by evil signs, sick, blind, hump-backed, halting, one-eyed. Others as dwarfs, or deaf, or dumb, feeble bodied, etc. Therefore must penances be performed by all means." The foregoing list contains the most interesting examples from this Sacred Book, and about two hundred and fifty penances are given for the offenders.

Among the three hundred and thirty duties of a householder there are some commendable ones, but not all, as those that forbid the man to eat with his wife, or tc look at his wife while she is eating.

In the chapter on "Criminal and Civil Law" there are many wise and just provisions for honesty and righteousness but a fine is imposed for killing birds, fish and insects, but none for burning widows alive. One of the severe ordeals compelled the one charged with guilt to carry in his hands a heavy red-hot iron ball some distance, and should his hands be burnt in the least he was adjudged guilty.

Under the head of funeral ceremonies it is said of the deceased: "Whether he has become a god, or stays in hell, or has entered the body of an animal, or of a human being, he will receive Sraddha offered to him by his relatives. He will not die before his time has come, even though he has been pierced by one thousand shafts; he will not live after his time is out, even though he has only been touched by the point of a blade of Kusa grass.

"As a man puts on new clothes in this world, throwing aside those which he formerly wore, even so the self of man puts on new bodies, which are in accordance with his acts in a former life."

The special thoughts given for the contemplation of the ascetic are not elevating but pessimistic, with a contempt for the body. However, there is a detailed account of the many different parts of the body, extending into the millions; for the atoms of the hairs of the body aggregate 546,700,000, whilst "the hair holes of hair of the beard and of the head" are placed at 300,000.

On several occasions I have referred to the Swamis who came to this country from India, of whom Vivekananda and Abhedananda have been the chief past-masters of their art in expounding their Vedanta philosophy that God and the soul are one, and all the world a delusive dream. The former says in his "Juana Yoga": "Talk not about impurity, but tell the mind we are pure. We have hypnotized ourselves into this thought that we are little, that we are born and that we are going to die, and into living in a state of constant fear. Why do we see wickedness? There was a stump of a tree in the dark at night. A thief came that way and said: 'That is a policeman.' A young man waiting for his beloved came that way and thought it was his sweetheart. A child who had been told ghost stories came out and began to shriek that it was a ghost. But it was a stump of a tree. We see the world as we are. Put on the table a bag of gold and let a baby be here. Let a thief come and take the gold. Would the baby know it was stolen? That which we have inside we see outside. The baby has no thief inside and sees no thief outside. So with all knowledge. Do not talk of wickedness of the world and all its sins. Weep that you are bound to see wickedness yet."

How the evil doers would welcome such a delusion among honest and decent people, for then there would be no arrests, no trials and public exposures, no fines and imprisonment; but the paradise which has been regained would be lost. The Swami himself has been completely hypnotized by his own delusive philosophy so that he mistakes sophistry for reasoning, and asks men to deny their senses as well as their intellectual and moral consciousness, and to brand conscience as an unscrupulous, irrepressible and unmitigated liar and which we must argue out of existence, as having no reality beyond our hypnotic state and which has been self-imposed.

The Bibles of the world as well as our moral convictions, laws and courts, make sin a real and terrible fact, one of the deepest and ineradicable realities of our being, which has caused the greatest individual and national sorrows that have come upon mankind. It is all nonsense to suppose that the human mind by any trick of any sort of legerdemain with words can persuade itself that all sin and evil doing, all theft and crime and wickedness are merely subjective, or mental delusion, and without moral quality or any actual reality. The fact is that the delusion only exists in the mind of the clever Swami, for according to his own illustration it was a thief that stole the bag of gold, and that the adult owner would suffer the loss even though the babe had not the sense to realize it. Moreover, a policeman is universally recognized as a stern reality and not an illusion or a mere inanimate stump and hence all evil doers fear him, for policemen do arrest thieves and they are put in real prisons and not into imaginary ones, for such an illusory imprisonment would only be conceivable for idiots and the hypnotized mind of the Swami. Our jails are constructed out of solid material, with iron doors, and if the Swamis who follow the teachings of their revered leader, Vivekananda, have persuaded themselves that these are all illusion, they might easily make a practical test.

In no country is the existence of evil more clearly recognized than in India with its ascetics and 5,000,000 religious mendicants, and the innumerable terrible hells for the offenders. The Swami's dreamland has no place in Hinduism. Unfortunately he succeeded in hypnotizing some Americans during his stay in our country but a visit to India would disillusion them, for they would behold the awful reality, for the appalling condition of the people would make them feel that evil has a real existence and that the world is not a dream. His ideal theories attracted some who were persuaded that India was a veritable paradise but if there is a paradise in India, it is Paradise lost! However, he is not expected to recognize the discrimination, for he declares that "Good and bad are never two different things; they are one and the same; the difference is not one of kind, but of degree." Hence there can be no essence in virtue and no ethical quality, and he knows it, for he declares that "to talk of evil and misery is nonsense, because they do not exist outside."

More startling statements follow in his declaration that the Vedanta seeks to teach "the deification of the world. See God in everything. It is He in the child, in the wife, etc. He in the good, He in the bad, He in the murderer, He in the sin, and He in the sinner, He in life and He in death. A tremendous proposal indeed!" I should say so; but what a confusion of thought, and jugglery of words, with high sounding terms. But he obscures thought and confounds reason by compounding the most diverse and contradictory ideas. He aspires still farther to reach the goal of his mental delusion as he exhorts his hearers: "Tell your own minds I am He, I am He. Let it ring day and night in your minds like a song, and at the point of death declare: I am He."

He furnishes additional evidence that he is in an illusive state when he boldly asserts that each one should repeat for himself the following: "I am the birthless, the deathless, the blissful, the omniscient, the omnipotent, ever-glorious soul." Of course there is no prayer, for that would be to recognize an imaginary being. "Where is there a more practical God than Him I see before me? For you are He, the Omnipresent God Almighty, the Soul of your Souls. If you are not God there never was any God, and never will be. You are

God and so am I; who obeys whom? Who worships whom? You are the highest temple of God. I would rather worship you than any temple or any image or Bible. What is more practical than worshipping you? I see you, feel you and know you are God. The Mohammedan says there is no God but Allah. The Vedanta says there is no God but man."

Again he says: "Who knows whether the ant is greater than man, or man than the ant? Who can prove one way or the other?" "It is the greatest of all lies that we are mere men; we are the God of the universe. Every man and woman is the palpable, blissful, living and only God." "The worst lie that you ever told yourself is that you were born a sinner." "If you are really pure how do you see the impure, for what is within is without. We cannot see impurity without having it first inside. This is one of the practical sides of Vedanta." What a trifling with moral values and with universal discriminations between morality and vice or righteousness and unrighteousness. We can see drunkenness without being intoxicated ourselves. The fact is that whilst this unique Swami befooled many people he had little regard for the statement of facts for he declared that "in India there are said to be three hundred millions of Vedantists," although he knew when he made that statement that the entire Hindu population of India at that time was then less than two hundred millions.

However, such slight discrepancies in the statement of facts do not disturb this Vedantist for it is a characteristic of his teachings, as he states, that "we had better remember here also that, through the Vedanta philosophy, there is no such thing as good and bad;

they are not two different things; the same thing is good or bad; the difference is only in degree, and that we see to be an actual fact." This is a sample of the logic by which he proves his facts: "The fire that warms us would also consume us." He should have no difficulty whatever in proving the existence of square circles, and white lampblack, for he identifies and harmonizes the most contradictory ethical terms and qualities, and transforms them in his potent alembic, for he says: "All the powers in the universe are already ours. The Vedanta says the man who does not believe in himself is an atheist. We who are fools cry that we are weak; we who are fools cry that we are impure. It recognizes no sin; it recognizes error and the greatest error, says the Vedanta, is to say you are weak, and a sinner. Instead of telling men they are sinners, the Vedanta takes the opposite stand and says you are pure and perfect, and all you call sin does not belong to you. Millions of years have passed since man was here and yet but one infinitesimal part of his power has been manifested." "Who cares whether there is such a thing as heaven or hell, who cares if there be a soul or not? Here is the world and it is full of misery. This world is a delusion; it is all Maya; whether you eat off the ground with your fingers or dine from golden plates, etc., death is the one result; it is all the same. So this Maya is what makes the difference between me and you, between all animals and man, between men and gods. It is again no theory, but a statement of facts."

He presents no proof for his assumed facts, but that they may not be true does not disturb his philosophy. In his subtle metaphysical speculations he ventures some bold and daring feats of mental gymnastics and which afford the reader an interesting example of sophistry, if not of intellectual exercise. I have given so much space to him and his teaching because of his prominence as the high priest of the Vedanta philosophy, and many still think that his teachings rival the Gospel. From these quotations the reader may judge for himself as to the quality and comparative value. In one place he is consistent with his philosophy that all is delusion or Maya when he makes this confession: "It may be an entire delusion in my brain. I may be dreaming all the time. We are walking in the midst of a dream. I am dreaming that I am talking to you, and that you are listening to me. No one can prove it is no dream."

No one knowing the Christian religion would confuse or identify it with the Vedanta as taught by Swami Vivekananda, who lost his bearings completely in departing so far from the ancient Veda. He flounders with words and ideas in the Slough of Despond, in his efforts to put forth an impersonal and godless God beyond the mere name. No one could mistake such mere verbal combinations for the conception of Deity expressed in our Bible. There is no note of indefiniteness, uncertainty, pessimism or despair in the New Testament, and its transcendent teachings of God and His relation to the world of humanity are without a rival among all the Sacred Books of the East. So vast is the difference that they can be more easily contrasted than compared.

John Fiske in closing his book on the "Idea of God" refers to "the great Teacher who first brought men to the knowledge of the true God. The infinite and eternal Power that is manifested in every pulsation of the universe is none other than the living God. The events of the universe are not the work of chance, neither are they the outcome of blind necessity. Practically there is a purpose in the world. . . . When from the dawn of life we see all things working together towards the evolution of the highest spiritual attributes of man, we know, however the words may stumble in which we try to say it, that God is in the deepest sense a moral Being. The everlasting source of phenomena is none other than the infinite Power that makes for righteousness. Thou canst not by searching find Him out; yet put thy trust in Him, and against thee the gates of hell shall not prevail, for there is neither wisdom nor understanding nor counsel against the Eternal."

Notwithstanding the appalling social and religious condition of India and the incomparably superior character of our country, Marie Snell, who spoke at the Parliament of Religions in Chicago, when returning to India gave them such a dark picture of our people that we may fail to recognize ourselves in it, for in speaking of our spiritual poverty she adds: "But in spite of the ignorance of the upper classes, and the savagery of the lower classes, there is a thirst for spiritual religion; a thirst that Hinduism and Swami Vivekananda are going to assuage." A gross slander of our people, but that is admissible, for it is inseparable from the hyperbole of the Oriental; but in the quotations from the Swami I have given his proposed panacea for assuaging the supposed American thirst. That oracle has signally failed in his strangely compounded panacea, and Swami Abhedananda has continued the undertaking. Unfortunately he fails to appreciate the moral integrity of the American missionaries, for he says of them, in his work on India: "If you wish to know the true condition of the women in India, you will have to reject ninety-nine per cent. of the statements which you hear from the missionaries or from Christian converts who come from India." He might as well have made a clean sweep of them instead of making an invidious distinction of ninety-nine per cent.

However, he is not infallible in his estimates nor unduly guarded in his statements and from what his predecessor published in India concerning the American women, we would deduct at least ninety-nine per cent. of his slanderous indictment, for he stated that "When the American woman tries her best to find a husband, she goes to all the bathing places imaginable and tries all sorts of tricks to catch a man. When she fails in her attempts, she becomes what they call an old maid, and joins the Church. Some of them become very churchy. These church women are awful fanatics. They are under the thumb of the priests there. Between them and the priests they make a hell of earth and a mess of religion."

"The Indian woman is very happy; there is scarcely a case of quarrelling between husband and wife. On the other hand, in the United States, where the greatest liberty obtains, scarcely is there a happy home. There may be some; but the number of unhappy homes and marriages is so great that it passes all description. Scarcely could I go to a meeting but I found three-fourths of the women present had turned out their husbands and children. It is so here and everywhere." These slanders of the women that he hypnotized were published in India in the *Madras Mail*, and the *Brahmavadin* respectively. Had he told his admirers to their face what he thought of them they might have turned him out also; at least he would have lost their further attachment.

I admire him for his boldness of speech to his own people at Lahore in denouncing certain evils and emphasizing the vastly superior character of the English. The contrast places them in a bad light, for he declared that "in England there is great love for their own people, for truth and justice, and charity for strangers at the door, and sympathy and rock bottom love. Where is the heart here in India to build upon? No sooner do we start a little joint stock company than we cheat each other and the whole thing comes down with a crash. Where are the foundations? Ours is only sand. There are two curses here. First, our weakness; second, our hatred, our dried up hearts." That confession shows the fruits of Hinduism after several thousand years.

Swami Abhedananda in his lectures on the Vedanta philosophy, of which we hear so much, says: "Love thy neighbour as thyself was taught by Christ, but why? The reason was not given by Hinduism. In the Vedas we find the reason: Thou shalt love thy neighbour because thou art thy neighbour in spirit. Thou art one with him." I have not found that saying in the Vedas but if the Swami has read it into the Vedas from the Gospel, he misconceives the spirit of Christ and gives a selfish reason for loving your neighbour and which practically amounts to loving your own self, "because thou art thy neighbour." But there is no such selfishness in the teaching of Christ, for we are to love our fellow men because we all are the children of God who is the Father of us all, and hence all are my brethren, as well as my neighbour, and the reason is plain why I should love him.

The same Swami writing for our people states that "Hindu minds are extremely logical. They will not accept anything that does not harmonize with logic and reason. For this reason Christian missionaries meet with the greatest opposition when they preach to the Hindus. True religion according to the Hindus does not consist in belief in a certain creed or set of dogmas, but in the attainment of God-consciousness through spiritual unfoldment. It is being and becoming God."

I showed that all this jugglery of words about God resolves itself into this—that the man hypnotizes himself into the arrogant belief that he is the only God there is, and that there is no God beside man, as Vivekananda declares. Yet, amazing as it is, this same Swami is blinding the minds of some by telling them that "it is a well-known fact that this religion of the Hindus surpasses Zoroastrianism, Judaism, Christianity and Mohammedanism in its antiquity, grandeur, sublimity and, *above all, in its conception of God.* The God of the Hindus is omnipresent, omnipotent, omniscient, all merciful and impersonally personal." That is not the God of the Vedantists. He employs the word, but without any regard as to our conception of God. Speaking of the images and symbols used in the temples, he states that the cross was a religious symbol in India long before Christ was born, but what did it signify? Not the Saviour of the world and man's redemption. But why did not Abhedananda describe some of the other religious symbols about the temple?

Because they were too obscene and too strong an indictment of Hinduism. It also requires Hindu logic to prove that the doctrine of the brotherhood of man and to "love thy neighbour as thyself" was taught by the Sacred Books of Hinduism that enjoined the practice of that inhuman caste system. No wonder that that eminent English jurist, Sir Henry S. Maine, characterized the Indian intellect as "elaborately inaccurate; it is supremely and deliberately careless of all precision in magnitude, number and time;—it stood in need, before everything else, of stricter criteria of truth."

National pride, ignorance and superstition have paralyzed the progressive spirit in the Hindu, and doomed India to remain stationary. As Monier Williams observes: "They have believed the whole circle of human knowledge to be contained in Sanskrit writings. To this very day the most bigoted are fully persuaded that to learn anything beyond the Shastras is quite useless." This statement is justified by a recent boast in the orthodox *Indian Mirror:* "Modern science is still very much in its infancy, and has yet to make much greater progress to enable it even to approach one-tenth part of the ancient philosophy of the East. Our modern scientists are not fit to hold a candle to some of these learned men of our country, who are well versed in scientific teachings of the East!"

Strange that sane men should be so blinded by prejudice to write contrary to the plainest facts in the case, and deal in such extravagant exaggeration. However, such unqualified statements are in keeping with the Hindu mind, for "time is measured by millions of the years, space by millions of miles, battles with millions of soldiers, elephants and horses," reincarnations or rebirths by eight millions, and their pantheon of gods by more than three hundred millions. Hence due allowance must be made when these Swamis deal in hyperbole and criticism of our missionaries and their noble work. Far more reliable is the testimony of Sir William Mackworth Young, lieutenant-governor of the Punjab, who said in a public address: "I take off my hat to the humblest missionary that walks a bazaar in India, because he is leading a higher and a grander life, and doing a grander work, than any other class of persons who are working in India."

I have referred to the two famous epics of India, both of which are remarkably popular and wield a powerful influence over the minds of the people, especially in the northern part where the Ramayana is their Bible, and at the close of the day they gather in large groups and listen to favourite portions read to them. But as an illustration of the origin and significance of the bed of spikes mentioned in my first chapter, and in order to give the reader some idea of the Homeric-like character of the Mahabharata and the nature of its moral and religious teachings, I shall quote some of the most thrilling lines of a story that recounts a terrific struggle of eighteen days in prehistoric times upon the battle-field near Delhi, where the slaughter was so great that the contending armies were practically annihilated.

It was a war of nations and the most sanguinary battle was the prolonged one of eighteen days, in which the commander-in-chief of one army was the ancient and mighty Bishma. Among the combatants were "god-born men of godlike grace," but "gallant godlike Arjun, born of mighty India, and with Vishnu's prowess filled," was the rival of the opposing forces. It was a war between kinsmen (the Pandavas and the Kauravas), and Krishna sought to dissuade the combatants from engaging in such a fratricidal war, and though he pled for peace and virtue his address prevailed not with the leaders of each hostile race. Even Bishma followed Krishna in an earnest appeal to his own king to yield and save his friends and kinsmen, "for sons and fathers, friends and brothers shall in mutual conflict die, kinsmen slain by dearest kinsmen shall upon the red field lie." But proud and wrathful Duryodhan was obdurate and unrelenting and would hold the empire undivided, and he concluded: "Town nor village, mart nor hamlet (help us, righteous gods in heaven!) nor spot that needle's point can cover shall not unto them be given."

Often there were scenes heartrending for the rival warrior's leaders as they beheld their revered elders whom they loved as fathers, and many of their dearest relatives and friends, but none the less, the ten days was an awful slaughter and the scenes of carnage covered the plain with the dead, for "ancient feud and deathless hatred fired the Brahman warrior bold," and

"Through the day the battle lasted, and no mortal tongue can tell
What unnumbered chieftains perished, and what countless soldiers fell.
And the son knew not his father, and the sire knew not his son,
Brother fought against his brother, strange the deeds of valour done.
Horses fell, and shafts of chariots shivered in resistless shock,
Hurled against the foeman's chariots speeding like the rolling rock.

Elephants by mahuts driven furiously each other tore,
Trumpeting with trunks uplifted, on the serried soldiers bore.
But as fire consumes the forest, wrathful Bishma slew the foe;
None could face his sounding chariot and his ever-circled bow.
Onward came the ancient warrior, and his path was strewn with dead,
And the broken Pandav forces, crushed and driven, scattered fled."

On the morrow the defeated "Sought the aid of gallant Krishna," and

"Onward came Kalinaga's forces with the dark tornado's night,—
Rose the shout of warring nations surging to the battle's fore,
Like the angry voice of tempest, and the ocean's troubled roar;
Darkly rode the tide of battle where Duryodhan's valiant son
Strove against the son of Arjun famed for deeds of valour done—
Godlike Krishna drove the coursers of resistless Arjun's car.
Forthwith rushed the fiery Arjun in his sounding battle-car,
And like waves before him parted serried ranks of hostile war—
Onward too came forth the Kurus by the matchless Bishma led.
Shouts arose and cries of anguish midst the dying and the dead.
Vainly too the Pandav brothers on the peerless Bishma fell;
Gods in sky nor earthly warriors Bishma's might could quell.

Morning saw the turn of battle; Bishma's charioteer was slain,
And his coursers uncontrolled flew across the reddened plain.
And with tears and soft entreaty thus the sad Duryodhan spoke,
'Bishma, on thy matchless powers Kuru's hopes and fates depend.
Gods nor men with warlike Bishma can in field of war contend.' "

But Bishma replied:—

" 'Vain, Duryodhan, is this contest, and thy mighty host is vain;
Why with blood of friendly nations drench this red and reeking plain?
They must win who, strong in virtue, fight for virtue's stainless laws,
Doubly armed the stalwart warrior who is armed in righteous cause.
Krishna now hath come to Arjun; Krishna drives his battle-car.
Gods nor men can face these heroes in the field of righteous war—
Bishma still will do his duty, and his end it is not far,
Then may other chieftains follow; fatal is this Kuru war.'
Dawned a day of mighty slaughter and of dread and deathful war.
Ancient Bishma in his anger drove once more his sounding car;
Morn to noon and noon to evening none could face the victor's wrath;
Broke and shattered, faint and frightened, Pandavs fled before his path.
Still amidst the dead and dying moved his proud resistless car,
Till the gathering night and darkness closed the horrors of the war.

Good Yudhishthir gazed with sorrow on the dark and
ghostly plain,
Shed his tears on chiefs and warriors by the matchless
Bishma slain.
'Vain this unavailing battle, vain this woeful loss of
life;
'Gainst the death-compelling Bishma hopeless is this
arduous strife;
As a lordly tusker tramples on a marsh of feeble reeds,
As a forest conflagration on the parched woodland
feeds,
Bishma tramples on my forces in his mighty battle-car.
God nor mortal chief can face him in the gory field of
war;
Nations pour their life-blood vainly, ceaseless wakes
the sound of woe.
Krishna, stop this cruel carnage; unto woods once more
we go.'
Sad, they held a midnight council and the chiefs in
silence met,
And they went to ancient Bishma, love and mercy to
entreat.
Bishma loved the sons of Pandu with a father's loving
heart,
But from troth unto Duryodhan righteous Bishma
would not part.
'Sons of Pandu,' said the chieftain, 'Prince Duryodhan
is my lord;
Bishma is no faithless servant nor will break his
plighted word;
Valiant are ye noble princes, but the chief is yet un-
born,
While I lead the course of battle, who the tide of war
can turn;
Listen more. With vanquished foeman, or who falls
or takes to flight,
Casts his weapons, craves for mercy, ancient Bishma
doth not fight.
Bishma doth not fight a rival who submits, fatigued and
worn;
Bishma doth not fight the wounded, doth not fight a
woman born.'"

HORSE COURT AT SERINGHAM

"Krishna deep and wise," by shrewdness took advantage of the solemn oath of virtue made by Bishma, and plotting his ruin said:

" 'Victim to the cause of virtue, he himself hath showed the way.'
And they faced the fiery Pandavs peerless in their warlike might.
Long and dreadful raged the combat, darkly closed the dubious fight;
Dust arose like clouds of summer, glistening darts like lightning played;
Darksome grew the sky with arrows, thicker grew the gloomy shade;
Cars went down and mailed horsemen, soldiers fell in dread array;
Elephants with white tusks broken and with mangled bodies lay.
And like sun from dark clouds parting, Bishma burst on Arjun's view,
And his eyes brave Arjun shaded at the awe-inspiring sight.
Half he wished to turn for shelter from the chief of godlike might.
But bold Krishna drove his chariot, whispered low his fatal plan;
Arjun the young Sikhandin in the deathful battle's van.
Bishma thought of word he plighted and of oath that he had sworn,
Dropped his arms before the warrior who a female child was born,
And the standard, which no warrior ever saw in base retreat,
Idly stood upon the chariot, threw its shade on Bishma's seat,
And the flagstaff fell dissevered on the crushed and broken car
As from azure sky of midnight falls meteor's flaming star.

True to oath and unresisting, Bishma turned his face away,
Turned and fell: the sun declining marked the closing of the day.
Arjun's keen and pointed arrows made the hero's dying bed.
Darker grew the gloomy midnight and the princes went their way.
On his bed of pointed arrows Bishma lone and dying lay!"

Bishma had been transfixed by such a multitude of arrows that when he fell from his chariot, instead of falling prostrate upon the earth, the shower of arrows that had pierced his body became an "arrowy couch" upon which he lay for many days, during which he counselled his king to

"'End this dread and deathful battle if thy stony heart can grieve;
Save the chieftains doomed to slaughter, bid the fated nations live.'
'Vain, alas,' the voice of Bishma like the voice of angel spoke,
Hatred dearer than his life-blood in the proud Duryodhan woke!
'Arjun is thy brother, Karna, end this sad fraternal war;
Seek not life-blood of thy brother nor against him drive thy car.'
Vain, alas,' the voice of Bishma like the voice of angel spoke,
Hatred dearer than his life-blood in the vengeful Karna woke!"

XI

CHRISTIANITY VERSUS OTHER WORLD RELIGIONS

TO judge the character, and estimate the actual content and inherent worth of the world religions in comparison with Christianity, we must not be influenced by biased or preconceived opinions nor captivated by mere verbal resemblances, but seek to discover the exact meaning that was originally embodied in those familiar terms, for they may not have conveyed to the followers of a particular religion the same qualities that we attach to them. Every day we hear misused words, as when some speak of "The awfully sweet child," and that it was "So sweet and awfully nice in you to write me, and I thought I would die when I read of the fun you were having." We have grown so familiar with such abused language that we make due allowance for the "marvellous" words, the hyperbole and confusion of terms, and we are not deceived by them. However, our reverence for sacred things restrains us from such a flippant abuse of words when speaking of the Almighty, and hence we were not prepared for the prevailing habit of the Swami to whom I referred in a preceding chapter, and who indulged in such a misuse of sacred terms that seemed incredible, for he knew that they were at direct variance with the meaning that he conveyed to his hearers, and many were misled by his cunning or unscrupulous jugglery of words.

Whilst attending the Christian College in Calcutta he had become thoroughly familiar with the content of the leading theological terms embodied in Christianity and which he employed subsequently in his public lectures, although he himself had eliminated the essence and essential reality of the fundamental and saving doctrines of the Christian religion, and was really feeding his hearers upon the mere husks or outward verbal forms of Christian belief. Many admirers were won by his clever sophistry in the misuse of sacred words, but they would have become disillusioned had they insisted upon his explaining just what he meant by the use of such words as "God," "Father God," and "Saviour God." Some at least would have been shocked and lost all their attachment for him to have learned from him that he even utterly repudiated the conception of such a being as a personal God, as well as the reality of all that is embraced in our most cherished religious convictions: our faith in God as our heavenly Father and Saviour, with our hopes of fellowship with Him after the close of this earthly life. Had the hearers understood the full significance of his belief, they would not have been led astray by the many attractive phrases abstracted from the Christian religion, but which he had divested of all their well-known meaning.

That which is of supreme importance and distinctive value in any religion is its conception of God. To get at the real essence and heart of any particular religion, or of the great world religions, we must inquire into their special conception or teaching concerning God.

What kind of a being is He? What is His character and attributes? What is His relation to man and His purpose in creating him, and what is to be man's destiny hereafter? In other words, is God an almighty, all loving, and merciful heavenly Father? Does He see, love, pity, and care for us, revealing Himself to us not merely through nature, but through the moral faculty of conscience, as well as through His Word, and especially as a person through His own Son Jesus Christ? Does He hear us when we pray and forgive us when we repent, and inspire us with lofty ideals?

This comparative study of religions is one of great practical value in view of its bearing upon Christianity, and which is gradually emphasizing the question: "What think ye of Christ?" That question is being forced upon us by the trend of recent critical historical studies and we cannot escape it. Inasmuch as contrast brings out in greater clearness the true values, we may hope for positive gain for Christianity by comparing it with the religions of the Far East.

The paramount importance of religion is unquestionable because of the powerful influence that it exerts over the individual and the community among every people and age since the early dawn of history, whilst anthropologists and archæologists have read in ancient remains the traces of evidence that confirms the prevailing influence of religion over the minds and habits of the races in prehistoric times, for it has profoundly affected the lives of all mankind.

In the comparative study of religions, the student is at times confined in his researches to monumental remains, and in many instances to rude objects without an inscription to record the exact meaning that was conveyed to the uncivilized races by those cultus designs. But in India all this is changed, for the contents of their Sacred Books take us far back to a period as remote as fifteen hundred years before the Christian era. In these Sanskrit writings may be studied the religious thought that controlled the minds and shaped the destiny of that early people.

I am not unmindful of the far older religions that have come down to us from ancient Assyria and Egypt, but the character of these brief inscriptions are not to be compared in fullness and clearness with the Sacred Books of India that were originally transmitted through many succeeding generations, until they were finally transcribed in permanent form upon the palm leaves. That religion has moulded and controlled the thinking of the unnumbered millions of the people, affecting their hopes and fears, their joys and sorrows, their manner of life, habits and social condition, through a period of about thirty-five hundred years. That is ample time for judging the character and merits of a religion by its logical fruits and direct effect upon its countless host of devoted followers.

After a long time in the study of the Sacred Books of the East, I had an ardent desire to visit India in order to see what their Bible had done for its adherents; in other words to see their religion in action as expressed in the daily practice of the people, and to study the effects of Hinduism by its fruits, for by its fruits among the people we may know its quality, and judge it accordingly. The conditions are particularly favourable among the Hindus inasmuch as they are intensely religious in thought and outward life, and as they believe and think concerning their gods, so they do. They give emphasis to the fact that man is not merely a religious being, but that his religious life, experiences and relation to God depend upon his conception of God, the character of that being and the relation that He sustains to us. These considerations determine man's mental attitude towards God, his moral consciousness, and peace of mind and inspiration for living according to the almighty and loving One in whom he believes and trusts. Man is conscious of his dependence upon some higher power, some superhuman help, for he often realizes his limitations and helplessness and hence the universality of prayer. "Oh, Thou that hearest prayer, unto Thee must all flesh come."

You will search in vain through the religious books of the East for the Christian's conception of God as our all-loving, heavenly Father, who declares to us: "I will be a Father unto you and ye shall be My sons and My daughters, saith the Lord God Almighty." "Like as a father pitieth his children so the Lord pitieth them that fear Him;" and "Like as one whom his mother comforteth so will I comfort you." "Call upon Me in time of trouble and I will deliver you." "Fear thou not for I am with thee; be not dismayed, for I am thy God; I will strengthen thee; yea, I will help thee; yea, I will uphold thee with the right hand of My righteousness."

The New Testament declares explicitly that "God is love," that "He gave His only begotten Son, that whosoever believeth in Him should not perish but have everlasting life" and "Herein was the love of God manifested in us, that God hath sent His only begotten Son into the world that we might live through Him." Among the many gods of the Vedas and Sanskrit writings none speak like the God whose we are and whom we serve. Those Sacred Books contain no such precious revelations to satisfy the deepest wants of the human soul, and those marvellous utterances from our Bible bear the unmistakable marks of divinity, and a God of infinite love alone could proclaim them.

We frequently hear men speak of the marked resemblances between our Bible and those of the Far East, and some have become disturbed in mind in possibility of a borrowing from those ancient writings, but there is absolutely no occasion for such suspicion as can be clearly seen by a careful comparison of the books in question. It is natural that the resemblances between Christianity and other religions should first attract the attention of those who have but a limited acquaintance with the Sacred Books of the East, for there is a psychological reason for this, and as experienced in daily observation.

We instinctively employ the comparative method by the irresistible law of association, and we are first impressed with points of resemblance, however vague and remote they may be. Thus we speak of a stranger as reminding us of some acquaintance, but the actual suggestions of resemblance may be of the most superficial character, perhaps in physiognomy, the particular contour of the face and expression or timbre of voice. With increased knowledge those seeming resemblances vanish because of the remarkable contrast revealed in the personality, moral and intellectual character of the men in question. The same is true in the study of religions and we must not allow ourselves to be carried away by mere superficial verbal resemblances, and overlook the vastly greater differences. We need to heed our Saviour's warning in this respect and "Judge not according to appearance but judge according to righteous judgment."

We welcome the rare gems of religious thought that are found in ancient literature, whatever people may have produced them, and in many of them we feel the heart throbs of universal humanity struggling between the burdens of life, and in its conscious weakness and sinfulness seeking to find help from the invisible God. "God made of one every nation of men to dwell on all the face of the earth;" and the Apostle Paul quotes from that remarkable hymn of Cleanthes, the Greek poet, and no one can read it without recognizing the fact that God never left the world without a witness of Himself, and that He is that "true light which lighteth every man coming into the world." This one God and Father of us all was always the same loving God and merciful heavenly Father, and He revealed Himself to His creatures in times and places so far as His children had the necessary mental and spiritual aptitude to receive Him.

Was not the soul of Cleanthes touched with the divine spirit as with the vision of the seer and moved by inspiration he uttered these words: "O Thou of many names, most glorious of immortals, Almighty Zeus, sovereign ruler of nature, directing all things in accordance with law; Thee it is right that all mortals should address, for Thine offspring we are, and alone of all creatures that live and move on earth have received from Thee the gift of imitative sound, wherefore I will hymn Thy praise and sing Thy might forever. No work is done without Thee, O Lord, neither on earth, nor in heaven, nor in the sea, except what the wicked do in their foolishness. Thou knowest how to make the rough smooth, etc. But do Thou, all bounteous Zeus, who sittest in the clouds, who rulest the thunder, save men from their grievous ignorance. Scatter it from their souls, and grant them to obtain wisdom, whereon relying Thou dost govern all things in righteousness."

Certain people have become unsettled by some startling discovery of unusual kinship with other religions, and not a few have gone to extremes in their endeavour to account for them. When the crosses at Palenque in Yucatan were discovered, the most sensational theories were advanced, and some over-zealous advocates jumped to the hasty conclusion that the prehistoric peoples who built the temples and carved the crosses upon them were Christian prophets, who with the vision of the seer penetrated the future and beheld the Cross that was to be raised on Calvary. The hasty and extravagant conclusions arrived at by some enthusiasts recall the story of a superficial traveller who found an old boot that had been washed on the shore of the Mediterranean, along the coast of Asia Minor, and which was marked with the letter J. At once his memory served him in recalling a familiar character mentioned in the Old Testament, and who had a most thrilling experience with the giant of the deep. He exclaimed: "Eureka! I have found the solution and the veritable boot of the disobedient prophet, for J. stands for Jonah, and the boot is the one that he lost in his desperate struggle to extricate himself from the jaws of the whale."

It is only a misconception of the rightful relation of Christianity to other religions that should cause any to be fearful of the comparative study, for its province is to discern the facts and truths and their relative values so as to discover the origin and meaning of certain religious phenomena, and their probable relation to other and later religions. There has been an evident growth or progress in religion, for God did not at once deliver to man the ready made plates for a book containing a complete revelation of Himself, and man's destiny here and hereafter, as has been claimed for the "Book of Mormon," for their leaders declared that they saw and handled with their hands the original metallic plates upon which in ancient writing was engraved the record that God Himself had prepared, and that He sent an angel from heaven to enlighten Joseph Smith, Jr., and to give him power to translate the mysterious writings.

Whilst the electrical forces and their wonderful possibilities always existed, it has only been in modern times that certain inventions and necessary adaptations have made their appropriation possible. Bacteria existed in the past as well as to-day and disastrous plagues followed, although men attributed the appalling ravages of disease to divine causes. In like manner God has ever been in the world and striving with man, although in primitive times man only apprehended in a very imperfect manner the Supreme Being from whom he could not escape. Hence it is not difficult to recognize the presence of God in other religions, as in the great reformers and seers of the Church.

One of the foremost scholars, Prof. Clement C. J. Webb, forcibly expressed this idea in his inaugural lecture: "I can probably count on the agreement of most of my hearers when I say that it is impossible for us to-day so to isolate any alleged system of Revealed

Religion from all others as to see in it nothing but what is divine, and in them nothing but what is human, or maybe diabolical. The marks of mutual kinship which all religions exhibit are too unmistakable; our conviction as men of science is too deep-rooted that such marks stamp them all as the issues of one process of evolution; while not less deep-rooted is our conviction as men of religion that we can recognize goodness where we see it, and that, wherever we see it, it must come from God." It is not too much to say that different religions arose in response to the profound wants and pressing needs of mankind in certain places and under special circumstances, whether we refer to Moses, Buddha, or Confucius.

Bearing upon this comparative study of religions, Professor Jastrow refers to the tendency of certain scholars in Germany "to trace the majority of the Hebrew traditions to Babylonian and Assyrian sources, to see in the myths of Genesis, in the legends of the patriarchs and even in the accounts of historical personages in the Old Testament, the reflections of an astral mythology and an astral theology which were developed in the priestly schools of the Euphrates Valley. It is no longer possible to question the kinship between certain elements of the Old Testament and what we find in the religion of Babylon and Assyria, and yet it is difficult to resist the conviction that its closeness has been exaggerated. Tempting generalities were hastily drawn of a direct borrowing by the younger civilization from the older. The thesis suggested by a more critical examination of the abundant material now at hand is that resemblances in myths and traditions are frequently as deceptive as resemblances in words of different languages." "The distinctive feature of Hebrew monotheism is its consistent adherence to the principle of a transcendent deity. No attempt was made at any time in Babylon and Assyria to set aside the cult of other gods in favour of Marduk."

It is well known that there are many splendid examples of lofty ethical teachings in the Sacred Books of the East, for all recognize the supremacy of that moral faculty which we call conscience and which is the common heritage of mankind. That inner and silent monitor which prompts us as to what we ought to do, and what we ought not to do, struggles to secure obedience and cannot be intimidated by threat nor silenced by sophistry and ruled out of court by legal technicalities, but it is its own defense, or accuser and prosecutor. It is the jury as well as the judge, and the decision is final and no appeal can reverse that decision. The guilty fully realize the supreme authority when unable to escape the inexorable penalty of a hell of remorse, even for the secret sin, for it has found out the evildoer himself, though he may have escaped the eyes of guardians of the law, and hence criminals have been forced by their own inner consciousness to confess their crimes, and to return conscience money.

Man may yield to temptation and be overcome of evil, but conscience will not accommodate the evil-doer by making an unconditional surrender its ethical standards, for with conscience, right is always right and never wrong, and wrong is always wrong and never right. In the universal presence of this dominant moral faculty among men we must also recognize the evidence of God's presence, who would confirm His children in the right and keep them from the wrong, for without conscience life would be intolerable, and society and state impossible. God must speak to men through their conscience, and hence the fact that beautiful moral truths have been echoed in other religions, and that even the Golden Rule had a place in the ancient sacred classics of China, does not in any way detract from Christ's teachings in the Gospel.

During a summer spent at Lake Mohonk, a young American who claimed to be a convert to Buddhism afflicted the peaceful minds of some of the guests by parading what he termed the gospel teachings of Buddha, and then embarrassed them by the suggestive question: "How do you account for the fact of the remarkable resemblances between Buddhism and Christianity: and inasmuch as Buddha came five centuries earlier than Jesus it is evident that he did not borrow from the latter, and how do we know that Jesus did not borrow from the former?" They were unable to give a satisfactory answer, for they were not acquainted with the teachings of Gautama, and they did not know that the differences were far more remarkable than the resemblances, and which must be taken into account. This will become evident to every one by reference to the earlier authoritative Buddhist writings. We recognize the noble and unselfish character of Buddha, who devoted himself to his mission, and by thoroughly ethical teachings condemning the excessive and soulless ceremonialism of Brahmanism, and enjoining the brotherhood of man. But alas, there was no Fatherhood of God in his teachings for the depressed and disconsolate ones of India, and here was an awful gulf between him and Jesus.

Moreover, Jesus was not an ascetic, and He claimed

to be far more than a mere human reformer. Whilst Buddha recognized no God in his mission among men, Jesus said: "I always do the will of My Father in heaven," and He also claimed oneness with God. "He that hath seen Me hath seen the Father, for the Father and I are One." "Abide in Me and I will abide in you, and My Father and I will come and take up our abode in you." "Peace I leave with you; My peace I give unto you; not as the world giveth, give I unto you. Let not your heart be troubled, neither let it be fearful."

In contradistinction to this, a mournfully pessimistic spirit pervades the teachings of Buddha, and which characterized his first sermon. We need but quote sentences that show the essence of his hopeless philosophy of life, and from which there was no escape. "Birth is suffering. Decay is suffering. Illness is suffering. Presence of objects we hate is suffering. Separation from objects we love is suffering. Clinging to existence is suffering."

From this mournful picture of life what a happy contrast is furnished by the message with which Jesus announces His mission. It was on the Sabbath day in the synagogue in Nazareth when He read from the book of the prophet Isaiah: "The spirit of the Lord is upon Me, because He anointed Me to preach good tidings to the poor; He hath sent Me to proclaim release to the captives, and recovering of sight to the blind, and set at liberty them that are bruised." Having read this message He said to the hearers: "To-day hath this Scripture been fulfilled in your ears." There is no note of pessimism or despair in the first sermon that Jesus preached in Nazareth as He proclaimed the purpose of

His mission; His words are full of hope and assured victory.

Buddha had not the lofty and extended vision of the inspired seer and the consciousness of divinity within himself as was true of Jesus, and in his deep personal interest for suffering humanity he even undertook the work without appealing to the almighty aid of a Supreme Being. Here was the lamentable hopelessness of his proposed system of redemption in giving to his followers that which by courtesy has been called a religion, but divorced from deity, and thus left without hope his system for human redemption was doomed to failure. In this atheistic teaching of Buddha, and which allowed man no recourse to prayer, we have an immeasurable difference between him and the founder of Christianity, and strange that any man should be blind to those marvellous contrasts, but be filled with enthusiasm respecting the most superficial resemblances.

In confirmation of these statements I would refer the reader to a recent Buddhist catechism, compiled from the sacred Buddhist writings for the use of Europeans by Subhadra Bikshu, and which contains the following: "Is Buddha a God, who has revealed himself to mankind? No. Or one sent by God into the world to bring salvation? No. Then he was a man? Yes; but a man far superior to ordinary men, one of a series of self-enlightened Buddhas." "There is no personal God Creator, on whose mercy and good will the universe depends. Human ignorance it is which alone invented a personal God Creator. The Buddhist utterly rejects the belief in a personal God." "Buddha cannot redeem us from the consequences of our guilt. Every one of us must become his own redeemer." "There is no heaven and no hell in the Christian sense." "But there are dark worlds or conditions of anguish and despair, where not a ray of hope and deliverance can penetrate, and where the sufferer has to remain until he has reaped the bitter fruit of his evil doings. There are equally bright worlds of joy." The upright and just man suffers for the wrong committed in his former life. The wicked and unjust often enjoy pleasures and honours in consequence of merit won in his former lives.

"The belief in an immortal, personal soul—that is, an indestructible and eternal separate substance which has only a temporary abode in the body—is regarded by Buddhists as a heresy. What is rematerialized in a fresh birth is not the soul, but the individuality, and this is not the soul, but the individuality, and this will assume, in accordance with its Karma, a new person. What we call a soul is dissolved after death into its constituent elements." "Reincarnation continues until perfect knowledge and Nirvana is attained." That "redemption is worked out by each one himself without any prayers, sacrifices and penances, without the ministry of ordained priests, without divine mercy." The Nirvana attained is not the same as the state of the Christian in heaven, for it is but "the continuance of individuality without an immortal soul, eternity, happiness without a local heaven." We must not fall into the error of some by making Nirvana a synonym for annihilation of being, or extinction of the soul in its complete entirety.

The Buddhism of to-day presents a variety of beliefs and is quite different in many respects from that which Buddha himself taught, and especially in that his followers have deified and worshipped him, for he acknowledged no deity and made no claim whatever to divinity for himself, but even disdained such divine honour and taught his followers to look to themselves alone for salvation after his departure. In spite of this fact to-day Buddha has been enthroned to a high seat among the gods, and he is associated with countless shrines, temples and statues, for no divinity in all the world has so many images raised to his honour. Some of the famous bronze Buddhas are of colossal proportions, and the excessive multiplication of his statues in some notable temples is amazing ; as though his virtues and powers were increased by this multiplicity.

We must distinguish between the purely legendary and the historical truth respecting the life of Buddha, for the Buddhist Bible or the whole of the Pitakas contain no life of him, and the only known biography of him was written two thousand years after his birth. Many unauthentic and unreliable statements have been made public by writers who drew upon their imagination for the picture that they presented, and many have been misled by those impressions. But fiction and legend, however interesting they may be, must not be seriously taken for fact. As an illustration, two university students, who had the ministry in view, called on me to tell of their serious doubts that had been aroused by reading Sir Edwin Arnold's "Light of Asia."

The marked resemblances that appeared between Buddha and Jesus were a shock to their faith, for knowing that the former's advent preceded that of the latter by some centuries, they suspected that Jesus had received His light from the "Light of Asia." To help them out of their perplexity I showed them the authoritative Sacred Books of Buddhism, and as the supposed wonderful resemblances vanished, and the marvellous differences appeared, their doubts disappeared also and their faith in Christ was restored. There is not the remotest reason for the fallacious charge that Christianity has been enriched by the writings of Buddhism or Hinduism. It would have been as reasonable had the explorer, who discovered the marble cross in the palace of Knossos on the Isle of Crete, proclaimed to the world that he had found the origin of the Christian's symbol, and that the inception of Christianity could be traced to that early people. Such a report might have produced a momentary sensation, but scholars would not have received it as reliable information.

Buddha, as Dr. H. Höffding states, "founded not a church but a monastic order. Buddhism became a popular religion only by means of the legends which wove themselves round the figures of Buddha, by the forms of worship which were adopted from the older religions of India, and, not least, by the strong emphasis of active love to man. Buddha's thoughts are like the grains of corn which, neither destroyed nor fulfilled, still lie in Egyptian graves as they were laid centuries ago. But the thoughts of Jesus have proved their fruitfulness. Buddha softened Asia, but Jesus taught Europe a great Excelsior." "Jesus wanted to purify and idealize men's wishes, not to do away with them," as was the method of Buddha. Fortunately whilst he banished the soul theory, he could not banish from man the soul fact, for that survived, just as God survived his atheistic theory."

Buddha could give no comfort to the father who

came bewailing the death of his son, but he gave all he had when he said to him, "Yes, so it is, my father. What a man loves brings him woe and sorrow, suffering and despair." No wonder that Höffding states that the "father turned from the Indian sage with an outraged heart, and he was right that a perfection won at such a cost is not able to express the highest personal value."

Unlike Jesus, Buddha had no solace for the bereaved, no balm for the broken-hearted, and when the young mother in great sorrow brought her dead child to him saying, "Lord and Master, do you know any medicine that will be good for my child?" he replied, "Yes, I know of some. Go get me a handful of mustard seed from a house where no son, husband, parent or slave has died." With a ray of hope awakened in her soul of agony by the promise that later proved but mockery, she hastened forth for the hope for remedy. But in those large Eastern homes where as many as four generations dwell together she found none into which death had not entered, and in despair she returned to her master with the sad story of her fruitless search. His only answer to that agonizing mother was: "You thought you alone had lost a son: the law of death is that among all living creatures there is no permanence."

Who knowing Jesus and Buddha would ever be troubled with their resemblances? Go with me to Nain, and stand by the bier with Jesus as He speaks the words of effectual comfort to the disconsolate mother and widow, "Weep not," and then dries her tears and rejoices her heart by restoring alive to her the son that they had been carrying to the place of burial. Or go to Bethany, to the home of Mary and

Martha, and follow them as they go to the tomb of their brother Lazarus to weep; and behold that scene as the divine and human meet, for no man ever spake like this Jesus of Nazareth. In deep sorrow of soul Martha says to Him: "Lord, if Thou hadst been here, my brother had not died." "Jesus saith unto her, Thy brother shall rise again. . . . I am the resurrection, and the life: he that believeth in Me, though he die, yet shall he live; and whosoever liveth and believeth on Me shall never die." Those words that brought life and immortality to light have echoed through the Christian centuries and no one can estimate their power in inspiring the bereaved with hope and consolation. Strange that any man should have an exaggerated vision for dark and superficial resemblances, and be blind to the marvellous differences that are as clear as the noonday sun.

When Buddha himself was nearing the end of his earthly journey he said to his beloved cousin: "O Amantha, my journey is drawing to its close. I have lived eighty years, and just as a worn-out cart can only with much care be made to move along. . . . In the future be ye to yourselves your own light, your own refuge. . . . Look not to any one but to yourselves as a refuge." Contrast such a confession of conscious human helplessness with some of the wonderful words of Jesus. "I am the Light of the world; he that followeth Me shall not walk in darkness." "I am the Way, the Truth and the Life; no man cometh unto the Father but by Me." "I came that they may have life, and may have it abundantly." "If any man keep My word, he shall never see death." "I give unto them eternal life," and "This is life eternal that they should know Thee the only true God, and Him whom Thou didst send, even Jesus Christ." "I am the living bread that came down out of heaven; if any man eat of this bread he shall live forever." "Destroy this body, and in three days I will raise it up again." To the sorrowing ones of earth He calls in words of sympathy and love: "Come unto Me, all ye that labour and are heavy laden, and I will give you rest; . . . and ye shall find rest unto your souls." "These things have I spoken unto you, that in Me ye may have peace. In the world ye have tribulation: but be of good cheer; I have overcome the world." "Let not your heart be troubled; believe in God, believe also in Me. In My Father's house are many mansions; if it were not so, I would have told you; for I go to prepare a place for you. And if I go and prepare a place for you, I will come again, and receive you unto Myself; that where I am, there ye may be also." "I will not leave you desolate: I come unto you. Yet a little while, and the world beholdeth Me no more; but ye behold Me: because I live, ye shall live also. In that day ye shall know that I am in My Father, and ye in Me, and I in you. He that hath My commandments, and keepeth them, he it is that loveth Me, and he that loveth Me shall be loved of My Father, and I will love him and will manifest Myself unto him." Buddha never spake words like these. His choicest gems do not bear even the remotest semblance to them, for he spake only as man and conscious of his own imperfections and limitations, whilst Jesus spake as the God-man.

I acknowledge that for the human mind there is unfathomable mystery in that eternal life which Christ promises, for death is universal and ends this earthly

MADURA TEMPLE

career, and we cannot penetrate the invisible Beyond. But life itself is a profound mystery, even that of the tiny seed, and with all the combined wisdom of scientific discovery, man has not been able to make a single one of these seeds. Man may imitate it so successfully in outward form as to deceive the eye, but he cannot deceive nature. You may plant that man-made seed in the richest soil, under the sunshine and showers of heaven, but it will not grow, for it lacks the essence and potency of life, and which God alone can give. In a world of such daily mysteries, we need not doubt Him when He promises eternal life to us who are His own children, and whom He made for fellowship for Himself.

Jesus in His farewell discourse to His disciples, referring to their sorrow, said, "But I will see you again, and your heart shall rejoice, and your joy no man taketh away from you." "These things have I spoken unto you, that in Me ye may have peace. In the world ye have tribulation: but be of good cheer; I have overcome the world." "Go ye therefore, and make disciples of all the nations, baptizing them in the name of the Father and of the Son and of the Holy Spirit: teaching them to observe all things whatsoever I commanded you: and lo, I am with you always, even unto the end of the world."

The transcendent character of Christ and the Gospel appear to advantage when compared with other religions, for contrast brings out the true and distinctive values as well as the comparative superiority or inferiority of the respective religions placed in comparison. It is still true that no man ever spake like Jesus, and we may safely challenge all the religionists of the

East to produce from their Bibles a passage comparable with that which Christ uttered when He declared that "God so loved the world that He gave His only begotten Son, that whosoever believeth in Him should not perish, but have everlasting life." In that brief declaration He gives us the Gospel in the concrete, revealing blessed truths, such as the world had never heard, and well might the Gospel of Christ be called good news. The greatest verities of human thought are contained in this brief message: God and man, and their relation to each other; earth and heaven; death and everlasting life. You cannot match it with any of the brightest gems culled from all the Sacred Books of the East, for it is unique, and bears the unmistakable stamp of divinity.

The human mind never conceived of such a revelation, for from the dawn of history we find man groping his way amid many and often degrading superstitions in his earnest efforts to find God, but now this order is reversed and God takes the initiative, and He comes through Christ to seek and to save the lost. That was God's own method and no such conception of Him had dawned upon the mind of man. To make such knowledge possible God must reveal Himself through a person, as He did through His own Son, and in this brief passage we have revealed the hope for the salvation of universal humanity. It reveals to us the boundless love of God, and is sufficient to save the world. In Christ we have our nearest and clearest view of God, and here is met the deep and universal need of the human soul as expressed by Philip when he made his appeal to Jesus: "Show us the Father, and it sufficeth us." Christ replied to him: "He that hath seen Me hath seen the Father, for the Father and I are one."

Whilst freely acknowledging all the intellectual difficulties involved in our belief in the doctrine of the incarnation, I am persuaded that the difficulties in the way of unbelief are still greater. If God is almighty, and our loving heavenly Father, then the fact of the incarnation, or God's interposition in our behalf, is reasonable as well as possible. But we must remember the character of that being for whom the great sacrifice was made, for it was man, the offspring of God, and who had been created in His own image. We know what sacrifice a mother will make even for an unworthy child, for often there seems to be no limit to the self-denial and suffering that she will endure for the sake of one that has gone astray, and will not the Infinite and all-merciful God and loving heavenly Father make infinitely greater sacrifice for the redemption of the countless millions of His own sons and daughters? Remember that God is our heavenly Father, and we are His children, however unworthy and estranged from Him we may have become. He has ever loved us as His own children, just as the wayward prodigal was still the son of his father. Man was no mere "grovelling worm of the dust" as some in their prayers have confessed him to be, but God's child, however much the divine image may have been effaced by sin.

On one occasion when purchasing a number of ancient coins that had been recently discovered, there was among them a tetradrachm of Alexander the Great, but so covered by a crust from the accumulation of many centuries as to be scarcely recognizable, except to a trained eye, and when that had been removed I had a beautiful silver coin, as bright and perfect as when it came from the ancient mint. The God of boundless love saw man's deplorable state, and in him He recognized His own child, and He could endure it no longer, but came to man's relief.

He could not be the God of love unless that love moved Him to action and to sacrifice for man's deliverance, for love is inseparable from sacrifice; it wants to do something and does not merely express itself in words. Hence "He who was rich, for our sakes became poor, that we through His poverty might be made rich."

There upon the cross we behold God's boundless love, not proclaimed merely in words, but in a sacrifice that speaks louder than words. That cross is the symbol of man's meeting place with God in a unique sense, for there in a preëminent degree God "was in Christ reconciling the world unto Himself," a fact that Jesus foresaw when He said: "If I be lifted up from the earth, I will draw all men unto Myself."

I have often been asked: "What impressed you as the most wonderful object that you saw in all your years of travel?" It was not our Western prairies; not the Yellowstone National Park, that Wonder-Land of the world; not the great volcanoes of the Hawaiian Islands; not the vast oceans, nor the Fjords of Norway and the midnight sun; not the Ganges, nor the Alps, nor the Kanchinjunga Range of the Himalayas, with Mt. Everest towering heavenward—almost six miles above sea level.

No, it was none of these physical wonders, nor yet the wonderful architectural creations that remain from ancient Greece and Rome, nor that unique Taj Mahal at Agra, nor any of the famous masterpieces of sculpture and painting; but the greatest object that I ever saw was man, God's greatest masterpiece, and made in His own likeness. This man was also far greater than any of his works, although he had often changed the face of nature, and tunnelled mountains, and connected lakes and the great oceans, and covered the plains and hillsides with towns and cities, and wrought out many startling inventions, and even brought the distant places of the earth within speaking distance. And yet it is not the wonderful inventions that we call the marvels, not that intricate mechanism of the modern printing-press, but the man who made it; not the machine that moulds the type and prints the paper, but that which is most marvellous by far is the man with the invisible mind who thinks out the contents of the newspaper and fills the homes and libraries and influences the thought of the world. No wonder that God was moved to a great sacrifice for this being, especially when his highest present and eternal welfare was involved, for this man was worth saving. Nor was that sacrifice made in vain, nor has the attractive power of the cross lost its influence in the world, but it continues with every age and people, and no name is so potent as that of Jesus.

When the leaders of the Jews threatened the Roman governor that if he released Jesus he was not Cæsar's friend, Pilate yielded, for he feared Tiberius who was the potentate of the great empire, although now without a single follower, and Jesus seemed helpless then as He went forth towards Calvary bearing His cross, for it looked like a lost cause, and yet contrary to all appearances, that crucifixion on Golgotha was to be His coronation, and would transform the despised Cross into the most precious and hallowed symbol in Christendom.

Graetz, the Jewish historian, admits this astounding fact, for in one of his volumes on the "History of the Jews" he states that Jesus is "the only mortal of whom one can say without exaggeration that His death was more effective than His life. Golgotha, the place of skulls, became to the civilized world a new Sinai. Strange that events fraught with so vast an import should have created so little stir at the time of their occurrence." But as an historian Graetz should have sought to discover the philosophy for this unique fact in all history, for there must have been a reason, since every effect has a cause. Had his religious prejudices not prevented him from searching the New Testament Scriptures, he might have found the reason clearly stated in the almost contemporaneous account of the life of Jesus as given in the Fourth Gospel; and which Christ Himself had foretold would come to pass when He should be lifted up from the earth and be crucified upon the Cross.

We know the impression that Christ created upon His immediate contemporaries, for this is stated in the Gospels and especially in the Epistles. Nor did His influence wane with the close of His life on earth, but through succeeding centuries He has met the profoundest aspirations of humanity and satisfied the deepest intellectual as well as moral and spiritual wants of mankind, in every age and country, and among people of the most diverse temperament, antecedents, environment and social life; and yet assimilating and regenerating them, and making them all new creatures in Christ Jesus, with changed thoughts and lives, hopes and joys, ideals, aspirations, conduct and service, with love to God and love to their fellow man.

Contrast to-day with the mighty influence of Christ Jesus, throughout the world, that of the entire pantheon of Greece and Rome. Gone is the power of all their gods and goddesses, and they have no place in the religious forces of to-day, except in the classics as so much ancient history, and in the comparative study of religions, for they have no living power in the hearts of men, no organized society of worshippers, and no temples devoted to their ancient cult. The fires of the Vestals, after having burned continually upon the altars for more than eleven centuries, finally died out forever, never again to be lighted, whilst Christ, the Light of the world, has lighted up the darkest places of the earth, and now encircles the globe with the most beneficent institutions for the healing of the nations.

I had a clear vision of this contrast the day I visited the ancient theatre in Ephesus, once crowded by the zealous followers of the Ephesian Artemis, who with a bedlam of voices cried out, "Great is Diana of the Ephesians," and it was not safe for Paul the missionary of Christ to enter, lest that angry mob should tear him limb from limb for daring to preach the Gospel in their city. With the background of history, and these local surroundings, in imagination I saw it all as an eye-witness, and how hopeless the cause of Christ seemed on that day, for then the preaching of Christ crucified was foolishness to the Gentiles; but how the situation has changed since then! That once great Diana, the Ephesian Artemis, whom they claimed that all Asia and the world worshipped, has not a single worshipper to-day. She is only survived by her marble, silver and bronze figures, and I have several exceedingly interesting contemporary numismatic monuments, containing the fine portraits of the Emperor Claudius and his wife Agrippina, whilst, on the reverse, is a splendid reproduction of the remarkable original image that they said fell down from Jupiter. What did Paul think as he looked upon this imperial authorization of Diana's worship?

Once the haughty Pharisees, with withering scorn, silenced the father of the boy whom Jesus had healed by replying to him in contempt: "Are ye also led astray? Hath any of the rulers believed on Him, or of the Pharisees?" They said it with a defiant boast, and felt that no one could challenge the truth of their statement, but how differently it has been answered during the history of the Christian centuries, and how abashed they would feel in the light of subsequent facts, for the greatest rulers of the world bow at the feet of Christ, and acknowledge Him as the King of kings, and the Lord over all.

Even the great Apostle to the Gentiles might be amazed at the progress, for once he wrote to the humble members of the church at Corinth: "For behold your calling, that not many wise after the flesh, not many mighty, not many noble are called." That is a contemporary picture of the social standing of the Church as Paul saw it, but it does not represent the Church of to-day that contains so many royal families, distinguished statesmen, judges, educators, scientists, and leaders in every department of society, as well as philanthropists, who bestow their many millions upon the various charities.

In the World's Exposition in Paris there was a great

collection of paintings from the leading artists of Europe and America, but among that number there were three that attracted the multitudes. As works of art they were not superior to many others, but it was their particular motive that held the thoughtful observer, and it was a significant fact that they were not only religious pictures, but in each instance the central figure was that of Christ, and I will give but a brief description of one of them: It was a large canvas, and in the foreground lay a French soldier across his steed, for both had been slain on the field of battle, and the brief inscription, "Pro Patria," told the sad story; he died for his country. The head of the patriot was resting against the foot of a cross and upon that cross was nailed the Christ of history, who died to save the world, and over His head was the significant inscription: "*Pro Humanitate.*" Christ died, not merely for His native land, but for all the nations of the earth, "for God so loved the world that He gave His only begotten Son, that whosoever believeth in Him should not perish, but have everlasting life."

It was that sacrifice upon the Cross that gave full proof of the infinite love of God, and His estimate of the worth of man; and it is this fact that touches and draws the human heart towards Him who first loved us. There is no power over the human heart like this matchless love of God, and we can trust Him amid the most trying experiences of life—when all things seem to go against us. It sustained the Apostle Paul, and he declared: "He that spared not His own Son, but delivered Him up for us all, how shall He not also with Him freely give us all things? . . . Who shall separate us from the love of Christ? Shall tribulation, or anguish, or persecution, or famine, or nakedness, or peril, or sword?" "God is faithful who will not suffer you to be tempted above that ye are able: but will with the temptation make also the way to escape, that ye may be able to endure it."

When a prisoner in Rome Paul tells us that: "At my first defense no one took my part but all forsook me. . . . But the Lord stood by me and strengthened me;—and I was delivered out of the mouth of the lion. The Lord will deliver me from every evil work, and will save me unto His heavenly kingdom."

Christ tells us that God so loved the *world;* that is, every race and people, and not merely the elect and favoured Jews who regarded themselves as God's chosen people, not only much dearer in His eyes than the greatest nations of the earth, but they excluded all other peoples from their holy temple in Jerusalem and thus denied them the blessings of religion. On the balustrade or wall around the temple, that separated the Gentile world from the favoured few, were placed oblong blocks of stone with inscriptions in Hebrew and Greek, warning all but Jews not to enter, on pain of death, which would certainly follow. In the museum in Constantinople I frequently looked upon that most interesting monument that has survived the temple in Jerusalem, and which Jesus must have seen, and the Apostle Paul no doubt saw it often, and had that same Greek inscription in mind when he wrote that Christ Jesus "made both one, and broke down the middle wall of partition," for that Jewish exclusion made a profound impression upon him when through Christ he learned of the Fatherhood of God and the brotherhood of man also.

Christianity has no middle wall of partition, for God

is no respecter of persons. There is no place for the caste system in the Christian religion, and Christianity is destined to become the one religion of mankind, for it appeals to the profoundest needs of universal humanity and from which there is no escape, and which are not provided for in other religions. Great changes will come with every succeeding generation, but man's religious nature will continue, and no advance in scientific research will quench its longings. At times when revisions of some individual cherished statement of belief become necessary, in view of the light and unquestioned knowledge gained from the revelations of science, some timid souls, with narrow vision, and who staked all their faith upon the preconceived views in vogue years ago, declare that if these things are true then the Bible is not true, and we may as well give up our Christian faith, for all is lost. But such reasoning is absurd, for, as an example, whilst the established facts of evolution and the origin and selection of the species have compelled us to abandon some former interpretations of the Bible, divine truth remains, and God remains and still manifests Himself to His creatures, and God's ways are better than ours.

The man who is persuaded by his moral and religious consciousness that Christ dwells in him, because of his transformed life and changed relation to Him and to the world, has a testimony that cannot be shaken. That conviction is as real to him as any of his five senses and no logic can disturb it. As well tell him that he cannot trust his eyes and that there is no starlit sky, but all is Maya, a delusion. We need different standards and methods for determining or testing certain qualities.

Love and moral character cannot be determined by examining the heart with a stethoscope, or Roentgen rays, nor the love and agony of a broken-hearted mother by a chemical analysis of her tears. It was the overmastering power of the profound personal conviction that Christ was with them that gave the disciples invincible faith, and they went forth like the immortals and with more than imperial power to conquer the world for Christ; and hence they refused to be silenced by the rulers and in defense replied: "We ought to obey God rather than man."

Some timid souls at times tremble lest religion has lost its supreme place in the world, in view of the restatement of certain religious beliefs made necessary by historic and scientific discovery, just as when men learned of the place that evolution had in the world, overlooking the fact of law and order in God's creation. The origin of the variations of types or species by the law or principle of natural selection, as well as the process of evolution, are well established truths, and why should any one be frightened at the discovery of God's own immutable laws? We should welcome such knowledge and willingly abandon our inherited erroneous views, for the ways of the Almighty are far better than what we once may have thought that they should have been. Some Christians insisted that the earth did not revolve on its axis around the sun, but that God made the sun to revolve around the earth, or, at least, should have done so. With the vote of the council to the contrary the earth still revolved. Others contended that it was a cardinal doctrine of faith that the Creator created the world in six days of twenty-four hours each, and that to deny it was to repudiate the

Bible and God's own testimony, and abandon faith in religion. But that was not the inevitable logic of the situation, for whilst every scholar has abandoned that erroneous theory, religion did not vanish when some of man's opinions were found to be erroneous, for man will never outgrow his religious nature no more than he will advance beyond his moral consciousness, and religion alone will satisfy the deepest needs of his being. Amid the dark experiences of life that try men's souls he will crave for that peace of God that passeth all understanding, keeping the heart and mind in Christ Jesus.

From age to age the world will advance in knowledge and outgrow many of the theories once defended by their advocates, but God will remain the same, although some of man's opinions and interpretations of the Being of God and His dealings with men must be changed. Whilst the genesis of many religious teachings and practices were divine, the verdict of history shows that certain ones were as certainly human, and a few of them even inhuman. The history of religions shows that no being has been so misunderstood and misrepresented as God our heavenly Father, and hence the great varieties and often most absurd vagaries of religious beliefs and practices. Even the Christian Church at times conceived of the Almighty, not as the God of love and all mercy, but of cruel hate towards mankind, and that Christ came and died on the cross in order that His blood might appease and reconcile God to us. The fact is that the very opposite is true, for man was estranged and needed to be reconciled and not God, and He was in Christ reconciling the world unto Himself. In truth God was unchanged. He was always our merciful and loving heavenly Father, and it was because He so loved the world that He gave His only begotten Son, and hence too we must not separate our heavenly Father from that sacrifice on the cross.

I can never look upon that famous fresco of the Last Judgment without a feeling of revulsion, for that horrible scene is not only appalling, but a caricature of the meek and lowly Saviour, who is represented as a Nero, and as though He found satisfaction in the tortures of the lost sons and daughters. No wrathful Jove displayed less feeling of sympathy and love than has been depicted in that face of Jesus. No wonder that institutions like the Spanish Inquisition were born and flourished when the fact of God's boundless love failed to be emphasized, and bigotry and hate gave rise to some of the saddest and blackest pages of history. All Christians of whatever name deplore the evils of that age, and it would be utterly impossible to repeat them, for the Church is more Christlike to-day, and never before in Christendom was the love of God so manifest in the lives of men, and never was the abiding sense of the brotherhood of man so strong and universally recognized in the common feeling of humanity—that there is but one God and Father of us all, and who revealed Himself to us through His Son.

At times the Church, in common with some scientists of the age, went astray in its teachings of science and made our heavenly Father responsible for many of the most dreadful sufferings that ever afflicted mankind. Being without the knowledge of the germ theory and the laws of sanitation, they attributed to the displeasure of the Almighty the chief evils of life, including disease, plagues, pestilence, fire and sword, with the appalling disasters on sea and land, not excepting earthquakes and tornadoes, as well as the shocking religious persecutions and slaughter of the innocent ones. No intelligent man to-day, suffering from typhoid fever, would look up into the face of Jesus and say, "Thou hast brought this affliction upon me," and yet such a blasphemous charge would be just what men once believed and taught.

Whilst freely confessing and deploring the shortcomings of the Church and many of which were the common product of the times, but none of which were the logical and legitimate fruits of the Gospel, we must not overlook the fact of the direct and inestimable blessings that have elevated humanity through the preaching of the Gospel. Through the centuries it has been good news to those who heard it, and made life worth the living by ennobling it, and showing its inseparable relation to the eternal future.

The question of the ages has been: "If a man die, shall he live again?" Men have speculated and hoped, but Christ not only proclaimed it in words, but gave full proof at Nain and Bethany, as well as on the third day when He Himself rose from the dead,—bringing life and immortality to light. He declares that "because I live, ye shall live also,"—and "I will come again and receive you unto Myself, that where I am, there ye shall be also." Since death is universal we cannot overestimate the comfort and sustaining power that has come from our assurance of a blessed and eternal existence. This enabled the Apostle after many years of severe trials and sufferings to exclaim: "Our light affliction, which is for the moment, worketh for us more and more exceedingly an eternal weight of glory; while we look not at the things which are seen, but at the things which are not seen: for the things which are seen are temporal; but the things which are not seen are eternal. For we know that if the earthly house of our tabernacle be dissolved, we have a building from God, a house not made with hands, eternal, in the heavens." That confidence made Paul the unconquerable hero, and he would have all believers share it with him as he writes to the Church at Thessalonica.

With such assurances of God's matchless love, and our eternal welfare, it is possible for us to endure and triumph, knowing that we are not left alone to our own strength, but that we are "kept by the power of God unto salvation," and He encourages us to cast all our care upon Him because He cares for us. The great Apostle to the Gentiles, with trying experiences that try the souls of few men, had an opportunity to make the most practical test of Christ's promised sustaining power. He had learned to know and trust Christ as he preached Him amid much persecution, but he declared with the conviction of certainty that had been born of years of antecedent experience in the service of his Master: "I can do all things in Him that strengtheneth me."

At times the professed followers of Christ and even leaders in the Church may have lost sight of their Divine Master, and turned from the ideals of His spirit and teachings, and brought reproach upon the Church; and yet making due allowance for the many and greatest evils committed under the sanction and authority of the Church, there is no institution on earth that is comparable with its unselfish character and lofty influence over mankind. It has been the foremost and mightiest moral and spiritual transforming power throughout the world, and as a sociological and economic agency among men it is invaluable to society and the state. It is not the cost of the Church that bankrupts and impoverishes the homes, but it is sin that destroys happiness, degrades and makes paupers, and robs men of everything that makes life worth the living, whilst the Church surrounds the young and families with safeguards, and ennobles them by giving lofty moral and spiritual ideals, and enjoining the conscientious fidelity to their neighbour and the state as well as to God.

Auguste Sabatier in his "Religions of Authority" has expressed in a most forcible manner his estimate of the supreme place of the Church and I quote it with hearty approval: "Taken all in all where shall we find a higher or more universal school of respect and virtue than in the Church, a more efficacious means of comfort and consolation than the communion of the brethren, a safer tutelary shelter for souls still in their minority? And what part played in history is comparable to that of the Church in the history of European civilization? On the other hand, what can we say of the Bible which would not fall short of the reality? It is the book above all books, light of the conscience, bread of the soul, leaven of all reforms. It is the lamp that hangs from the arched roof of the sanctuary to give light to those who are seeking God. The destiny of holiness on earth is irrevocably linked with the destiny of the Bible. Christianity can neither realize nor propagate herself without the Church; the Church cannot live without the Bible, that original source and classic norm of religious life as it is manifested in the Church itself. These are potencies of fact, of historic authority."

Christ committed the spread of the Gospel, and the redemption of the world, to the Church, and as you follow the faithful and devoted Christian missionary around the world, you will see the blessed fruits of the regenerating, civilizing and uplifting power of Christianity in every land and among every people who have accepted the Gospel of good news. Wherever the missionaries have extended their influence there has been an awakening of the conscience, followed by social transformation of character in the individual as well as in society. Intellectual activity and industrial improvements have followed, for the highest civilization is inseparable from Christianity. Hence degrading superstitions, idolatry and barbaric practices have disappeared, and a transformed as well as enlightened people have appeared, for old things have passed away and they have become new creatures in Christ Jesus. Heavy and grievous burdens have been removed, higher ethical standards substituted for the old, with more refined and cultured manners, with educational advantages provided for all.

With a changed and ennobled religious consciousness, their new conception of God as their loving heavenly Father, their mental attitude and relation to Him became changed; and they have come in possession of new ideals, motives, inspirations, aspirations, hopes and joys in the knowledge of being the sons and daughters of God, and brother or sister to their neighbour. With such a moral consciousness they found themselves living in a different world, and that they themselves were nobler beings, and with a higher and more glorious destiny on earth than they ever conceived of until Christ, the Light of the world, came to them, and inspired them with new hopes. Many have risen in their might and are now filling important stations and rendering valuable service to their people.

As an example I need but mention the familiar name of Panditi Ramabai, once the mournful Hindu widow, but whom Christ transformed into a new creature, fitted for a wonderful mission in behalf of the oppressed widows of her own people, and to-day the best known woman in India, and no Hindu woman in all the history of that country has done so much for the unfortunate women of India. Never shall I forget the impression made upon me when we met her at Khedgaon and saw her great and far-reaching work, not merely among the thousands whilst connected with that remarkable institution, but they have gone forth throughout the land, and leavened tens of thousands of homes with messages of Christ's love.

I recall another example of which I learned when travelling in that country where woman has not received her own. In this instance it was a poor little orphan girl from the outcastes. There was something about her deplorable condition that attracted the special attention and sympathy of the wife of a missionary, and she was taken home, placed under Christian influences and educated. Later she graduated in medicine, and displayed unusual qualities, and that once neglected and despised outcaste orphan girl was then at the head of the woman's department of one of the leading government hospitals in India. That showed what Christianity could do for the women of India, and that was sufficient to justify the hopes of those engaged in the work to evangelize that people.

Hinduism in forty centuries failed to produce one

such example in all India, and there is no hope for the countless millions without Christianity, for Hinduism has been tried and found wanting. With the progress of the Christian missionaries marvellous changes have taken place, and boys from the once hopeless outcastes that had been abandoned by Hinduism have been trained in the mission schools, and some of them who later entered the universities even carried off some of the highest honours.

I witnessed an impressive illustration during the commencement exercises of the Forman Christian College at Lahore in the Punjab; and I had similar impressions when visiting the flourishing college at Guntur. Some of the most convincing apologetics for Christianity may be found in the missions in India. In confirmation of my estimate, Sir Wm. Mackworth Young, lieutenant-governor of the Punjab, writes: "As a business man, speaking to business men, I am prepared to say that the work which has been done by missionary agency in India exceeds in importance all that has been done, and much has been done, by the British government in India since its commencement." Sir Augustus R. Thompson, lieutenant-governor of Bengal, says: "In my judgment Christian missionaries have done more real and lasting good to the people of India than all other agencies combined. They have been the salt of the country, and the true saviours of the empire."

The same is true of the power of the Gospel in whatever country the missionary may have preached it, and Mr. Charles Darwin, the renowned naturalist and traveller, adds his high testimony as the result of personal observation: "The success of the mission in

Terra Del Fuego is most wonderful and charms me, as I always prophesied utter failure. I could not have believed that all the missionaries in the world could have made the Fuegians honest. The mission is a grand success." "The lesson of the missionary is the enchanter's wand." "Remember that human sacrifices and the power of an idolatrous priesthood—a system of profligacy unparallelled in any other part of the world—infanticide a consequence of that system—the bloody wars, where the conquerors spared neither women nor children—that all these have been abolished, and that dishonesty, intemperance, and licentiousness have been greatly reduced by Christianity." And all this had been accomplished within a comparatively brief period of not many years, and what better defense for the Gospel can be offered, and what mightier credentials for the divine origin of Christianity can be presented than the marvellous fruits that have followed the preaching of the Gospel by the Christian missionary in the march of Christianity around the world during the nineteen centuries?

The Hon. Charles Denby, LL. D., who for thirteen years was United States Minister to China, was generous in his praise of the missionaries and their work in that country, and he declared that the converts were "morally, mentally and spiritually benefited by their teachings." "If the missionaries had done nothing else for China, the amelioration of the condition of the women would be glory enough. It is said that 15,000 converts were killed during the riots, and not as many as two apostatized." That was proof of their genuine character, and that they were not merely "rice Christians," as the enemies of foreign missions sneeringly call them. United States Minister Denby says that the missionaries are benefactors of humanity and deserving our support. "Civilization owes them a vast debt. They have been the educators, physicians and almoners of the Chinese. They are the early and only translators, interpreters and writers of the Chinese. To them we owe our dictionaries, histories and translations of Chinese works. They have scattered the Bible broadcast, and have prepared many school-books in Chinese. Commerce and civilization follow where these unselfish pioneers have blazed the way. Believe nobody when he sneers at the missionary. The man is simply not posted on the work."

Major Edwin H. Conger, United States Minister to China, and whom I heard at the Convention of the General Synod, bears this high tribute to the missionaries: "They are the pioneers in all that country. They are invariably the pioneers of Western civilization. It is they who, armed with the Bible and school-books, and sustained by a faith which gives them unflinching courage, have penetrated the darkest interior of the great empire, hitherto unvisited by foreigners, blazed the way for the oncoming commerce which everywhere follows them. It was they who first planted the banner of the Prince of Peace in every place where now floats the flag of commerce and trade. The dim pathways which they travel, sometimes marking them with their blood, are rapidly being transformed into great highways of travel and trade, and are fast becoming lined with schoolhouses and railway stations, where heretofore were found only idolatrous shrines and lodging houses for wheelbarrow men and pack-mules." The missionaries have not been the cause of

JUGGERNAUT CAR AT SERINGHAM

THE GOPHURA AND TEMPLE TANK

trouble in China as charged by some of their enemies, and the Hon. John Barrett, United States Minister and Consul General to Siam, says: "In my experience as United States Minister, one hundred and fifty missionaries, scattered over a land as large as the German empire, gave me less trouble in five years than fifteen business men or merchants gave me in five months."

I have often been asked how I account for the contradictory reports concerning the missionaries, and in reply I cannot do better than to quote from the Hon. Charles Denby: "In general, the tourists who spend a few days or weeks in China sneer at the missionaries or damn them with faint praise. . . . Tourists who never put foot in a missionary compound have written books, nevertheless, teeming with criticism on the work of missions. I recall two prominent instances. One of the two was a distinguished American, who stayed three weeks in my legation. I particularly invited him to visit the mission stations in Peking, but he declined to do so. He knew absolutely nothing of missionary work, but in his book he derided the whole system. The other gentleman was a celebrated Englishman, who has filled the highest offices under the Crown. He bitterly attacked the missionaries one day in conversation with me. I asked him if he had ever visited or inspected any mission compound. He said he never had."

I heard the common stereotyped criticisms from various foreigners living in the Eastern ports, who volunteered to prejudice me against the missionaries, but they were manifestly unfair and unreliable, as I learned from personal observation among the many missions in Japan, Korea, China and India. Some of the reasons for their attack were highly suggestive, and the situation may be partly illustrated from a remarkable incident of history from the Hawaiian Islands. During the weeks spent there, I had many interviews with prominent people who had spent their lives on the islands.

I gathered much important information from some of the distinguished children of the early missionaries, including Dr. Alexander, the historian, the venerable scholar, Dr. Hiram Bingham, and Mrs. Persis G. Thurston Taylor, daughter of the Reverend Thurston who was one of the first two missionaries to these islands of the Pacific. She was born at Honolulu within a year after they landed, and she had the distinction of being the first child of white parents born on the islands of Hawaii, and as she had passed more than fourscore years I appreciated my opportunity for gaining valuable information bearing upon the history of Christianity on those islands. I was also deeply impressed with the fact that she was the sole existing living witness from those early times, and the only connecting link between the planting of the mission and its succeeding growth to the present time. With her advent every Hawaiian was a pagan, but she lived to see the day when they had become so transformed by the Gospel that there were no longer any pagans among them.

However, we must not repeat the erroneous and general impressions that the native Hawaiians, or Sandwich Islanders as they were once called, were cannibals, for the fact is that cannibalism was not one of their barbarous practices, but they regarded such a shocking custom with horror and detestation. They had enough sins of pagan degradation to answer for and I was grateful to learn that cannibalism was not one of them. Perhaps the impression grew from the disposition that was made of the body of Captain Cook, and the accidental eating of his heart by a native, who stole it from a tree where it was suspended to dry, he supposing it to be the heart of a swine. According to their custom with celebrities, the body had been boiled in a calabash, not to feed the warriors, but that the flesh might be removed from the bones and burned, whilst the bones were to be preserved and deified.

My aged informer knew very well and had often conversed with several of the Hawaiians who had been present at the time of the tragic death of Captain Cook, who really suffered the penalty of his own sins, committed against that superstitious and idolatrous people. He took undue advantage of that ignorant people by posing as a god, and receiving divine honours, for "he moved among them as an earthly deity, observed, feared and worshipped." On one occasion he was received with much religious pomp, and the "priests made offerings and prayers to their supposed patron divinity," whilst the king was overawed in the presence of the incarnation of the god Lono, as they mistook him to be. They not only worshipped him with solemn ceremonies and prayers, but the king on entering the shrine or tent of the strange god acknowledged him with proper obeisance, and removing his own magnificent feather helmet and cloak, composed of the rarest and most beautiful feathers, placed them upon the head and shoulders of the famous navigator who was now assuming the new rôle of a divinity. He practiced the deception well, and a half dozen more of the costly feather robes were laid at his feet by the King Kalaniopuu, whose confidence Captain Cook had won and abused. The estimated value of these gifts might be reckoned by thousands of dollars, and as a return for these munificent royal presents, the foreign god took the king and his chiefs on board his ship, and presented the king—shame to say—with a linen shirt and a cutlass, a gift scarcely in keeping with the supposed wealth and generosity of a local god.

With all our admiration for Captain Cook as a navigator we must condemn his inexcusable conduct among the Hawaiians, and I had no sentimental tears to shed when visiting his lonely grave on the shore of the bay where a suitable monument marks the resting place of a remnant of his bones obtained from the natives. Dr. Alexander, the historian, as well as Mrs. Taylor received their information from eye-witnesses, including the widow of King Kalaniopuu whom Captain Cook had attempted to entice on board, but she fearing some treachery kept near her royal spouse. Chiefs who suspected the plot prevented his yielding to the overtures from the foreigners and after the death of several, a warrior thrust a spear through the body of the great navigator and he fell dead.

I have introduced this episode as an example of the baneful moral influence that many foreigners from Christian lands have exerted upon the pagan world, and against the progress of Christianity, for the natives are confused by immoralities which they abhor; for they often fail to discriminate between a Christian and a man from a Christian country, and the two are not necessarily synonymous. Too many foreigners in the East, separated from father and mother, and with the lowering of ethical standards and living the life of a prodigal in a strange land, have become the enemies of those men and women who condemn their sins. These moral degenerates are generally the missionary detractors, and who declare that foreign missions are a failure, and that "the native religion is far better for the people than Christianity, which inevitably makes them hypocrites and worse than they were before their conversion."

Unfortunately they prejudice certain hurried tourists who have neither time nor inclination to visit the mission fields. It was the Europeans and among them the sailors of Captain Cook who inoculated the Hawaiians with nameless fatal diseases that have spread with fearful mortality in their ineradicable transmission from generation to generation, and which have doomed the native Hawaiian race to final extinction according to the belief of some physicians. No such marvellous work of the Gospel among a basely degraded pagan people had been witnessed since apostolic times.

As the Gospel spread it grew with accumulated power, and like a great tidal wave it swept with irresistible force over the islands, and idolatrous practices and still worse forms of disgusting vice disappeared. It was evident in the transformed and ennobled lives that a divine regenerating power had come among them, for the people themselves were the unmistakable witnesses, and they knew as well as others that they were new creatures in Christ Jesus. Within a few years had been accomplished that which men would have said was impossible. Homes were refined and purified, thousands became faithful members of the Church, and large houses of worship were erected, one with a capacity of five thousand souls, and it was often crowded with earnest worshippers.

All honour and gratitude are due to the unselfish and consecrated band of missionaries who went out from our country to save the degraded Hawaiians who were perishing from their shocking vices—and had been left without hope and without the knowledge of God. The missionaries appealed to their conscience and preached Christ unto them,—condemning their sins and pointing the way of salvation. With quickened and enlightened conscience they responded to the appeals and accepted the gospel message with its ideals. Their moral character and lives were elevated, their homes purified, as they became restored to right relations to God and to their fellow men.

And yet, strange to say, some of these same self-sacrificing and devoted missionaries met with strong opposition and were bitterly persecuted by some godless foreigners who had been accustomed to land with their seamen and corrupt the natives still more, and afflicted them with the horrible diseases that have threatened the extermination of the Hawaiian race. The moral reforms of the Christian missionaries stood in the way of the ruinous immoral license practiced by the foreign crew up to this time, and when the missionaries denounced their shameful vice and appealed to the local powers to prevent its continuance, they were attacked, severely punished and barely escaped with their lives. No doubt these same enemies of God and the Hawaiians became missionary detractors after that event, and told Europeans that the work of the American missionaries was another failure and that the people became worse after their conversion to Christianity.

I admit that some of the criticisms in reference to certain missionaries and missions are true so far as they relate to particular instances, but they are unjust and misleading because of lack of discrimination, and the proper sense of proportion, for their reports are made to reflect upon the work of foreign missions as a whole. I well remember what the Prime Minister of Japan, Count Okuma, said to me in a long interview in his home, during which I asked him many questions concerning Christianity in Japan. To a certain question he replied: "Yes, send us many more missionaries, for we need them for the moral elevation of our people, but send us only good and able ones, for you have made some great mistakes in this respect." He had special reference to some years gone by, and the mistakes were not repeated, for the missionary cause had suffered.

At times there have been some ill-advised methods pursued that tended to denationalize and Westernize the converts, and which naturally tended to prejudice the spirit of patriotism and national pride against the missionaries as well as their converts. But much has been learned from experience, and a more rational and sympathetic attitude has proved more successful, by recognizing all that is best in their religious beliefs, and then seeking to adapt our religious and moral conceptions to their modes of thought so as to win their acceptance of the essence and cardinal truths of the Gospel, and trusting to its divine power to transform their lives and practices, instead of divorcing them from the things that are distinctly national, and which must remain Indian.

We cannot, and we should not attempt to transplant all the human infirmities and man-made peculiarities that characterize the various opposing sects of the Western world with some peculiar forms, and then set them up in India, and build a high stone wall around its compound, thus separating itself like a high caste from the poor natives, as well as from the many different sects or denominations that claim priority, and which greatly confuses the mind of the natives. I acknowledge that there have been some mental and moral weaklings, some adventurers and irresponsible men and women among the great army of missionaries, who by their indiscretions brought reproach upon the cause, but their number is rather limited. I have known a few erratic ones who claimed that the Lord called them to go into the Far East, and before they had learned the language or rendered any practical service, they received another call to return home; but no sane man will charge the Lord with such contradictions.

I found many representative people connected with the great mission fields, and among them were some of God's noble men and women, of sterling character, and with great minds and hearts. Some were even labouring at their own expense, but like many others being wholly constrained by the love of Christ for humanity to labour for the highest welfare of an unfortunate people. Never shall I forget the impression made upon me when we met that heroine, Dr. Rijnhart, on the Yangste, near Nanking. Her husband had been basely murdered in Thibet where she had previously lost her only child, and amid terrible hardships and dangers she left the country and returned to her own home in America to recuperate a shattered constitution. She was cast down, but not forsaken, and having recovered her strength, we found her journeying north ward through China, to enter alone once more that forbidden country, but cheered and sustained by an invincible faith.

We must keep the great, heroic and consecrated men and women in mind when we are told of some individual failures, for some ministers and Churches at home have failed, but Christianity in America has not failed, and the same is true of the history of Christianity around the world, in every land and on every isle of the sea where it has been established, for it has been for the healing of the nations through the centuries, and the marvellous results abundantly prove that the Gospel is the power, has been, and is still the "power of God unto salvation to every one that believeth."

In contrast with the hope and certainty of the Christian religion and the triumph of Christianity, compare the hopelessness and despair of Hinduism, as expressed by Sir Alfred Lyall in "Meditations of a Hindu Prince":

"All the world over, I wonder, in lands that I never have trod,
Are the people eternally seeking for the signs and steps of a God?
Westward across the ocean, and Northward across the snow,
Do they all stand gazing, as ever, and what do the wisest know?

"Here, in this mystical India, the deities hover and swarm
Like the wild bees heard in the tree-tops, or the gusts of a gathering storm;
In the air the men hear their voices, their feet on the rocks are seen,
Yet we all say, 'Whence is the message, and what may the wonders mean?'

"A million shrines stand open, and ever the censer swings,
As they bow to a mystic symbol, or the figures of ancient kings;
And the incense rises ever, and rises the endless cry
Of those who are heavy laden, and of cowards loth to die.

"For the Destiny drives us together, like deer in a pass of the hills;
Above is the sky, and around us the sound of the shot that kills;
Push'd by a power we see not, and struck by a hand unknown,
We pray to the trees for shelter, and press our lips to a stone.

"The trees wave a shadowy answer, and the rock frowns hollow and grim,
And the form and the nod of the demon are caught in the twilight dim;
And we look to the sunlight falling afar on the mountain crest,—
Is there never a path runs upward to a refuge there and a rest?

"The path, ah! who has shown it, and which is the faithful guide?
The haven, ah! who has known it? for steep is the mountainside,
For ever the shot strikes surely, and ever the wasted breath
Of the praying multitude rises, whose answer is only death.

"Here are the tombs of my kinsfolk, the fruit of an ancient name,
Chiefs who were slain on the war-field, and women who died in flame;
They are gods, these kings of the foretime, they are spirits who guard our race:
Ever I watch and worship; they sit with a marble face.

"And the myriad idols around me, and the legion of muttering priests,
The revels and rites unholy, the dark unspeakable feasts!
What have they wrung from the Silence? Hath even a whisper come
Of the secret, Whence and Whither? Alas! for the gods are dumb."